Praise for *The Violent Take It by Force*

"With its meticulous research, lively writing, and exceptionally nuanced analysis, *The Violent Take It by Force* pulls back the curtain on the radical religious movement once occupying the fringes of American Christianity but now situated within reach of the centers of American power. This book should be required reading for anyone seeking to understand Christian nationalism and the threat it poses to American democracy."

—**Kristin Kobes Du Mez**, *New York Times* bestselling author of *Jesus and John Wayne*

"A timely insight into the New Apostolic Reformation, one of the most significant movements in the United States today. Thoroughly researched and highly accessible, *The Violent Take It by Force* is essential reading for anyone who wants to learn about the religious ideology and key figures that helped foment January 6, and how Christian supremacy is set to continue to shape the United States."

—**Elle Hardy**, author of *Beyond Belief: How Pentecostal Christianity Is Taking Over the World*

"Since the January 6 insurrection, a growing number of Americans are realizing we need a better understanding of far-right Christian nationalism. And since most of us are not religious scholars, we also need an interpreter. Dr. Matthew Taylor provides that in *The Violent Take It by Force*, a meticulously researched, cogently explained translation of the often-unintelligible language of this movement, including the shadowy networks of apostles and prophets that use strategic spiritual warfare, ancient symbols, and unique theologies to support an agenda of authoritarianism and global Christian supremacy. Whether you are a policy maker, a student of religion, or a citizen who simply values separation of church and state, you will find *The Violent Take It by Force* illuminating, authoritative, and compelling."

—**Congressman Jared Huffman** (D-CA), co-chair, Congressional Freethought Caucus

"In this critical book, Matthew Taylor gives us a harrowing tour of the once-fringe charismatic forces that have coopted and upended the contemporary

Christian Right political movement, infusing it with an anti-democratic theology of spiritual warfare that is increasingly spilling over into political violence. For anyone who has been perplexed about the dangerous, carnivalesque marriage of Trump's MAGA movement and Christian nationalism, this well-written book helps dispel the confounding mist."

—**Robert P. Jones,** *New York Times* bestselling author
of *The Hidden Roots of White Supremacy and the
Path to a Shared American Future*

"An essential book for understanding the role of religion in twenty-first-century American politics. Matthew Taylor has written a page-turning account of a small group of leaders, hucksters, and activists who once were on the fringes of US culture, but recently exerted influence on the highest office in the land—and may yet again. A thorough study and a thoroughly unnerving warning, *The Violent Take It by Force* should be required reading for anyone concerned about the future of our democracy."

—**Peter Manseau**, author of *One Nation, Under Gods:
A New American History*

"Matthew Taylor shines a bright light on a dark corner of American Christianity, depicting its role in the ascendency of Donald Trump, the January 6 insurrection, and the 'holy violence' it is bringing to our political life. In brisk, engaging prose, he portrays the leaders and the followers of a movement that threatens to replace rational public discourse with strident demonology, endangering the future of our democracy."

—**Anne Nelson**, author of *Shadow Network*

"The New Apostolic Reformation is one of the most influential and dangerous Christian nationalist movements in the United States—and beyond. Matthew Taylor is the world's leading scholar of religion on the New Apostolic Reformation. In *The Violent Take It by Force*, he clearly and succinctly explains how the NAR grew from the work of C. Peter Wagner and flowered into a present-day spiritual and political juggernaut. Taylor has the training to notice broad trends, to place the NAR in historical context, and to articulate its theological avenues. But he also has the patience to follow every NAR prophet and apostle to the corners of their ministries, locating them on the ground in congregations and communities across the world. This is what makes *The Violent Take It by Force* one of the most important books on religion to appear in the last several years. Every once in a while a book comes along that changes not only its field, but how many of us understand the past and future of the United States. This is one of those books."

—**Bradley Onishi**, author of *Preparing for War* and host of the *Straight White American Jesus* podcast

"The New Apostolic Reformation is filled with characters, and in *The Violent Take It by Force*, Matthew D. Taylor brings major figures of the movement—their spirituality, their political ambition, and their proximity to the January 6 insurrection—to life. Taylor's work illuminates the NAR's aim to shape religion and politics in the 2024 election cycle and beyond."

—**Leah Payne**, author of *God Gave Rock and Roll to You*

"If you think you've already read everything you need to understand American Christian nationalism, think again. The movement is more diverse than many realize. And nobody knows its charismatic and violent elements better than Matthew D. Taylor. The cynical should pay attention. At the center of this movement aren't politicians parroting empty rhetoric; they're soldiers at war, with cosmic stakes. And these aren't leaderless mobs of rioters; they're organized, playing the long game. If you find this book disconcerting, you are paying attention."

—**Samuel L. Perry**, author of *Taking America Back for God* and *The Flag and the Cross*

"Matthew Taylor has written an essential guide to the radical charismatic Christian movement that catapulted from the fringes of evangelicalism to the center of Republican politics in the Trump era. *The Violent Take It by Force* takes us deep inside this fantastical world of spiritual warfare by self-declared prophets, with a vivid portrait of how these Christian supremacists market themselves to pews and politicians, and how their radical goals pose a dire threat to democracy."

—**Sarah Posner**, author of *Unholy: Why White Evangelicals Worship at the Altar of Donald Trump*

"As Matthew Taylor details in his fascinating and revelatory book, Independent Charismatic religious leaders, who twenty years ago would have been shunned by the mainstream Christian Right, are now front-line captains in the American culture wars, offering biblical rationales for the embrace of radically theocratic, authoritarian agendas. Taylor's sensitively reported exploration is a vital contribution to our understanding of the crisis facing democracy."

—**Katherine Stewart**, author of *The Power Worshippers*

"This astounding book is the inside story of the theology that both undergirded and inspired the January 6 insurrection and has continued to grow into the greatest religious threat to democracy this election year. Beyond the importance of politics, we need to change the 'faith factor' at this urgent moment. Only a good theology of democracy can replace the idolatrous false worship of Christian nationalism, which turns a distorted concept of spiritual warfare into political violence. Matthew Taylor's brilliant work here is a great place to start in our understanding of how bad religion must be replaced by true faith."

—**Jim Wallis**, director of the Center on Faith and
Justice at Georgetown University and author of
*The False White Gospel: Rejecting Christian Nationalism,
Reclaiming True Faith, and Refounding Democracy*

"Matthew D. Taylor's work is a gift. He has given us an empathetic, fair-minded, highly intelligent, and eminently readable story that explains one of the most important religious movements in modern America. Most people don't even know what the New Apostolic Reformation is, much less that it has been a driving force of Christian Trumpism. *The Violent Take It by Force* will change that."

—**Jon Ward**, author of *Testimony* and *Camelot's End*

THE VIOLENT TAKE IT BY FORCE

MATTHEW D. TAYLOR

THE VIOLENT TAKE IT BY FORCE

THE CHRISTIAN MOVEMENT THAT IS THREATENING OUR DEMOCRACY

Broadleaf Books
Minneapolis

THE VIOLENT TAKE IT BY FORCE
The Christian Movement That Is Threatening Our Democracy

29 28 27 26 25 24   2 3 4 5 6 7 8 9

Unless otherwise indicated, passages from the Bible are taken from the New King James Version®. Copyright © 1982 by Thomas Nelson. Used by permission. All rights reserved.

Early drafts of some of these chapters appeared on the Charismatic Revival Fury audiodocumentary series of the *Straight White American Jesus* podcast, https://www.straightwhiteamericanjesus.com/.

Library of Congress Cataloging-in-Publication Data

Names: Taylor, Matthew D., author.
Title: The violent take it by force : the Christian movement that is
  threatening our democracy / Matthew D. Taylor.
Description: Minneapolis : Broadleaf Books, 2024. | Includes
  bibliographical references and index.
Identifiers: LCCN 2023053477 (print) | LCCN 2023053478 (ebook) | ISBN
  9781506497785 (print) | ISBN 9781506497792 (ebook)
Subjects: LCSH: Evangelicalism—United States—History—21st century. |
  Evangelicalism—Political aspects—United States. | Presidents—United
  States—Election, 2016. | Capitol Riot, Washington, D.C., 2021. |
  Voting—Religious aspects—Christianity. | Trump, Donald, 1946-
Classification: LCC BR1642.U5 T45 2024 (print) | LCC BR1642.U5 (ebook) |
  DDC 322/.10973—dc23/eng/20240323
LC record available at https://lccn.loc.gov/2023053477
LC ebook record available at https://lccn.loc.gov/2023053478

Cover image: © 2023 Getty Images; Rear view of young women protesting for equal rights while marching in city/1146162874 by Maskot © 2023 Getty Images; Rainy day on a street leading to the United States Capitol, Washington, DC, USA/1461207519 by Marc Guitard © 2023 Getty Images; Cheering crowd during concert/979493964 by Stephanie Canarte © 2023 Getty Images; Concert Hands In Air
Cover design: Broadleaf Books

Print ISBN: 978-1-5064-9778-5
eBook ISBN: 978-1-5064-9779-2

In proportion as a nation assumes a democratic condition of society, and as communities display democratic propensities, it becomes more and more dangerous to connect religion with political institutions; for the time is coming when authority will be bandied from hand to hand, when political theories will succeed each other, and when men, laws, and constitutions will disappear, or be modified from day to day, and this, not for a season only, but unceasingly. Agitation and mutability are inherent in the nature of democratic republics, just as stagnation and inertness are the law of absolute monarchies.

If the Americans, who change the head of the Government once in four years, who elect new legislators every two years, and renew the provincial officers every twelvemonth; if the Americans, who have abandoned the political world to the attempts of innovators, had not placed religion beyond their reach, where could it abide in the ebb and flow of human opinions? where would that respect which belongs to it be paid, amidst the struggles of faction? and what would become of its immortality, in the midst of perpetual decay?

—Alexis de Tocqueville

CONTENTS

CONTENTS

INTRODUCTION

WHEN THE RIOTING started in earnest, the Christian leaders mostly held back. Bundled in parkas and hats against the frigid January air, they knelt and prayed with fervent tones and feverish emotion. Some participated in prayer conference calls on their cell phones or live streamed the frenzy and fury around them. A few joined the expletive-screaming throngs forcing their way into the Capitol Building, but most waited outside with the restive crowds.

These Christian leaders weren't passive so much as expectant—waiting for God to show up. They prayed. They worshipped. They decreed and declared and sang and beseeched. They did battle in the spirit realm. There on the sprawling Capitol Grounds, they prepared for God's promised deliverance. They pined for a miracle that did not materialize.

We Americans have spent years now grappling with the aftermath of January 6, 2021—the day American democracy came to the brink of collapse. There have been endless reports, thousands of legal proceedings, congressional hearings, and media investigations of the insurrection. We think we know the story: Donald Trump refusing to concede the 2020 election; his legal team trying dozens of ways to litigate his frivolous claims, all unsuccessfully; and his call for crowds of supporters to descend on Washington, DC, on January 6 to prevent the final certification of the election. We know the shape of that day, its contours: Trump instigating the crowds to "fight like hell" at a rally on the National Mall and then those crowds storming the Capitol, led by Proud Boys' and Oath Keepers' shock troops.

But a crucial side of that story has not been fully told. Christian symbolism, Christian prayers, Christian music, and Christian citations of the Bible were rife among the riotous crowds. And this seemingly jumbled array of Christian symbols and utterances, dispersed around the besieged Capitol, baffled and disoriented many who noticed it. Who can forget the QAnon

Shaman—a quixotic American religious figure if there ever was one—
tattooed, shirtless, bellowing, then courteously removing his bull-horned
hat to pray an overtly Christian prayer in the Senate chamber? Or the "Jesus
is my Savior, Trump is my President" flags? Or the Proud Boys kneeling in
prayer before stomping off to crack some skulls? As Peter Manseau, curator
of American Religious History at the Smithsonian, put it, religion was not
a piece of the story of that day; it was "*the* story of what happened" on
January 6.[1]

But that true statement raises many questions: Whose religion? What
sort of religion? What genre of Christianity was on display? How did religion
serve as a propellant for a patently political rebellion that sought to overturn
a national election?

In *The Violent Take It by Force*, you'll read about a particular form of
American Christianity whose escalating radicalization poses a real and immi-
nent threat to pluralism and democracy. Leaders from this group inspired
many of the visible expressions of Christian piety and forged the Christian
ethos of January 6. In these pages, we will investigate the Christian leaders
and the theological ideas that kindled the Capitol Riot.

If "follow the money" is a good journalistic dictum, "follow the theology" is an important corollary here. I'm less preoccupied with the foot-
soldier Christian believers who were among the hundreds of rioters entering
the Capitol or the thousands in the supportive crowds surrounding the
building. I want to understand the ringleaders, the instigators: the people
I'm calling the principal theological architects of the Capitol Riot.

None of the major characters of this book—all of whom were either
present at the riot or whose ideas were widely invoked that day—have faced
any legal prosecution or congressional scrutiny for their role in January 6.
If anything, these leaders' radicalism, their power, and their influence have
grown since that day. And even if you are an avid religion-news consumer,
you may have never heard of them. They aren't among the A-list celebrities
of the religious right, like Phyllis Schlafly, Jerry Falwell, James Dobson, or
Tony Perkins. These are not household names outside of a certain niche of
American Christianity. But their ideas helped whip up an insurrection, and
their reach among devoted Christians is growing both in the United States
and globally.

The movement I track in this book is called the New Apostolic Reformation (NAR), and it has thrived in relative obscurity. This little-known but potent network of Christian leaders built the theology of Christian Trumpism and then inspired thousands of Christians to show up on January 6 to fight for Donald Trump. Further, the NAR's theological ideas around politics and spiritual warfare are increasingly setting the agenda for the religious right in America and quickening our polarized, zero-sum political environment.

The NAR is organized around a highly networked but loosely affiliated pantheon of charismatic preachers, pastors, celebrities, nonprofit leaders, and international entrepreneurs who understand themselves to be recreating the energy and vitality of the early Christian church. They believe that the church has languished for centuries in feebleness and aimlessness, led by timid pastors and functionary priests—until now. Now, they believe, in these momentous latter days, God has reinvigorated the church through the Holy Spirit-backed renewed leadership of apostles and prophets. They believe that Christians need to conquer the high places of influence in society and govern from the top down. Engaged in a cosmic spiritual war against the forces of darkness, they believe God has mandated them to use spiritual violence to defeat Satan and then build the kingdom of God on earth.

I have spent months and months immersed in the data of January 6, including legal filings and massive databases of social media posts and videos from that day. Digging deeply into the social networks and ideational formation of hundreds of Christians who were there, I have tracked more than fifty charismatic Christian leaders to Washington, DC, on January 6. *Charismatic* here does not mean "appealing" or "magnetic" in personality; I use it here as a technical term of Christian belief and practice that emphasizes the supernatural dimensions of Christian experience. Some of these charismatic Christian leaders from the Capitol Riot are local pastors or heads of small ministries, and some are international Christian celebrities. Among the January 6 religious celebrities in attendance was a cadre of top NAR leaders you will get to know in this book.

So while images of the Q Shaman may be burned into our collective memory, when you dig a bit deeper, you'll see signs of charismatic influence everywhere on January 6:

- Many in attendance that day were doing a "Jericho March." They saw it as the culmination of a series of dozens of such Jericho Marches in the preceding months. Like January 6, these previous events entailed intercessory prayers, worship music, shofar-blowings, and marching around government buildings in swing-state capitals and in Washington, DC.[2]
- Dozens of people arranged themselves in choir formation and sang Christian praise songs, a cappella, just yards from the besieged Capitol. "The Lord will fight the battle for his people when we cry aloud unto him," they sang, as onlookers listened and live streamed, "and he will crush the enemy."[3]
- A troupe of prophets roved through the enraged crowds at the steps of the Capitol, prophesying "against communism and against a spirit, a demonic spirit that wants to be unleashed in this country."[4]
- A pastor offered personalized prayers and blessings to people who had broken into the Capitol and who witnessed the shooting of Ashli Babbitt: "God, Lord, protect this soldier for you, this man that was brave. Father, Lord, I just declare right now [over] this lionheart that angels of God be protecting over him."[5]
- Many people in different parts of the surrounding crowds, evidently unrelated, made no attempt to enter the Capitol but repeatedly shouted or sang, "The blood of Jesus" toward the building.[6]
- Dozens of white flags emblazoned with a simple green pine tree and the phrase "An Appeal to Heaven" punctuated the roiling crowds. This flag, as we'll see, has become a totem for a prophetic movement to reconstitute America.[7]

You may not have noticed those manifestations of religion in the coverage of January 6. Or if you did, you might not have seen them as pieces of one coherent expression of American Christianity. But they are.

What Does Christian Nationalism Look Like?

Christian nationalism, the belief that America was founded by and for Christians, has become a catchall designation for the Americanized spirituality we saw on January 6. But there are many compartments and subdivisions of American Christian nationalism, and the broad-strokes label gets applied to a warren of different communities, ideologies, and theologies. Some of what gets called "Christian nationalism" is deadly serious, and other manifestations are actually fairly benign and sentimental. I'm a religion scholar, and the fact that some churches sing historic Christian nationalist hymns like "God Bless America" or the "Battle Hymn of the Republic" doesn't keep me up at night. Such mashups of piety and patriotism aren't my cup of tea, but neither do they pose a grave hazard to American democracy.

Other versions of American Christian nationalism are overtly racist and white supremacist or misogynistic and, clearly, are not benign at all. Those are real and malignant forms of Christian nationalism. However, those openly racist and misogynist tendencies are not precisely what I have in view here either. Indeed, this investigation into the NAR and the broader phenomenon of what we might call *the Independent Charismatic style of Christian nationalism* may surprise readers who come with a strong prior impression of what Christian nationalism looks like.

First, outside observers of Christian nationalism often assume that it is a uniformly white, racialized phenomenon, bound up with American racism and nativism; hence, many analysts prefer to write about *white Christian nationalism*.[8] The Independent Charismatic corner of American Christianity, as we will see, is highly multiethnic and even transnational in its orientation. Indeed, among the religious leaders who were designated advisers to Donald Trump, almost all the Christian leaders of color in those circles were Independent Charismatics.[9] This is not to say that race and racism are not relevant here; they certainly are. But it's a more perplexing picture of race and religion than one might surmise at first glance.

Second, observers frequently draw an explicit connection between Christian nationalism and patriarchy. As sociologists Andrew Whitehead and Samuel Perry write, "Christian nationalism advocates for a particular social order that lionizes hierarchies between men and women."[10] This is broadly true, and Independent Charismatic leaders and communities certainly do have strong views on gender and gender-attuned topics like abortion. But we'll also discover their surprisingly egalitarian sensibility when it comes to gender and leadership, with women moving within every echelon of charismatic religious leadership in a way that scandalizes other Christian nationalists and many other Christian traditions.

Third, it is commonly asserted that Christian nationalism is detached from Christian belief. As one popular resource claims, it is "a cultural framework . . . [that] is more about identity than religion," implying that Christian nationalists subordinate theology and biblical interpretation to more mundane political interests.[11] But I'm going to argue that the NAR's long-standing alliance with Donald Trump (not to mention their mobilization for January 6) has been every bit as much about theology and biblical interpretation as it ever was about politics.

I raise all this not to invalidate or undermine existing conversations about American Christian nationalism but to illustrate why we need more in-depth examinations of the strands and subcurrents within it. The predominant form of Christian nationalism that generated the Christian countenance of the Capitol Riot was not simply reducible to racist, misogynistic, or abstract political motivations. The Capitol Riot was also propelled by potent theological ideas.

The Charismaticization of Right-Wing Politics

Beyond the Capitol Riot and its Independent Charismatic Christian instigators, this is a book about a series of tectonic shifts that have occurred in recent decades, a subterranean yet exceedingly significant revolution in the leadership of the religious right in America. We will explore this little-understood world of Independent Charismatic Christianity, an ethos and a segment of evangelicalism that is rapidly expanding both nationally and globally. Through interviews with dozens of NAR and other Independent Charismatic leaders, some of whom were there on January 6, and through archival research, I have gained an unprecedented level of access to how they understand themselves, the relational and social dynamics among these leaders, and what motivates them.

The spaces, networks, and ideas that we'll explore in these pages are among the most poorly understood domains of Christianity by outside observers. A diagram can offer a simple taxonomy for locating these groups in the larger landscape of American Christianity. While it's not meant to be

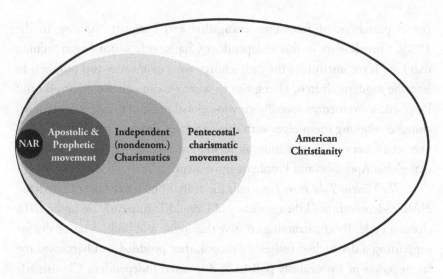

Fig. 0.1 Taxonomy of Independent Charismatics and the New Apostolic Reformation within American Christianity.

proportional, this can illuminate the way the leaders and ideas in this book are nested within larger movements.

Many observers are accustomed to sorting American Christianity into simple buckets such as Catholic, evangelical, mainline Protestant, Historically Black Protestant, and Orthodox. But as I'll lay out with more complexity in the first chapter, the world of the Pentecostal-charismatic, sometimes just called *charismatic*, movements overlap with all those categories. In conversations with some American religion reporters, several of them have told me that these Pentecostal-charismatic folks are the most difficult to write about and report on because, while demographically sizable and important, they hold supernatural beliefs and practice a mystical spirituality that are peculiar and virtually unintelligible to outsiders.

And even within the mélange of Pentecostals and charismatics, the action of this book takes place among the amorphous nondenominational segment of charismatic Christianity, where there are few boundaries or overarching institutions. This is a distinct subculture *within* the evangelical subculture—the realm of nondenominational megachurches, of televangelism channels, of prophecy conferences, of healing revivals and prosperity gospel preachers, of free-range evangelists and exorcists. Starting in the 1980s, some leaders in this Independent Charismatic sector began arguing that God is reconstituting the early-church roles of apostles and prophets to lead the modern church, giving rise to what we can call the Apostolic and Prophetic movement, a speedily growing global trend of nondenominational churches aligning themselves with these apostles and prophets. The NAR is one set of networks—the most influential and controversial one—within that global Apostolic and Prophetic movement.

The Violent Take It by Force tells the story of how a cohort of respected NAR leaders embraced the candidacy of Donald Trump early on in the 2016 election cycle. By constructing creative theologies and biblical rationales for supporting a debauched real-estate mogul, they prodded and harnessed the latent power of a previously politically disjointed Independent Charismatic world. These seemingly fringe theologies—some with catchy titles like the Seven Mountain Mandate or the Cyrus Anointing—have leached into broader American evangelicalism, engendering aggressive and chauvinistic visions of Christian supremacy.

The events I describe in these pages have brought about a sea change in the leadership of right-wing Christianity in America. Independent Charismatic leaders, who twenty years ago would have been mocked by mainstream religious right leaders, are now frontline captains in the American culture wars. Amid the 2016 campaign and Trump's victory, George W. Bush's former chief of staff, Andrew Card, commented that "the rug of American politics used to have more rug than fringe. Today, the rug seems to have little rug and a lot of fringe."[12] Card was describing the radicalization of politics on the right in general, but we could use the same analogy to describe the radicalization and charismaticization of the religious right. Indeed, by the time Trump was inaugurated and running the country, the fringe had become the carpet.

My narrow focus on what used to be the evangelical fringe— Independent Charismatics and the NAR—is not intended to excuse or exonerate broader American evangelicalism for its authoritarian turn. Rather, it is to narrate the route by which a once purportedly principled and values-driven evangelical religiopolitical movement became obsessed with an autocratic and principleless individual. These are the leading-edge charismatic pastors and leaders who threw open the doors of evangelicalism to Trump. They have served as the early adopters, most ardent advocates, and die-hard avengers of Christian Trumpism. And the NAR leaders' militant theologies, violent rhetoric, and Christian mobilization efforts were inextricable from the happenings at the Capitol Riot.

Entry Points

While I didn't grow up in the NAR circles per se, I was raised next door to them theologically. The first thirty years of my life were spent as an evangelical in Southern California, caroming around among the same set of institutions that gave rise to the NAR, so I couldn't help but catch the edges of these leaders' influence. I have friends, acquaintances, and family members who've joined some of the churches and networks described in this book. I have seen firsthand how alluring and mesmerizing they can be.

After college, I went into evangelical Christian ministry, spending seven years working with college students, unwittingly sharing some of the same charismatic experiences and theologies I later discovered emerged alongside and through the NAR. I earned a master's degree in theology from Fuller Theological Seminary in Pasadena, California, the social and academic space in which the NAR was first conceived and incubated. Then I left that evangelical world and moved to Washington, DC, to Georgetown University, where I earned a PhD in religious studies with a focus on modern religious movements and Muslim-Christian relations. I also discovered a great affection for that historic, beautiful, and complicated capital city. I thought I had left behind the slightly idiosyncratic and hard-to-explain charismatic Southern California evangelical environment in which I came of age.

Then, on January 6, 2021, I watched with revulsion as the symbols and scriptures of evangelical Christianity were used to endorse a violent, antidemocratic attack. I cringed, trying to keep my preschool-age children from noticing the raging events on the TV, unable myself to look away as mobs of Christians overran some of the locations of my treasured memories of Washington, DC.

As someone who grew up proximal to this NAR movement and who has the theological and academic background to make some sense of it, I felt a certain responsibility to write this book. My analysis is rooted in the disciplines of religious studies, theology, and history, and I make every effort to be even-handed. But these pages do not contain some dispassionate, arms-length rendering. The book's very title should signal that I am out to warn against these ideas and the hyper-politicization of charismatic theology as a civic menace to American democracy. Yet I do not disdain these leaders. Given my background, I sympathize and even, on some level, identify with the NAR leaders and followers. I know how electrifying and life-altering an exciting new theological paradigm or charismatic experience can be. I understand how perceived manifestations of the supernatural—as mediated through truly captivating and talented human beings—can inspire deep-seated devotion.

If you read what critics write online about the NAR, you'll soon discover ill-informed opinions galore. Some people depict the NAR leaders as a kind of charismatic Illuminati, spookily manipulating American politics. Some Christians think the NAR leaders are heretics, others a cult. Still other commentators will say that the NAR leaders are frauds—hucksters out to grab power and money. I disagree with all these assessments. The NAR, and the broader Independent Charismatic arena in which it operates, offers a very plausible, popular, and even evangelical interpretation of Christianity. You will find the characters of this book citing the Bible with a facility and familiarity that rival most other Christian leaders. To many of their followers and fans, the characters of this book have unparalleled access to the mind and power of God.

My hope is to humanize these leaders—in both directions. That is, to their admirers and devotees, I try to situate them historically, locating their ideas and their supernatural claims within the realm of social forces and human motivations. But to their legion of critics, I'm also attempting to make intelligible a set of beliefs, practices, and ambitions that frequently seem bizarre to the uninitiated. I hope by the end of this book, you both understand what motivates the NAR leaders and recognize the grave peril their theological vision poses to pluralism and democracy in the United States and around the globe.

In this book, we'll ask: How does a group of talented, intelligent, and very capable people get religiously and politically radicalized? How do they come to believe they are God's anointed leaders in our time, hearing directly from God and battling against the devil? How do millions of people trust such leaders, even to the point of mobilizing to storm the US Capitol? And could they do it again?

The Violent Take It by Force

Littered among the endless scroll of social media posts about January 6 from charismatic Christians who were present at the Capitol or cheering them on at a distance are thousands of prophecies, exhortations to stand with Trump, and Bible verses. So many Bible verses. One of the most repeated biblical citations you can find there, appearing in post after post, is the passage in which Jesus said, "From the days of John the Baptist until now the kingdom of heaven suffers violence, and the violent take it by force" (Matt. 11:12).

Christian commentators disagree mightily about how to interpret this verse. Some argue that Jesus is lamenting the persecution of Christians by "the violent," a lá Herod executing Jesus's cousin, John the Baptist. In other words, they maintain that Jesus is being descriptive rather than prescriptive. Others argue that Jesus is using a positive metaphor of violence to describe the passionate intensity in laying spiritual claim to the kingdom of heaven

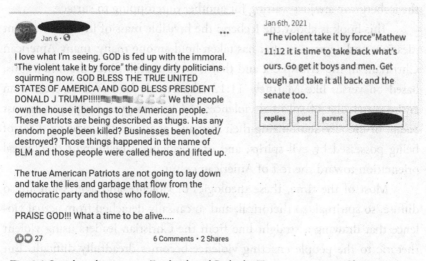

I love what I'm seeing. GOD is fed up with the immoral. "The violent take it by force" the dingy dirty politicians squirming now. GOD BLESS THE TRUE UNITED STATES OF AMERICA AND GOD BLESS PRESIDENT DONALD J TRUMP!!!!! ████ ██ ██ We the people own the house it belongs to the American people. These Patriots are being described as thugs. Has any random people been killed? Businesses been looted/destroyed? Those things happened in the name of BLM and those people were called heros and lifted up.

The true American Patriots are not going to lay down and take the lies and garbage that flow from the democratic party and those who follow.

PRAISE GOD!!! What a time to be alive.....

Jan 6th, 2021
"The violent take it by force" Mathew 11:12 it is time to take back what's ours. Go get it boys and men. Get tough and take it all back and the senate too.

Fig. 0.2 Social media posts on Facebook and Parler by Trump-supporting Christians on January 6, 2021.

"by force." Still others, like the NAR leaders we'll encounter in this book, understand this verse as a mandate, from the mouth of Jesus himself, for Christians to employ spiritual violence to advance the kingdom of God on earth.

Some Trump-supporting Bible-quoters, in the lead-up to January 6, amended their citations of the verse with one word: "the violent take it *back* by force." *Make America Great Again* became synonymous with the flourishing of the kingdom of God.

Experts in political violence and democracy tell us when a surge in violence threatens the democratic order, as we saw on January 6, that violence is merely the tip of the iceberg. The relatively small group of people who actually commit violence is only the visible outcropping, one that indicates the existence of a much larger mass of people who participate in the discourse of violence, believe violence is necessary, imagine and cheer on that violence, and support the people who commit it.[13] In short, if we stop our analysis of January 6 at the people who beat Capitol Police officers or trashed the seat of Congress, we miss the bigger picture of what transpired that day. For every person who assaulted the Capitol Building, thousands more were praying for and urging them on, either in person in the surrounding crowds or online at a distance. The rule of law involves the prosecution of those who commit antidemocratic political violence. But if we don't acknowledge and deal with the iceberg, we are just waiting for another outcropping to surface.

This book is about the iceberg: the invisible mass of invective, violent ideation, and aggression that has taken hold among many, many American Christians in the Trump era and that is with us still. Since the mid-1990s, based on verses like Matthew 11:12, charismatic leaders have created an entire vernacular of spiritual violence: of Christian war campaigns against Satan, of literally demonizing their human opponents by accusing them of being possessed by evil spirits, and of advancing a belligerent theological orientation toward the rest of American culture.

Most of the time, these theologies of violence and aggression are so diffuse, so spiritual, so rhetorical, and so causally detached from actual violence that drawing a straight line from the Christian leaders using violent rhetoric to the people enacting violence becomes dreadfully difficult. But the Trump administration and the aftermath of the 2020 election were crystallizing events—a turbulent microcosm that mirrored our embedded forms of extremism back to us. What had been subtext became text. What had been innuendo became a riot. The forcible discourse of spiritual violence tipped over into actual violence before our very eyes.

Just as we have been able to determine who the political and practical ringleaders, schemers, and organizers of January 6 were, we need to recognize the religious leaders who helped push our politics to the precipice. Which leaders inspired masses of Christians to show up on January 6? What symbols did they innovate and theologies did they operationalize? What epistemic assumptions and ecstatic visions drove the principal theological architects of January 6 to do what they did?

When you seek out the underlying leaders and the theologies that spurred thousands of Christians to pursue the illegitimate reinstatement of Donald Trump, you inevitably come to the people mentored and the ideas propagated by a renegade evangelical seminary professor, C. Peter Wagner, the "intellectual godfather" of the NAR.[14] Even though Wagner died in 2016, more than four years before the Capitol Riot, the unique group of leaders who amassed around him would create one of the major trajectories converging toward January 6 and become a profoundly aggravating force in America's polarized politics.

Yet before we meet Wagner and his disciples, we need to reckon with one of their most prominent allies: Paula White. This self-described "messed-up Mississippi girl" turned powerhouse preacher has helped to facilitate a massive reconfiguration of power in the religious right in the past decade. She gained a level of political influence during the Trump administration that was virtually unparalleled for any American religious figure in recent memory. Understanding her odyssey from obscurity to the halls of power and the Independent Charismatic world that has shaped her will set the stage for the rest of our investigation. Indeed, when the definitive history of Christianity in twenty-first-century America is written, Paula White will be, for good or for ill, a central character in that story.

❦ 1 ❦

A TELEVANGELIST IN THE
WHITE HOUSE

ON NOVEMBER 4, 2020, the day after the presidential election but before news outlets had officially called the race for Joe Biden, a pastor led a prayer service at her Florida church. Pastor Paula White rhythmically intoned prayers, imploring heaven to give Trump victory. She interspersed these prayers with speaking in tongues, a practice in which a charismatic believer utters ecstatic sounds that participants believe to be a heavenly language. White said, among other things:

> I hear a sound of abundance of rain. I hear a sound of victory. The Lord says, "It is done . . ."
>
> For angels have even been dispatched from Africa right now. . . . They're coming here. They're coming here in the name of Jesus from South America. . . .
>
> Angelic reinforcements, angelic reinforcements. For I hear the sound of victory. . . .
>
> We break and divide every demonic confederacy against the election, against America, against who you [God] have declared to be in the White House.

Short clips from that infamous service would soon sweep across You-Tube, social media, and news broadcasts. In the intense season surrounding the election, these clips were mocked mercilessly and held up as exhibit A to prove that Trump-supporting Christians had come unhinged.

White's words generated contempt for several reasons. First, for most Americans and, indeed, for most Christians, speaking in tongues, though written about in the Bible, is a foreign experience. Many assume speaking in tongues to be on the fringes of Christian expression or spirituality.

Second, beyond the fact that most people don't share White's worldview—about angels who can transfer intercontinentally by request—many critics detected something invidiously racist about her prayers. Asking for angels from Africa and South America to come and bolster a white American president—one whose administration had often made common cause with white nationalists—sounded all the wrong notes.

Third, many Christians are uncomfortable—theologically and culturally—with women preaching. So White's rhythmic and ecstatic delivery that day got filtered through latent misogyny and disdain for women religious leaders.

And the fourth reason she was so roundly criticized was, at the time that she prayed this, Paula White was a White House employee. She was the central spiritual adviser to President Trump. So these words were not emanating from some obscure pastor in a tiny church in the middle of nowhere. They were spoken by one of the most prominent Christian leaders in the country.

While this chapter focuses on Paula White, it is equally about the distinct Independent Charismatic Christian subculture in which she has grown up—a subculture that she, above all others, dragged from the margins into the mainstream of conservative American Christianity. No matter how you evaluate her sincerity or her character, White has served as the first female primary spiritual adviser to a US president, the first female clergy member to pray at a presidential inauguration, and the first pastor to officially preside over an American insurrection. But we'll get to that.

Paula White is the fulcrum on which an epochal shift in American religious politics tilted. Yet she inhabits a style of Christianity that is still opaque to many Americans. So learning about her life and ministry will familiarize you with that world, its history, its social dynamics, its celebrity culture, and how that celebrity culture got wrapped around Donald Trump and changed the political dispositions of millions of American Christian voters.

On our way to understanding Paula White's world, though, let's look at a conceptual model for understanding American Christianity, one that might help us keep straight where all the vivid characters of this book fit.

The Four Quadrants

The typical buckets into which we sort American Christians—evangelical Protestant, mainline Protestant, Historically Black Protestant, Catholic, and others—aren't so helpful for thinking about the leaders and followers who are at the heart of this book. Pentecostal and charismatic networks and streams simply cut across all these boundary markers. I propose we look at the landscape of American Christianity as four quadrants, determined by the answers to two questions: Does the individual Christian or community belong to a *denomination*? And is the Christian or community *charismatic*? Let me explain.

Denominations evolved to manage Protestant sectarianism. One of the core features of the Protestant Reformation in the sixteenth century was a renewed focus on reading and interpreting the Bible. But the early "Protestants"—they didn't all call themselves that—discovered that an "anyone can interpret the Bible for themselves" approach quickly gives way to an "everyone will interpret the Bible differently" reality. So the Protestant movements were highly schismatic from the start, disagreeing over matters of interpretation on topics sublime and mundane. They fought over how the church should be governed, what was happening theologically in the Lord's Supper, whether people should be baptized as infants or adults, and on and on. As these different versions of Protestantism crossed the Atlantic into the American colonies, the bureaucratic institutions we know as denominations emerged, as practical modern governance structures, to manage and contain this factionalism. *Protestant* became the umbrella term, with different Presbyterians, Lutherans, Baptists, Methodists, Episcopalians, and others enshrining their differences through denominations.

The term *charismatic* comes from a biblical idea contained in the writings in the New Testament that depict an early Christian church filled with supernatural manifestations and divine interventions. The Greek word *charisma* (plural *charismata*), which could literally be translated as "gifts" or "graces," was used among the early Christians to describe these extraordinary endowments from God, given to the church through the Holy Spirit. There are different lists of these *charismata* in the Bible, ranging from speaking in tongues, prophecy, miracles, and healings, on the flashy side, to more prosaic gifts like administration, teaching, and mercy. For most of Christian

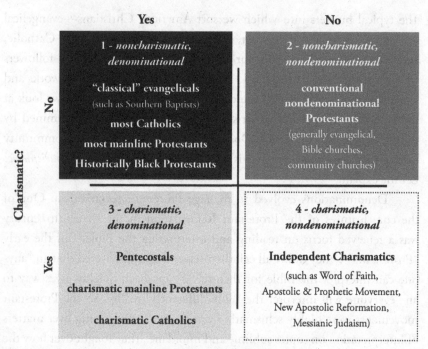

Denominational?

	Yes	**No**
No	1 - *noncharismatic, denominational* "classical" evangelicals (such as Southern Baptists) most Catholics most mainline Protestants Historically Black Protestants	2 - *noncharismatic, nondenominational* conventional nondenominational Protestants (generally evangelical, Bible churches, community churches)
Yes	3 - *charismatic, denominational* Pentecostals charismatic mainline Protestants charismatic Catholics	4 - *charismatic, nondenominational* Independent Charismatics (such as Word of Faith, Apostolic & Prophetic Movement, New Apostolic Reformation, Messianic Judaism)

Charismatic?

Fig. 1.1 A four-quadrant model of American Christianity.

history, most believers assumed that the more supernatural of these gifts either had been a special dispensation in the era of the early church or else were exceedingly rare. This assumption was thrown into question during the twentieth century, when multiple charismatic movements, starting with Pentecostalism, blossomed, premised on the idea that these dormant supernatural dimensions of Christianity were reappearing.

So we can map these two questions onto a two-axis grid to come up with four quadrants of American Christianity.

The first quadrant (noncharismatic, denominational) includes how most American Christians from the nineteenth century to the present would think of themselves: comfortably identifying with a denomination—or with the Roman Catholic Church, although my Catholic friends sometimes bristle at having the Protestant concept of a "denomination" applied to them. Among American Christians, this first quadrant is by far the largest.

Mainline Protestants are by definition denominational because to be mainline, historically, was to belong to one of the mainline denominations: Presbyterian Church (USA), Episcopal Church, United Church of Christ, and
so on. This quadrant is also where many Historically Black Protestants are.
And this is where I would put what I'm calling "classical" evangelicals: evangelicals who align with a denomination, such as the Southern Baptists, and
who might be open to some charismatic expressions or practices but do not
see them as an essential part of faith and practice.

The second quadrant (noncharismatic, nondenominational) represents a deep-rooted countervailing tendency in American Christianity.
Shortly after the American Revolution, some American Christians began
looking askance at denominational structures. When they read the Bible,
they didn't see anything like denominations bureaucratically managing congregations and shoring up theological divisions. Instead, they embraced a
restorationist model, intended to recover the authentic heart of the early
Christian church, and they jettisoned denominational distinctions in favor
of independent communities that could read the Bible for themselves and
govern themselves. People who belong to these communities typically identify as evangelical. Today many Christians are gravitating toward this nondenominational approach, and many congregations are choosing to disaffiliate
from their denominations. A 2020 survey of congregations found that, for
the first time in the history of the survey, nondenominational congregations
outpaced the largest Protestant denomination (Southern Baptists). More
than twenty-one million Americans identified as nondenominational Christians; that's 6.4 percent of the entire US population.[1] That survey didn't
delineate which of those nondenominational churches were charismatic, so
those twenty-one million people would be spread between the second and
fourth quadrants, making these two the smallest quadrants.

The leader who most typifies this second quadrant in my mind is John
MacArthur. MacArthur is famous for an austere theology, a willingness to
denounce anyone who disagrees with him—especially charismatics—and
leadership of a Christian college and seminary, his own little nondenominational fiefdom.

The third quadrant (charismatic, denominational) encompasses a
range of Christians who blend denominational belonging and charismatic

expressions. Most prominent in this quadrant are the Pentecostals, participants in a charismatic revival movement that broke out in the early twentieth century. The Pentecostals famously reinvigorated the practice of speaking
in tongues in the modern world, but they were also interested in other *charismata* like prophecy and healing. Fairly early on in Pentecostalism, the
movement leaders—who, like other Protestants, were prone to schism and
disagreements—appropriated the denominational model. Today most people who'd call themselves Pentecostals in the United States belong to one
of the Pentecostal denominations: the Assemblies of God, the Foursquare
Church, and the Church of God in Christ, among others.

Pentecostalism was racially diverse from the start, but the early Pentecostal interracial solidarity dissolved into division and strife, so most
American Pentecostal denominations today are coded as either primarily
Black or white. In the mid-twentieth century, the energy and dynamism
of this Pentecostal style of worship and prayer spread outside of the Pentecostal denominations into mainline Protestant and Catholic congregations. This shift was called the Charismatic Renewal at the time, and still
today, you can find small pockets of mainline churches that are spiritually
charismatic. Moreover, a huge swath of global Catholicism today is charismatic, with an estimated 215 million charismatic Catholics, mostly clus-
tered in the Global South (Africa, Latin America, and Asia).[2] US Supreme
Court Justice Amy Coney Barrett was raised in a charismatic Catholic
community.

The fourth quadrant (charismatic, nondenominational) is where this
book largely takes place. These are the so-called Independent Charismatics—
sometimes labeled "neocharismatics" or "neo-Pentecostals"—who enthusiastically embrace and pursue the supernatural expressions of Christianity
while also rejecting the bureaucracy and constraints of denominations. This
is the amorphous, tumultuous Wild West of the modern church. Fast-paced
and energetic, it is ethnically diverse and globally connected. It is also the
fastest-growing segment of Christianity in America.[3] Up until very recently,
these Independent Charismatics, to the degree that anyone thought of them
at all, were considered marginal, ostentatious, and kooky—until, that is,
Paula White and the other leaders we'll meet in this book took the Independent Charismatics mainstream.

This four-quadrant model illustrates how complicated American evangelicals are. A casual news consumer, particularly one with no personal experience of evangelicalism, might be tempted to think that evangelicals are a homogeneous group of conservative white Christians who all vote the same way and worship the same way. It's true that there are some common features among evangelicals: most share a love of direct Bible interpretation, an impulse to evangelize nonbelievers, certain theological emphases, and a generally conservative political outlook.

But if you look at the diagram, you'll see that there are people who call themselves evangelical in each of these four quadrants, yet they represent very different flavors of evangelicalism. *Evangelical* in the United States is a coalitional umbrella term, describing a heterogeneous mix of denominational and nondenominational churches and charismatic and noncharismatic spiritualities.

First-quadrant evangelicals inhabit denominations and will frequently identify as much with their denomination—"I'm a Southern Baptist," or "I go to a PCA (Presbyterian Church of America) church"—as they do with the title "evangelical." Second-quadrant evangelicals, who aren't interested in either charismaticism or denominations, will often say, "I'm just a Christian," or "I'm nondenominational," signaling that they don't want to play the first-quadrant identity-parsing game. Third-quadrant evangelicals, though they're often labeled "Pentecostals," usually are also keen to identify as evangelicals, although noncharismatic evangelicals have tended to treat tongue-speaking Pentecostals like weird cousins you pretend not to know. A recent study by sociologist Ryan Burge showed that the Pentecostals were more likely than any other denominational Protestants to identify as "evangelical or born-again," with 94 percent of Assemblies of God members and 91 percent of other Pentecostals saying they are evangelical.[4]

Fourth-quadrant evangelicals, the focus of this book, might share a lot of theology and political persuasions with other evangelicals, but they often experience a sense of alienation from their fellow evangelicals, particularly the first- and second-quadrant types. They feel a strong charismatic kinship with Pentecostals, even if they ultimately reject the denominational elements of American Pentecostalism.

Put simply, as important as knowing that someone is classified as an evangelical is understanding *what sort of evangelical they are.* We return now to the story of Paula White, but as you read the remainder of this book, this conceptual model will help you understand the oft-diverging impulses and identities within evangelicalism.

Paula White's Origins: "Messed-up Mississippi Girl"

Paula White's early life was marked by devastating trauma and suffering. She was born Paula Michelle Furr in Tupelo, Mississippi, in 1966. Her doting father and entrepreneurial mother owned two toy and craft stores, and Paula and her older half brother—a son her mother had with a high school sweetheart—felt the security to grow and enjoy life. Paula was an outgoing, precocious child. "She was born breech and she hasn't slowed down since," her mother reflected in one interview. "She interacted with everyone she came across. . . . She was very tenacious in whatever she decided to do."[5]

But her father had a gambling problem, began drinking heavily, and struggled to hold down a job, until finally her mother took the two kids to Memphis when Paula was five. Paula's father followed them to Memphis and showed up at their door one stormy night, frantic, drunk, and demanding that he take Paula with him or he'd kill himself. He got violent, shoving her mother into a wall, and her mother called the police, who took him to the station to sober up. Inexplicably, the police released him early, and Paula's father died while driving back to Tupelo later that same night when his car went into a sharp curve and crashed into an embankment.[6] Everyone, including Paula, assumed it was suicide, just as he'd threatened.

Her tragedies and traumas compounded in the wake of her father's death. In her grief, her mother began drinking heavily, and young Paula was often the one having to clean up her mother's messes and get her into bed. Starting in the first grade, Paula was repeatedly molested by a babysitter and the babysitter's boyfriend. She describes being "sexually and physically abused numerous times in horrific ways" by caregivers, relatives, and neighbors before she turned thirteen.[7]

Her mother married again to a military man who would eventually become a two-star admiral in the navy, so the family moved around a lot.

Unlike many of her carefree friends in high school, Paula never got into par-
tying or drinking because she didn't want to lose control the way her parents
had. But she developed bulimia, which contributed to a deep depression.
She describes herself at eighteen as "an old soul," blind to all but "the hope-
less carnage of today."[8]

As a desperate, serially abused teenager with an eating disorder, Paula
met and fell in love with Dean Knight, the charming lead singer in a local
band in Maryland, where Paula's family was living. It was Dean's uncle, who
lived out of state but was visiting one day, who first shared the gospel with
Paula. After explaining concepts like Jesus and sin and salvation, Dean's
uncle prayed a very charismatic prayer over her: "Please, Lord, let Paula
know she's not a victim of the things that have happened to her, that she's
not to blame. . . . Deliver her from the demonic torment of her past. Lord,
fill her now. Wash her in Your precious Holy Spirit. Show her who you are."[9]
This encounter was a transformative experience, and Paula describes feeling
as though years of burdens, pain, sin, and depression were being lifted.

Then, unexpectedly, Dean and Paula conceived a child out of wedlock.
Immediately Dean proposed, and they married hastily. The son they had
together, Brad Knight, is Paula's only biological child.

Paula and Dean joined the Damascus Church of God, a Pentecostal congregation where Dean had been raised. She remembers how striking
it was to see people speaking in tongues and doing a Jericho march, an
occasional Pentecostal-charismatic practice of marching around the church
praying, singing, and shouting for God's deliverance. All of this was new for
Paula, and she found it raw and exciting and liberating. She decided, "*This
is me.*"[10]

She threw herself into church life, volunteering to teach Sunday school
and joining in trips to feed the homeless in nearby Washington, DC. When
the church janitor quit, she volunteered to clean the church, eager to con-
tribute in whatever way she could. She began to attend Bible school at the
denomination's National Church of God in the nearby Washington, DC,
suburbs.[11] There at the Damascus Church of God, as she became increasingly involved, she met a man who would alter the trajectory of her life:
Randy White, a fifth-generation Pentecostal preacher.

This part of Paula's life story is complicated and contested, but it's also
the inception of her career in Christian leadership. The version Paula and

Randy would tell was that Paula was already separated from Dean and on the way to being divorced before she became involved with Randy, who was also separated from his wife and on the cusp of divorce. The Church of God denomination frowned on clergy being divorced, and Randy had stepped away from ministry to work at the US State Department. They started dating in 1989 for just a few months, married after their divorces were finalized, and moved to Tampa, Florida, in 1991. There they founded a new church.[12]

The story some of White's friends and fellow church members from that time tell is quite different. They say that Randy, eight years Paula's elder, was firmly in place as the associate pastor, with his father serving as the lead pastor, when they "became romantically involved" in 1987.[13] News of their relationship leaked out in the small church community, and one church member even publicly called out Pastor Randy and Paula's affair in the middle of a church service. This, friends say, led to Randy and Paula moving to a nearby town together, divorcing their spouses in 1989, and marrying each other in 1990. When challenged by reporters with this alternate version of her marriage's origins in 2008, Paula responded, "We cannot control the way our story is or has been reported, nor can we control gossip, innuendo, or other people's memories of events twenty years ago."[14]

What is clear is that her marriage to Randy White not only initiated a lasting surname change for Paula but also launched her into a career in charismatic ministry. It would become evident later that while Randy had the pastoral training and pedigree, Paula had the talent and driving ambition. With their move to Tampa, Florida, they were moving states—and, within our working model of American Christianity, we could also say they were switching quadrants. Randy had grown up within, and Paula had come to faith in, denominational Pentecostalism. But then they discovered firsthand how the strictures and accountability of denominationalism carried a real sting, with higher-ups frowning on Randy's divorce and pushing back on their remarriage. Denominations have rules and bylaws, standards, and disciplinary procedures for wayward clergy.

When they went on to found a new church in Tampa, they decided to have it be both charismatic and nondenominational. They were migrating into the fourth quadrant. They wrote on their new church's website, "Determined to make a difference, together both Randy and Paula rid themselves of denominational restraints and in 1991 with 5 founding members they launched a ministry of 'Evangelism and Restoration' known as South Tampa Christian Center."[15]

Paula White is certainly a singular figure, but her career is not without precedent. Let's pause the narrative of White's life for a moment and consider the life of another woman, one whose work still reverberates throughout the world of Pentecostal-charismatic Christianity.

Echoes of Aimee Semple McPherson

Part of the reason that Paula White, as a woman, could become a minister in the first place, let alone rise to the heights of religious leadership in the United States, was that she entered Christianity through Pentecostalism. Most evangelical churches in the first and second quadrants—that is, non-charismatic churches—still do not ordain women or allow them to serve in pastoral leadership roles. Mainline Protestant denominations have been ordaining women since the 1940s or 1950s, but Pentecostals were ordaining and elevating women in ministry forty years before that. Indeed, in classical Pentecostal history, the first person to speak in tongues in the modern era was a woman, Agnes Ozman, on January 1, 1901.

But the iconic Pentecostal woman who laid the track for Paula White is Aimee Semple McPherson. McPherson did for Pentecostalism in the early twentieth century what Paula White would do for Independent Charismaticism in the twenty-first: usher a fringe spirituality into the mainstream. McPherson wrote the script for how a talented woman wielding charismatic celebrity and media savvy could electrify America.

Raised in Ontario, Canada, Sister Aimee, as her devoted followers called her, caught the Pentecostal fire in 1907, at the age of seventeen, when an Irish Pentecostal preacher named Robert Semple came to town sermonizing about revival and being filled with the Spirit. Aimee was taken with both the message and the messenger, and after being baptized in the Spirit at the gathering, she married Robert Semple in 1908. Early Pentecostalism was fixated on spreading the Holy Spirit outpouring through overseas missions, and the young couple embarked for China as missionaries two years after they married, only to encounter tragedy. They both contracted malaria there, and Robert died.

Sister Aimee remarried shortly thereafter, to mild-mannered accountant Harold McPherson in Rhode Island, but Aimee's sense of calling and ambition to spread the kingdom of God led her to preaching at tent revival meetings to thousands of ardent converts. Her success and independence proved a source of real tension. The couple separated in 1918, and their messy divorce was finalized in 1921.

McPherson moved to Los Angeles in 1918 at the end of World War I and on the cusp of the Roaring Twenties. Despite her troubled marital status and her lack of formal ministry credentials, Sister Aimee promoted herself and her trendy version of Pentecostalism there via her entrepreneurial spirit, incalculable charm, organizational fortitude, and preaching panache. Over the decade of the 1920s, Sister Aimee would build her own five-thousand-seat megachurch, called Angelus Temple, where she preached three services on Sundays to packed-out crowds. She built and led her own Bible college, her own radio station, and her own denomination, the International Church of the Foursquare Gospel. In the words of McPherson's excellent biographer, Matthew Sutton, "Dazzling religious theatrics and a penchant for publicity made McPherson one of the most famous American personalities of the interwar years. . . . She combined the old-time faith, show biz sensibilities, marketing savvy, and passionate Americanism" to popularize her Pentecostal-style evangelicalism.[16]

Like Paula White, McPherson was a controversial and polarizing character in her time. Critics argued that Sister Aimee promoted flash over substance, bringing too much Hollywood show business flair into religion. She was a fashion icon in her time, rubbing shoulders with Hollywood celebrities. Moreover, her very public and messy divorce, as well as rumors of affairs, generated accusations of hypocrisy.

Then, in May 1926, Sister Aimee disappeared. Beachcombers and deep-sea divers at the beach in Santa Monica where she was last seen searched in vain for her body, and after several weeks, her family held a memorial service. Three days after her funeral, Aimee mysteriously turned up in Arizona, with a wild tale of having been kidnapped by a nefarious couple, smuggled into Mexico, and finally escaping her captors to freedom. The press rabidly covered this dramatic saga, making it front-page national news. Los Angeles prosecutors and many in the broader public remained skeptical, and a grand jury was empaneled to investigate whether McPherson had lied and committed perjury. She was put on trial, but prosecutors eventually dropped the case.

Though not overtly partisan, McPherson also threw herself into local and national politics. She opposed both communism and fascism. But she also argued for a robust and charismatic form of Christian nationalism and against the separation of church and state, believing that "only a national revival led by born-again Christians baptized in the Holy Spirit could restore the United States to its privileged position as God's modern-day holy land." When Sister Aimee launched a nationwide preaching tour, calling the nation "back to the Faith of Our Fathers," more than two million people—that's 2 percent of the entire nation—came out to attend one of the meetings, and millions more listened on the radio.[17]

As Aimee Semple McPherson's career shows, charismatic Christianity could open up incredible opportunities for resourceful female religious leaders. But the celebrity that comes with such leadership is a double-edged sword. Streetwise charismatic leaders must be entrepreneurs, creating their own mythology and history in real time. The qualities that constitute charismatic leadership—an air of mystery and supernatural power and insight—must be sustained over a long period of time, requiring a tightrope walk for anyone bold enough to seize the chance. Pentecostalism, from its earliest origins, was more gut level than cerebral. In essence, if people are showing up not out of some deep confessional loyalty or sense of traditional belonging but to be entertained and offered new experiences, well, that is a beast that must always be fed. Otherwise, it can turn unruly.

Paula White's Career: A Televangelist Therapist

When Randy and Paula White started South Tampa Christian Center in 1991, the church met in a small storefront that could barely seat fifty people. The couple was so poor and so invested in the church that they reportedly "lived on government cheese and peanut butter" some weeks.[18] But the Whites were full of gumption and willing to experiment. They built a portable stage on the back of a truck and took it all over Tampa's impoverished housing projects, conducting outdoor services. Their church motto was "We're the perfect church for the people who are not."[19] Their church grew so quickly that, within a few months, they had to move out of their original storefront location to a school cafeteria. By the end of 1991, the church had seven hundred members.[20]

In 1997, they changed the church name, ditching the humdrum "Christian Center" for the more universal and iconic "Without Walls International Church." The name was partly a joke; the church was growing so fast, they couldn't find a building to accommodate the five thousand weekly attendees. So by that time, they were meeting in a giant air-conditioned tent—literally, a church without walls. It was also remarkably racially diverse, at 30 percent white, 30 percent Latino, and 40 percent Black. Asked about the secret of their success, Paula responded, "When a church begins to get beyond its comfort zone, out of its four walls, it's going to grow because people are hungry. . . . The reason you're seeing the moving and growing of the Pentecostals is that there's a sense of belonging; we're meeting needs and we're saying to the community 'Hey, here's the Gospel, and it can be relevant to you.'"[21]

As remarkable as the success of the Whites' Without Walls Church was, it was part of a burgeoning trend: the megachurch movement. Megachurches—defined as Protestant congregations with more than two thousand people consistently attending weekly services—were almost unheard of when Aimee Semple McPherson was building Angelus Temple in the 1920s. But by the 1990s, they were big business. Scott Thumma, a scholar who studies megachurches, estimates that there were maybe ten megachurches in the United States in 1900. By 1980, it was 150. By 1990, it was 310. And by 2005, it was 1,210.[22] While megachurch numbers are difficult to compare with each other because of varying ways of counting "members" and "attendees," the Whites' Without Walls congregation was, by the early 2000s, regularly making top-ten lists of the largest churches in America. The congregation passed the twenty-thousand-member mark around 2006 when Paula was forty years old.[23]

Throughout this period, as her profile grew, Paula White began traveling the country to lead evangelistic services. A huge boost to her career came in the late 1990s when T. D. Jakes, one of the rising star Independent Charismatic Black preachers in the United States, endorsed her ministry and began to mentor her. He invited her to speak at his blockbuster conferences catering to women. With her ministry in Tampa, White had already established a strong power base among Black Pentecostals, and Jakes's support grew her influence even further. They became so close that White started calling him her "spiritual father."[24] This language of "spiritual father" or "spiritual mother" is very common in Independent Charismatic leadership circles, where, without the structures of denominational leadership hierarchies and seminary training, ambitious leaders defer to familial models of being raised and apprenticed.

In 1998, Paula approached Randy to say she felt God was calling her to begin a television ministry. He agreed to support it, and they discovered there was an early morning time slot available on Black Entertainment Television (BET). So Paula—a petite white woman from Mississippi—signed up to lead a Christian talk show on a cable channel for Black audiences. They cobbled together some rented furniture, a spare room in the church, a single TV camera, and a homemade black backdrop. She joked, "I'm the producer, the talent, the director, and just about everything else that goes into making a television program."[25] This is the beginning of Paula's independence from Randy.

As with many areas of her career, Paula proved to be phenomenally adept at being a Christian talk show host. Many televangelists' style of presentation is merely upbeat and promotional: they're always pitching a new message, a new fundraising drive, a new prophecy, a new lifestyle enhancer. But Paula White discovered the effectiveness of a more therapeutic posture. She could take her own trauma and heartache and poor life decisions and empathetically draw those same deep hurts out of her guests to get them talking. In one of her early shows, a religious leader panelist broke down crying when Paula asked about her father. The film crew's instinct was to stop shooting, but White signaled to them to continue recording. She recognized the power of emotional vulnerability to surface our common humanity.[26]

Sociologist Shayne Lee and historian Phillip Luke Sinitiere, who have studied White closely, argue that she represents "a nonconfrontational style of postfeminist leadership."[27] Through her talk show, they claim, White became "the 'Oprah' of the evangelical world by tackling the nitty-gritty, day-to-day realities of life and by finessing dialogues with celebrities and experts concerning various facets of self-actualization."[28] Other televangelism executives quickly began to recognize that Paula had a unique appeal, and her show began airing on other networks.

Through T. D. Jakes's sponsorship, her multiethnic congregation, and her popular show on BET, Paula White became especially famous within Black Pentecostal and charismatic communities. Her preaching style and cadence have clearly been shaped by the call-and-response, musicality, and physicality often associated with Black preaching. As her son, Brad Knight, once summarized, "The black community told her, 'You're a white girl who preaches black.'"[29]

Part of what made Randy and Paula White such a success was that they were preaching something called the *prosperity gospel*, or the *health and wealth gospel*. To be clear, virtually no one goes around saying, "I preach the prosperity gospel," and you won't find that phrase in White's books or her sermons. It's a polemical label, leveled as an accusation. Indeed, there are many different prosperity gospels, many contributing Christian theologies about wealth, health, and wholeness that get critiqued as teaching prosperity. Most of what gets called *prosperity gospel* today originates from within the Independent Charismatic sector into which Paula and Randy White had migrated in the early 1990s. So before we go much further in Paula's story, let's consider the social world and ecosystem in which she was operating. This is the historical backdrop for how Paula White—and all the major characters of this book—became so popular and influential.

Three Revivals That Defined the Independent Charismatic Sector

From the very start of the Pentecostal revivals in the late nineteenth and early twentieth centuries, some charismatic churches have remained independent, refusing to conform to denominational regulations and oversight. But for most of the twentieth century, these churches were relatively small, disconnected, and marginal.

In the post–World War II era, three important mutations to Pentecostalism realigned this peripheral Independent Charismatic world. All three are what Pentecostals and charismatics call *revivals*: intense, timebound, and geographically localized outbursts of piety and charismatic activity that they understand to be specially ordained manifestations of the Holy Spirit's work.

The first, which came to be called the Healing Revival, broke out in the 1940s and 1950s through a group of itinerant Pentecostal healing evangelists. By the late 1940s, Pentecostalism was due for a revival. The first-generation Pentecostal leaders were dying off—Aimee Semple McPherson died in 1944—and the younger Pentecostals were longing for renewal. Enter William Branham, an esoteric and eccentric preacher. In 1946, Branham was traveling around the Midwest, preaching and reportedly healing the sick and performing other miracles. Branham claimed that an angel traveled with him and healed people through him, and he evidently had supernatural insights, correctly identifying people's illnesses at a glance before, purportedly, healing them.

Though healing evangelists were often caricatured as scheming charlatans by outsiders, within the Pentecostal subculture, news of these healings spread rapidly and magnetized people with longing for similar revival experiences. Soon Branham had many imitators: upstart revivalists who wanted to travel, preach, and perform miracles. Despite the fact that Branham was, in historian C. Douglas Weaver's phrase, the "pacesetter for the revival," after the widespread movement started, Branham himself was plagued with health issues and accusations of fraud, diminishing his popularity.[30] His theology, followed by a small but ardent company of devotees, became more fringy, extreme, misogynistic, and racist, up until his death in 1965.

If Branham was the pacesetter, Gordon Lindsay was the publicist of the revival. A young Assemblies of God pastor, he came alongside Branham in the 1940s to coordinate and broadcast the revivals led by Branham and the other faith healers. As historian David E. Harrell Jr. summarizes the fruit of Lindsay's efforts, "By the early 1950s scores of healing evangelists filled tents and auditoriums around the country, attracting tens of thousands of people, reporting thousands of healings and other miracles, and collecting millions of dollars in contributions from supporters."[31] Lindsay would also go on in the 1970s to found Christ for the Nations Institute (CFNI), an unaccredited Pentecostal-charismatic training institute in Dallas, which will feature significantly in chapter 7. The year 1956 marked the apex of the revival, with nearly fifty of these traveling healing evangelists traversing North America and hundreds of thousands of people attending the meetings.

The most popular of the healing evangelists was Oral Roberts, a Pentecostal Holiness Church preacher. From 1947 to 1968, Roberts led more than three hundred multiday healing crusades and personally laid hands on and prayed for millions of people. But in 1955, Roberts made his most important contribution to Pentecostal-charismatic culture by creating a national weekly television show where he brought his healing message to distant millions who could never attend his meetings. Within two years, Roberts was appearing on enough networks to reach 80 percent of the American television audience.[32] He was the first major Pentecostal-charismatic televangelist, and he pioneered the genre of televised charismatic theology and faith application that Paula White would master in the following century. Roberts brought awareness of Pentecostal healing practices to many Americans who would never have darkened the flaps of a revival tent. By 1980, when Gallup conducted a survey of the best-known religious figures in America, they found that 84 percent of the American public knew who Oral Roberts was.[33] In 1965, Roberts founded an eponymous university in Tulsa, Oklahoma. Oral Roberts University is still an anchoring educational institution for Pentecostal-charismatic Christianity in the United States.

One of the itinerant healing evangelists from the 1950s who joined up with Lindsay's promotional efforts was a preacher named Kenneth Hagin. In 1966, Hagin would set up shop in Tulsa alongside his friend Oral Roberts and begin teaching about what was called the Word of Faith doctrine. He emphasized the need for bold faith, God's desire to heal and prosper devout Christians, and the need to speak your blessings into reality. These gut-level Word of Faith concepts and ideas proliferated out into the loose Independent Charismatic networks. This decentralized Word of Faith movement is where most of what is today called the *prosperity gospel* originates.

The healing revivalists became so popular, the historian Harrell writes, that their independent ministries "came to rival the Pentecostal denominations in size and world-wide influence."[34] This created obvious tensions between denominational Pentecostalism—then roughly half a century old, with established institutions—and the more freewheeling and largely unaccountable traveling healers. As the Pentecostal denominations denounced or distanced themselves from the new, controversial public faces of "Pentecostalism," the healing evangelists increasingly drifted into more welcoming and unregulated nondenominational charismatic spaces, what we're calling the fourth quadrant.

The second major Pentecostal revival was operating contemporaneously. A group of Pentecostal teachers at a Bible school in Saskatchewan were so taken by the healings and other charismatic experiences they witnessed at one of Branham's revivals that, in 1947, they began praying for revival at their school too. Through their prayers and revival meetings, a different awakening broke out in Saskatchewan, quickly spreading to other parts of Canada and the United States. This group called itself the Latter Rain, or, sometimes, the New Order of the Latter Rain. So from 1948 to the mid-1950s, two sweeping revivals were reconfiguring fourth-quadrant Christianity in America.

The Latter Rain name was a biblical reference to the distinct weather patterns in Israel, where the rainy season begins with heavy rain in October (the former rains) and ends with heavy rain in May (the latter rains). For Latter Rain theologians, the highly charismatic early church represented the former rains, and they believed they were prophetically living into the latter rains: an end-times deluge of the Holy Spirit. Similarly, they sensed that God was revealing that the task of the church was not merely rejuvenating ancient spiritual practices that had fallen by the wayside in Christian history, like the Pentecostal focus on speaking in tongues. No, the Latter Rain folks also believed that the world was on the cusp of a global Christian revival once the proper government of the church was restored.

Frustrated with slow-moving and bureaucratic denominations, the Latter Rain leaders especially fixated on passages in the book of Ephesians, including Ephesians 2:20, which says that Christ's church is "built upon the foundation of the apostles and prophets," and Ephesians 4:11, where the author describes five leadership gifts Jesus bestowed on the church: apostles, prophets, evangelists, teachers, and pastors. The Latter Rain mystics believed that, although the roles of supernaturally guided apostles and prophets had died out after the early church era, giving way to centuries of bureaucratic bishops and timid pastors, God would soon commission new Spirit-filled apostles and prophets to lead God's people and bring about an end-times victorious church.

This Ephesians list of five gifts, and the aligning of church leadership around them, is often called the *fivefold ministry* model by proponents, and it usually includes an emphasis on the centrality of apostles and prophets. Slowly, over the next few decades, these fivefold teachings and prophecies spread into the diffuse Independent Charismatic networks. The Latter Rain teachings, though not enfolded into a single denomination or statement of faith, saturated many of these loose networks of nondenominational churches, forming what Mark Chironna, who has spent most of his life navigating those networks, calls "part of the subcultural language" binding them together.[35]

The third revival came in the 1960s and 1970s and was centered in California. This revival is usually called the Jesus People or the Jesus Movement. Not all Jesus People communities were charismatic, but most were, so that the movement, in historian Larry Eskridge's words, "seemed to be awash in a Pentecostal ethos of glossolalia [speaking in tongues], prophecy, 'words of knowledge,' 'singing in the Spirit,' and divine healing."[36]

Many of the Jesus People were hippies or ex-hippies, with an aesthetic akin to the 1960s countercultural movement. They emphasized Jesus as an iconoclastic, revolutionary figure, and they scorned more established mainline and evangelical churches as being hopelessly conformist. They sought mystical experiences through Christian worship and the new genre of Christian rock and roll they helped invent. In their suspicion of established practices, the Jesus People converts were particularly attracted to churches that were both nondenominational and charismatic. It's also worth noting that many of the excited new converts among the Jesus People were Jewish, and they wound up taking over or building new Jewish-Christian institutions that led to the creation of the concept and movement of Messianic Judaism: a controversial, predominantly Independent Charismatic movement of ethnically Jewish and theologically Christian people.

These three revivals, spanning four decades, shaped the Independent Charismatic sphere in the United States. All these overlapping waves of revivals and the networked-but-nondenominational character of the Independent

Charismatic space have created a distinct leadership culture, within which all the characters of this book have proven quite skilled navigators.

The Culture of Independent Charismaticism

Charismatics are among the most innovative, media-savvy, and pathbreaking Christians out there. Every new technology—from magazines to radio to television to music to Facebook to YouTube—has been utilized by charismatics to drive their message home. Independent Charismatic worship music provides the soundtrack for other evangelicals. Additionally, the past fifty years have witnessed the growth of a colossal Independent Charismatic media sphere, one that most people outside that world are barely even aware of: charismatic news sites and magazines like *Charisma News*; charismatic television networks, such as Trinity Broadcasting Network and GOD TV; charismatic YouTube channels where prophets post their sometimes daily prophecies; and innumerable websites and social media pages that promote the charismatic celebrity class. And that's just in the United States. Dig even an inch into these media, and you will find webs of communication and relationship that span the globe and touch every continent.

Independent Charismatic leaders are entrepreneurial, whether they brand themselves as pastors, prophets, apostles, worship leaders, Messianic rabbis, evangelists, revivalists, faith healers, or spiritual life coaches. They are autonomous, managing their own ministries and churches, but they are also supremely collaborative. Over the past fifty years, certain social conventions have been established in these elite charismatic circles: go along to get along; you don't have to agree with someone 100 percent to be partners; develop your own schtick, and don't steal someone else's; respect your elders; lend your credibility to friends or future friends when you're on a stage with them; find spiritual fathers and spiritual mothers who will sponsor your rise; and, most of all, remember the goal: revival, revival, revival.

As much as these rules might seem calculating or cynical, I believe most of these leaders are utterly sincere and just following the incentives and laws of nature within the Independent Charismatic ecosystem. This is not a world of distinct boundaries, agreed-on statements of faith, or purity tests; that's what denominations are for! All roles are open to men and women and people of any race as long as they've got the gifting. Formal, accredited training is rare, so most Independent Charismatic leaders, like Paula White, apprentice themselves to people they want to emulate. If you read an Independent Charismatic leader's bio, you likely won't find academic credentials but accomplishments, mentors, and stylistic branding.

Depending on their background, Independent Charismatic leaders will sometimes speak of themselves as continuationists—as in the supernatural gifts of the Spirit continue today—and sometimes as evangelicals, or Pentecostals, or Spirit-filled. Those are all acceptable forms of identification. Independent Charismatic leaders may also speak about evangelicals as a group that they are *not* part of—meaning, particularly, first- and second-quadrant, noncharismatic, "mainstream" evangelicals. Yet I would argue that they are undeniably part of the broader phenomenon that we call *evangelicalism*.

Three brief analogies may help us make sense of this unusual religious leadership and social culture. First, it's a lot like Hollywood. The path to success is celebrity, and celebrity often depends on lucky breaks and who you know. New projects, new conferences, new concepts are constantly being put forward and assembled by entrepreneurial leaders. In Hollywood, fans don't have to choose between their love for Natalie Portman and their love for Gwyneth Paltrow; similarly, Independent Charismatic followers generally do not feel the need to follow only one apostle or megachurch pastor. Instead, Independent Charismatic leaders form different clusters and constellations of support and fandom.

Second, Independent Charismatic leadership culture is like a marketplace. In fact, it literally *is* a marketplace, in which huge sums of money flow through merchandising, ministry donations, worship-music sales, and television channels. But it's also a marketplace of ideas, where each leader is finding their style or signature idea and promoting their brands and their memes. Leaders are always looking for their angle, the message or meme that will make them iconic.

Third, we could say that Independent Charismatic leadership culture is, ideologically, a lot like a lava lamp: you can distinguish certain movements—they prefer the language of "streams"—but those movements are constantly combining and recombining. It is not contradictory to simultaneously call yourself a pastor, an apostle, a Word of Faith preacher, a revivalist, and a social media personality. The NAR's ideology is hard to track precisely because it is suspended within this ooze, along with so many other Independent Charismatic streams, endlessly merging within individual figures and ministries.

So now we can see more plainly why Paula White has had such phenomenal success. White was part of the first generation of Independent Charismatic leaders who navigated—and shaped the rules for navigating— the emerging internet and social media landscape. She proved herself to be extremely flexible and adept at playing this unique game by its unique rules, far more so than her husband, Randy. White assembled a distinct brand: white woman skilled in the idiom of Black Pentecostalism and vouched for and mentored by Black leaders like T. D. Jakes; therapeutic preacher with some Word of Faith / prosperity teachings in the mix; megachurch pastor; and "Oprah" to evangelicals.

Independent Charismatic celebrity culture mingles very well with other forms of celebrity. Independent Charismatic leaders often have tens or hundreds of thousands of fans clamoring for their attention. They're scrappy and entrepreneurial, and other celebrities apparently sense an affinity with them. In Paula White's case, hosting a Christian talk show meant she was hobnobbing with a lot of famous guests.

As Without Walls International Church became one of the largest megachurches in the country in the late 1990s and early 2000s, professional athletes, including football star Deion Sanders and baseball star Darryl Strawberry, started attending. Paula was invited to lead a Bible study with any interested New York Yankees players when she was in town. This opened doors to similar opportunities with the New York Mets and then other NBA and NFL teams. When Michael Jackson was in crisis in 2003, having been charged with sexually abusing a boy, Paula was invited out to Jackson's Neverland Ranch to personally minister to the pop star. At one point in 2004, supermodel Tyra Banks, a friend of hers, gave Paula a fashion photo shoot, and some of the photos ran in *Maxim* magazine with the headline "Sexy Televangelist." White also became the personal pastor of the performer Kid Rock and officiated his short-lived marriage to model Pamela Anderson in 2006.

This is the context in which Paula White, in 2002, out of the blue, received a phone call from Donald Trump.

Paula White's Growth: Becoming Apostolic

To hear White tell the story, Trump is quite the preaching connoisseur. On the phone that day, the real-estate tycoon told White that he had seen her talk show and some of her sermons on TV while staying at his Mar-a-Lago estate, and he told her, "You have the *it* factor." She offered the half-joking rejoinder, "Sir, we call that the anointing."[37] Trump then recounted to White, point by point, three of her sermons on "the value of riches" that he had particularly appreciated.[38]

Trump had spent years watching preachers on TV and evaluating their techniques, according to White, and he spent the rest of the phone call discussing and dissecting his favorite preachers' styles. He loves Billy Graham and Jimmy Swaggart, and he reserves a special place of affection for the famed Manhattan pastor Norman Vincent Peale. Peale was famous for his "power of positive thinking" approach to the gospel, which is a kind of noncharismatic version of the prosperity gospel. Trump had attended Peale's church for years, and after Peale's death, he struggled to find other sermonizers who could rival the Manhattan preacher.[39] Indeed, author Christopher Lane writes, "Trump [has] named Peale and his writings among his strongest influences."[40]

White describes a feeling she got from God as their friendship developed: "that Trump is 'a spiritual assignment for me,' that I am to pray over him daily and show him God. So I do."[41] Trump would later be a featured guest on White's talk show, and she wound up purchasing a $3.5 million condo in Trump Tower in New York. So while many Americans outside of charismatic circles had never heard of her before 2016, Paula White has served as Donald Trump's personal pastor for more than twenty years.

When it comes to her marriage and ministry, Paula White avers that she was never in it for the money and fancy lifestyle. If anything, that was more Randy's fixation. In her 2019 autobiography, Randy comes across as the villain. He's the one who initiated their romantic relationship despite their existing marriages; he had affairs during their marriage; he was obsessed with money and fame; he was emotionally abusive and controlling; he sometimes threatened suicide in desperation. Many of Paula's critics are suspicious of this narrative, but the tawdry or exculpatory details of their marriage are not the point here; by 2004, it was clear that they were headed for divorce.

Then in 2006, Randy's eldest daughter from his first marriage, Paula's stepdaughter, was diagnosed with terminal brain cancer at the age of twenty-eight. This crisis and her eventual death a year and a half later, both delayed and cemented their impending divorce. Divorce is almost always messy, but this was worse than most: they were co-pastors of one of the largest churches in the United States, and they were both religious celebrities.

On the heels of their divorce announcement in 2007 came more devastating news for White. Senator Chuck Grassley revealed that the Senate Committee on Finance was opening an inquiry into the tax-exempt status of certain religious organizations: namely, six ministries led by Independent Charismatic prosperity preachers. The Whites were on the list. These triple crises brought about a destabilizing season for Paula as she tried to simultaneously divide up the ministry empire with Randy, skirt a congressional investigation, and grieve the loss of her stepdaughter.

By 2011, Without Walls International Church's property was under foreclosure, and it was forced to vacate its massive building, eventually entering into bankruptcy. Also in 2011, Senator Grassley published a scathing report on the Whites', and the other televangelists', decadent lifestyles and corrupt financial practices, although there were no penalties or ensuing prosecutions.[42] Randy White disintegrated under the compounding pressure and retreated from public view.

But Paula White landed on her feet. In 2011, she moved to Orlando and engineered herself into the role of senior pastor of a majority Black, prosperity-oriented, Independent Charismatic church called New Destiny Christian Center. This is also a muddled transition story involving the promising, dynamic, young Black founding pastor, Zachary Tims, whom Paula called a "spiritual son," dying of a drug overdose that year; Paula coming in as interim pastor, eventually being asked to stay on permanently; and Tims's ex-wife accusing White of manipulating the situation.[43] These are the sorts of thorny situations that denominations were created to avert or manage.

A subtle shift in White's status and theology emerged during this time, and that shift interests me more than the relational drama of these years. Somewhere in this liminal season, Paula White began picking up those old Latter Rain ideas about modern-day apostles. The process and timing of this theological evolution are not clear, and many sources are possible since these apostolic and prophetic ideas had been percolating for decades in Independent Charismatic networks.

One factor in the emergence of apostolic language in Paula White's ministry might be that New Destiny Christian Center, White's newly acquired church, had already embraced the Latter Rain concept of "fivefold ministry" before White got there.[44] A significant portion of charismatic Black fivefold ministries often get classified as part of "Black Pentecostalism" when they are actually nondenominational. In other words, observers assume they are part of denominational charismaticism (third quadrant), but they belong more properly in the fourth quadrant of my model. It's possible White was simply adopting the existing frameworks and theology of the new community.

Yet more influential than the church she took over leading, I believe, was the new spiritual father she found. Archbishop Nicholas Duncan-Williams is an Independent Charismatic Ghanaian apostle, part of the proliferation and flourishing of charismatic Christianity in Africa. He's sometimes referred to as the "Apostle of Strategic Prayer" for his emphasis on prophetic spiritual-warfare prayer.[45] But starting in 2012, alongside her entry into leading New Destiny church and right up to the present, Paula White, a white televangelist from Mississippi, has been looking to this Ghanaian apostle as her mentor and spiritual father. This is what I mean when I say that these Independent Charismatic (fourth quadrant) dynamics are transnational and involve webs of relationships that span the globe.

So in 2012, we find Paula White introducing herself to her new church and preaching about the need to move into an "apostolic reformation" and that "the prophetic always has to go along with the apostolic."[46] As an aside, some eager analysts have used this shift into apostolic language to claim that White was part of the NAR, but, as we'll see, the NAR was a set of networks built around C. Peter Wagner and his cohort of disciples. She did not, as far as I can find, even know Peter Wagner. White seems to be getting her own understanding of fivefold ministry and "the apostolic" through Duncan-Williams, whose intellectual lineage does trace back to some Latter Rain groups. He is part of the broader global Apostolic and Prophetic movement but is not directly tied to Wagner's NAR groups.[47]

Since at least 2012, through this Ghanaian apostle, Paula White has added "apostolic leader" to her brand. It was Archbishop Duncan-Williams who presided over Paula White's third marriage in 2014, this time to the keyboardist from the famed rock band Journey, Jonathan Cain. In 2019, Paula White would announce that she was renaming New Destiny Christian Center as City of Destiny church and that she was handing off pastoral leadership to her son, Brad Knight, so that she could serve as the church's "apostolic overseer" while also focusing on planting new churches.[48] This latest charismatic-apostolic rebranding of Paula White occurred just a few months before she officially became a White House employee.

Donald Trump and the Independent Charismatics

How did Donald Trump, a thrice-married, notoriously reprobate, real-estate tycoon and television personality win over millions of evangelical voters and gain their undying loyalty in the 2016 election and since? There are many ways to answer this question, but my argument in this book is that it had everything to do with Paula White and her Independent Charismatic celebrity class. I asked Stephen Strang—who, as founder and CEO of Charisma Media, which publishes *Charisma News* and *Charisma* magazine, is the headmost media mogul of the Independent Charismatic world in the United States—"Why do you think there has been so much alignment between Donald Trump and charismatic evangelicalism?" His response: "I can say it in just one word, or, I should say, one name: Paula White."[49]

Not widely known is the fact that Donald Trump had flirted with the idea of running for president in the 2012 election cycle. According to White, Trump reached out to her in 2011, asking her to gather some Christian leaders to advise him and pray over whether he should run. So Paula convened a group of about thirty pastors and televangelists to meet with and intercede about Trump's presidential ambitions. As she tells it, she wound up advising Trump against running that cycle, and he ultimately agreed.[50] Ralph Reed, a leader of the religious right who was also discussing the run with Trump at the time, has an alternate theory about this decision-making process, noting that NBC "threw an unbelievable sum of money at him" to do another season of *The Apprentice* and that Trump simply couldn't refuse.[51]

By the time the 2016 campaign season rolled around, Trump was unequivocally running, and White writes that he asked her to "be in charge of reaching out to the evangelicals."[52] She agreed, but there was a hitch. The superstructure of the religious right in the United States, since the 1980s, was predominantly built by first- and second-quadrant evangelicals: denominational leaders, the Roman Catholic hierarchy, institutional players, networked activists, and those in similar circles. But that was not the Pentecostal-charismatic crowd that Paula White ran with. As Strang, who lives in Florida and who has known Randy and Paula White since the 1990s and tracked their ministry for decades, detailed for me, "Paula's a wonderful person, but she does not move in evangelical [as in first- and second-quadrant evangelical] circles. . . . In fact, the evangelicals don't like her because she preaches like a house on fire, and she's not dignified . . . and a lot of them don't believe in lady preachers."[53]

Instead of trying to cultivate the old guard of the religious right, Paula White reached out to the people she knew and began arranging meet-and-greets for different groups of Independent Charismatic leaders and Trump. Whether this strategy—reaching evangelicals through cultivating Independent Charismatic celebrities—was a stroke of genius on Trump's part or simply something he stumbled on accidentally, it worked.

These initial Christian leaders to meet with Donald Trump in 2015 were not your typical neighborhood-church pastors or religious right VIPs. No, it was televangelists, apostles, prophets, megachurch pastors, Messianic rabbis, faith healers, and prosperity gospel preachers—the entrepreneurs of the Independent Charismatic celebrity class—who got in on the ground floor of the Trump movement. This would eventually engender a revolution in the configuration of power in the leadership of the religious right.

Paula White was becoming Trump's evangelical translator and chaperone, briefing him before these gatherings about each of the people who would be there. These meetings are the genesis of a whole genre of photos: groups of religious leaders praying over or blessing Trump. And given that these were not the stoic and staid evangelical leaders of old, things sometimes got raucous, with prophets prophesying over Trump and Word of Faith pastors naming and claiming blessings on his behalf. These charismatic religious leaders would even sometimes, as they were accustomed to doing in their churches, lay hands on the famously germophobic Trump, inadvertently proving just how far he would go to curry their favor.

Early in the 2016 campaign, most respectable evangelical leaders would not have wanted to lay hands on Donald Trump with a ten-foot pole. What these mainstream evangelical leaders were slow to realize at the time was that rank-and-file evangelicals loved Trump. From the summer of 2015 to the end of the primary, Trump was consistently winning a plurality of evangelical support, even if it was frequently a very small plurality. Members of the respectable evangelical class from the first and second quadrants were endorsing Ted Cruz, Marco Rubio, Mike Huckabee, Mike Pence, or Ben Carson throughout the primary. But the Independent Charismatic leaders, led in no small part, as we shall see, by NAR networks, became the vanguard of Christian Trumpism.

As these dynamics became clear—elite evangelical derision, grassroots evangelical fervor—Trump started getting more and more faith-related questions from reporters. He made several high-profile faux pas—telling a group that he'd never asked God for forgiveness, pronouncing Second Corinthians "Two Corinthians." Paula White, seeing these gaffes pile up, decided to intervene. She and Mike Huckabee sat down with Trump, and she said, "Sir, I suggest you make a decision whether you go public with your faith or whether you keep it very private and hold it close to your chest."[54] She told him that these theological zingers would keep coming as long as he was willing to take public questions on his religious identity. So Trump opted, on White's recommendation, to be candid about faith in private, with small groups of leaders, but to publicly offer only vague platitudes. This meant that Paula White became Trump's spokesperson on matters of faith. She became the one to vouch for his sincerity and piety, and she became the gatekeeper for religious leaders wanting access to him. This had the added benefit of making Trump's personal spirituality a Rorschach test, of sorts, which different Christian audiences could interpret variously.

Over the course of the Republican primary, as Trump's rivals dropped out one by one and as his evangelical base remained unwavering, the old-guard leaders of the religious right slowly realized that Trump was going to be the nominee—and also that they had no relationship with him. Soon, as Strang puts it, "these evangelical hot shots"—most of whom had scoffed at the brash real-estate tycoon and his prosperity-gospel-touting female pastor—"had to go hat in hand to this thin little blonde lady who looks more like a fashion model than she does a preacher."[55]

In a turn that no one could have predicted even two years earlier, Paula White and her coterie of televangelists, prophets, and charismatic mega-church pastors were suddenly *the* Christian face of the Republican presidential ticket. Many have asserted that Donald Trump selected Mike Pence as his running mate to "win over" or "secure" the evangelical vote. But I would argue that Pence's elevation to the ticket in 2016 had much more to do with smoothing things over with the noncharismatic evangelical elite. Trump had already locked down the support of the evangelical multitudes.

We see this tension reflected among the people selected as Trump's formal, and sometimes informal, circle of evangelical advisers. Relatively few of those people are first- or second-quadrant evangelicals, and the lion's share are fourth-quadrant charismatics. There are various lists of these evangelical advisers from the 2016 campaign, the Trump administration, and the 2020 campaign; the group seemed to have a strong core with a more fungible periphery. Some of the people on these lists are exactly who longtime watchers of the religious right would expect: James Dobson, Ralph Reed, Franklin Graham—the usual suspects. But on all the lists I can find, Independent Charismatics make up at least half of the group, with Paula White serving as the chair and convener. There are also people on the list who might fit squarely in the first quadrant (denominational and noncharismatic), like Robert Jeffress, the well-known pastor of First Baptist Church of Dallas. Their access to that cohort seemed to originate in the fact that they also had shows on televangelism networks, making them part of White's social—if not theological—circle. The Trump campaign also, evidently, utilized the ethnic diversity of the fourth quadrant as nearly all the Christian leaders of color who were advising Trump were Independent Charismatic leaders.

In her public remarks about advising Trump, leading his evangelical advisers team, and brokering smaller-group gatherings of religious leaders with him, White returns again and again to the image of being a bridge builder. In September 2017, she would tell a room of religion journalists, when asked about her role as Trump's spiritual adviser, "I say I'm a construction worker . . . it is building bridges. It is putting people around him, putting those men and women of God, which so far has totaled more than 400 men and women of God."[56] But the most important bridge that White built from 2015 to 2020 was a bridge between the previously isolated and irrelevant Independent Charismatic celebrity class and the leadership eche-lon of the religious right.

Along the way, Paula White has accomplished a number of notable firsts. In 2016, she became the first woman to offer a benediction at the Republican National Convention:

> We believe in faith that it's time for darkness to be dispelled.
>
> It's time for this nation to live out its holy calling in the world,
> And it is time for us to bridge the divide and become one again.
>
> We believe in faith that it is time for us to become the light that this world so desperately needs.[57]

She also became the first female clergy member to pray at a presidential inauguration:

> Let your favor be upon this one nation under God. Let these
> United States of America be that beacon of hope to all people and
> nations under Your dominion, a true hope for humankind.[58]

She even managed to finagle having her spiritual father from Ghana, Archbishop Nicholas Duncan-Williams, pray at the private church service for Trump and Pence before the inauguration. He was, as far as I can find, the first African religious leader to do so.

A Televangelist in the White House

Through Paula White's closeness to Trump, her vast network of relationships among charismatic evangelicals, and her willingness to insert herself into Trump's—at the time preposterous—presidential campaign, Independent Charismatics moved from the margin to the center of right-wing Christian politics in America. The fringe became the carpet.

And toward the end of the Trump administration, Paula White—the "messed-up Mississippi girl" turned televangelist who hitched her wagon to Donald Trump's political ambitions—fully moved inside the administration. After years of informally advising Trump and convening and chairing his circle of evangelical advisers, sometimes as the only female religious leader in the room, she found, in 2019, her path finally cleared to take on an official role as a White House staffer in the Office of Public Liaison, running the administration's Faith and Opportunities Initiative. Having segued into more of an apostolic role a few months earlier, she was ready to lay aside her speaking, talk-show facilitating, and pastoring to focus on advancing Trump's agenda.

A few days after White assumed this new role, while the news was still fresh that a charismatic televangelist had joined the White House staff, I helped to gather a group of Jewish and Christian Baltimore clergy and congregational leaders on the completely unrelated question of congregational security. This was in the wake of a growing number of shootings at synagogues and churches, and we thought it important for pastors, priests, and rabbis to think collaboratively about issues of congregational safety during a rising tide of violence and attacks.

A friend and colleague of mine, a Black Independent Charismatic bishop who leads a network of congregations, attended the event, and his response to the safety prompt took me aback: "Our Black congregations don't worry too much about violence and attacks. We're Black people in Baltimore: we live with the threat of violence every day. What really worries people in my congregation right now is Paula White."

I wasn't sure what he meant, so I asked him to elaborate. "The people I minister to have spent years and years watching Paula White, following her ministry, and learning from her," he told me. "Now she took this White House job, working for that man, and my people are in a genuine crisis of faith. I have congregation members in tears telling me, 'I thought Paula was filled with the Spirit of God, but if she can go and serve Trump, I don't know what it means to be filled with the Spirit of God.'" As far as I can tell, these small pockets of predominantly Black Independent Charismatic communities have been the only significant chunk of the fourth quadrant that's resisted Christian Trumpism.

But Paula White was, in many ways, *not* the first televangelist to get a job in the White House. The first, I would argue, was Donald Trump himself, who had entered the White House two years earlier. In the picture that Paula White paints, Trump has long been an assiduous student of TV preaching, particularly what's propagated by prosperity preachers and positive thinkers. With his oddly coiffed hair, his formative Norman Vincent Peale theology, his salesmanship, his bombastic oratory, and his unflinching personal schtick forged out of years of celebrity and television savvy, Trump has pantomimed the televangelists. His celebrity could easily mingle with Paula White's clique of entrepreneurial charismatic celebrities because Trump's whole brand is made of similar material. For what is "Make America Great Again" if not a gospel? It's a nationalistic prosperity gospel, to be sure, mixed with a few "American carnage" fire-and-brimstone threats if Trump's ways are not followed. Coached by Paula White, Trump has now mastered the religious dimension of his own televangelism career, riding evangelical support all the way to the White House.

There was only one official White House-sanctioned prayer offered on the morning of January 6, 2021. It was led by Paula White. On that cold January morning, before Donald Trump's speech at the Ellipse telling the lusty crowds to "fight like hell," before Rudy Giuliani shouted for "trial by combat," and before the crowds began marching across the National Mall to threaten lawmakers into reneging on American democracy, an invocation from Paula White opened the event.

> Let us pray, because God is going to be in today. We believe in miracles. . . .
>
> So let every adversary against democracy, against freedom, against life, against liberty, against justice, against peace, against righteousness be overturned right now in the name of Jesus . . .
>
> God, we ask right now in conclusion for your provision, for your protection, for your power, for an outpouring of your Spirit like never before. I secure POTUS [President of the United States]. I thank you for President Trump. I thank you

that he has stood with Israel; he has stood with life; he has
stood for righteousness. . . .

He has walked in your ways. And as you have allowed me to
have a relationship with him and his family for twenty years,
right now, as his pastor, I put a hedge of protection around him.
I secure his purpose. I secure his destiny. I secure his life.[59]

This tenacious, talented, tragic, triumphant woman—someone who
has broken every glass ceiling she came up against—became the first pastor
to offer an official blessing over an attempted American insurrection.

It's true that Paula White has built bridges. She built a bridge that
allowed her fellow Independent Charismatics to enthusiastically join the
inner circle of power within the religious right. She built a bridge across
a major divide in American evangelicalism between charismatics and non-
charismatics. And she built a bridge between the Independent Charismatic
celebrity class and the White House.

These bridges proved strong enough that the leaders of the NAR,
and other ambitious charismatic leaders and networks, could link arms
with other Christians and Trump advisers in an attempt to overthrow our
democracy, all under the banner of Christian unity and revival hope. So it's
time that we meet one of the most pivotal leaders in constructing modern
fourth-quadrant Christianity, the renegade seminary professor who became
an apostle: C. Peter Wagner.

2

THE GENESIS AND THE GENIUS OF
THE NEW APOSTOLIC REFORMATION

SO MUCH OF how you understand history depends on where you start telling the story. Many analysts of the January 6 riot have located its beginning in a gonzo, six-hour meeting held on December 18, 2020, at the White House, where then-president Donald Trump squabbled with lawyers and advisers including Rudy Giuliani, Sidney Powell, and Michael Flynn. That meeting reportedly involved screaming matches, airing of conspiracy theories about foreign governments interfering in the 2020 election, and heated arguments about whether Trump had any options left in contesting the election. Just hours after that meeting, in the early morning of December 19, Trump would send his inciting tweet: "Big protest in D.C. on January 6th. Be there, will be wild!"[1]

The congressional January 6th Committee begins its narrative a month and a half earlier, on the morning of November 4, as the election count from the day before was beginning to point toward Joe Biden. That was when Trump, anticipating the voters' verdict, spoke to the press, saying, "This is a fraud on the American public. . . . Frankly, we did win this election."[2]

Or you could locate the genesis of January 6 even earlier—say, during the 2020 campaign, when Trump began floating ideas about voter fraud and questioning whether the election was rigged. Or what about starting with Trump's inauguration in 2017, another cold January day that Trump declared, on the very steps of the US Capitol, was "the day the people became the rulers of this nation again. The forgotten men and women of our country will be forgotten no longer. Everyone is listening to you now"?

In truth, January 6 had many origin points. It represented a confluence of forces—populist sentiments, anti-Black and nativist racism, political grievances, conspiracy theories, pandemic exhaustion, MAGA belligerence,

Christian nationalist rage. In this book, we look at the spiritual origins of January 6. Where did the assertive, optimistic, angry, shofar-blowing, worship-music-singing, dramatic prophesying Christian energy on display that day originate?

For that story, I'd suggest that we begin twenty-five years earlier, in 1996, at a meeting of pastors and a seminary professor in Los Angeles. Out of that meeting emerged a phrase and a movement that would leave an indelible mark on the religious disposition of the insurrection.

In the previous chapter, I proposed a model for locating this burgeoning Independent Charismatic subdivision of Christianity. C. Peter Wagner was the esteemed theorist of the growth of the fourth quadrant, arguing forcefully to his fellow evangelicals that they should embrace this unregulated and exciting new Independent Charismatic sector as the hotbed of God's work in the world.

Wagner's ideas, filtered through his closest followers or his prolific writings, have taken hold among a significant segment of these charismatic evangelicals today, and the people he mentored wield astounding influence over hundreds of thousands, sometimes millions, of followers. The remaining chapters introduce the cohort of Wagner's mentees, but in this chapter, we focus on Wagner himself. This diminutive, avuncular, and unpretentious professor with a signature goatee promoted and platformed a set of leaders and ideas from the margins of American Christianity—leaders and ideas that proved instrumental in mobilizing and inflaming Christians to be ready to rumble at the Capitol on January 6.

A Passion for Cows and Church Growth

Charles Peter Wagner—his friends all called him Peter—had an unusual profile for someone bound to become a seminary professor. Born in 1930, he grew up in New York City in the midst of the Great Depression, but he spent a lot of time with his grandmother, who lived in a small farming community upstate. There he developed a lifelong love of cows and farming equipment. His friends would later laugh at how he could identify any breed of cow by sight and offer an impromptu lecture on the finer points of cattle husbandry. Late in life, he would collect antique tractors, though he didn't own a farm. His family was irreligious, hardly ever attending church except for weddings and funerals. They didn't even own a Bible.

Peter enrolled in a college agriculture program and shortly thereafter met Doris Mueller, the daughter of local farmers and a recent convert to evangelical Christianity. Enamored with Doris, Peter began reading the Bible at her urging, and five months into their relationship, he decided to become a Christian. Doris, suspicious that his conversion might be prompted by a desire to marry her, cautioned him that she had promised God that she would become a missionary to Africa. Peter's response was, "Do they have cows over there in Africa?"

Later, in his memoir, he wrote, "When she assured me that they did, I told her that I would like to be a missionary too. So I accepted Christ and dedicated my life to be a missionary the same night."[3] This mixture of expeditious decision-making, utilitarianism, and willingness to radically rearrange his views and life plans would become a hallmark of his career.

The couple married ten months later, and Doris Wagner became Peter's lifelong partner in ministry and academia. After he graduated from college, the couple moved to Southern California so that Peter could attend Fuller Theological Seminary in Pasadena, a recently founded transdenominational school. Fuller was a big-tent evangelical institution and one of the main venues where the modern identity of being "an evangelical" emerged in the middle of the twentieth century.[4] Fuller—my own alma mater, though I didn't overlap with Peter Wagner there—remains one of the largest and most influential evangelical seminaries in the United States. Doris enrolled as an undergraduate at the nearby Biola College, now Biola University.

As a newcomer to evangelical Christianity and theology, the farm-minded Peter found many of his seminary courses too abstract and full of "irrelevant material."[5] But he managed to finish at Fuller, and then the couple pursued their vision of becoming missionaries. Instead of going to Africa as Doris had originally imagined, they spent sixteen years as missionaries in Bolivia. Their time there was devoted to raising their three daughters and attempting to start evangelical churches in the face of local Catholic opposition. In the process, Peter began teaching some classes at local Bible institutes, which led him to discover his love of instructing and mentoring younger people in ministry. During their years in the mission field, Peter

Wagner also discovered a passion for writing. He would ultimately write hundreds of articles and dozens of books, many of them translated into multiple languages.

Peter returned to Fuller to do another master's in missiology, the study of missionaries and missionary work. While there, he was introduced to a groundbreaking, buzzy field of study in the late 1960s called church growth. Church growth, which was pioneered by Wagner's professor and mentor at Fuller, Donald McGavran, aimed to blend the hard-nosed data of sociology with evangelical theology. Church growth theorists were convinced that all the new learning coming out of the social sciences, if applied strategically, could accelerate the evangelizing work of the church. Instead of missionaries or churches merely aiming to convert individuals, they could target whole people groups, affinity clusters, and cultures.

This church growth concept spoke deeply to Wagner's pragmatic streak and zeal for success and results, and in 1971, he and Doris chose to move back to Southern California for him to teach at Fuller, alongside McGavran. McGavran and Wagner were both faculty in Fuller's newly created School for World Mission, a division of the seminary dedicated to training missionaries.

The Wagners' return to Fuller inaugurated the second major stage of Peter's career, and he would serve on the Fuller faculty from 1971 to 1999. Back in California, Peter also completed a PhD in social ethics from the University of Southern California. His dissertation offered a contrarian take on Martin Luther King Jr.'s famous lament that "11 am Sunday morning is one of the most segregated hours in Christian America." Wagner asked what if that human instinct toward segregation into homogeneous groups could be "a dynamic tool for assuring Christian growth"?[6] In other words, he claimed, it's natural for birds of a feather to flock together, so grouping people accordingly would be a more effective strategy for the church than focusing on integrating everything.

Renegade Seminary Professor

We have already seen how the theology and practice of being charismatic—building one's spirituality around supernatural experiences and extraordinary gifts given through the Holy Spirit—has created divisions in modern

Catholicism, mainline Protestantism, evangelicalism, and Historically Black Protestantism. In formal theological terms, this is often talked about as the divide between "continuationists" and "cessationists." *Continuationist* is a synonym for *charismatic*: the belief that the extraordinary elements of early Christianity continue today. Cessationists are not anti-supernatural or anti-miracles per se, but they argue that those supernatural aspects of Christianity largely ceased to manifest after the founding of the early church— that they were a special dispensation for a special time.

Peter Wagner was not terribly invested in this argument early on in his career. The churches he joined after his conversion, Biola College (where Doris attended), and Fuller Seminary were all broadly cessationist in their orientation, so Wagner writes, "When I went to Bolivia as a missionary, I was a convinced cessationist."[7] But the Wagners happened to be in Bolivia when a wave of Pentecostal revivalism was sweeping through South America. According to Wagner, in 1950, roughly 20 percent of the churches in Latin America were Pentecostal, but by 1970, they made up 70 percent of the churches.[8]

At first, the Wagners joined their fellow cessationist missionaries in dismissing these rival Christians as uncouth and irrational. Wagner would later marvel, "I felt I was serving God by denouncing Pentecostals!"[9] But then Bolivians they knew and respected claimed they had experienced physical healing at Pentecostal revival services, and Wagner's interest was piqued.

By the time he started gravitating toward the church growth framework, Wagner's pragmatism outweighed his cessationism, and he became fascinated with the astounding growth of Pentecostalism. If growth signaled the blessing of God on a movement, as he believed it did, then clearly God was blessing the Pentecostals. The first book Wagner wrote after joining the Fuller faculty was provocatively titled *Look Out! The Pentecostals Are Coming*, and, in it, he argued that Pentecostalism was the wave of the future. This, naturally, was very well received by the Pentecostals and other charismatics, who now felt that they had an ally among the predominantly cessationist faculty at Fuller. This was the context in which Peter Wagner met John Wimber.

A quarter century after his death, John Wimber still looms larger than life. He was a member of the band that became the Righteous Brothers, though he left before they took that name or became truly famous. Wimber left his literal rock-star life, converted to Christianity, and became a rock-star pastor. He came to Fuller as a doctoral student and took one of Peter Wagner's church growth classes in 1975. Wagner recognized that while he might have many theoretical ideas about church growth, John Wimber was "a bona fide practitioner."[10] Every church or ministry Wimber touched seemed to grow exponentially. So Wagner hired Wimber to come and help lead the seminars and consulting side of his church growth work, training pastors and ministries in data-driven growth strategies.

In 1978, Wimber stopped working with Wagner at Fuller to start his own church. There Wimber began experimenting with charismatic expressions in the services. Wimber's motto was "doin' the stuff," as in we're just doing the stuff that Jesus did in his ministry, such as healing the sick and casting out demons. Wimber offered a more toned-down form of charismaticism that Wagner and other evangelicals found very appealing. In 1982, John Wimber became the leader of a blossoming movement of charismatic churches called the Vineyard, with already more than thirty churches in it, and Wimber's church, the Anaheim Vineyard, became the flagship of the movement. That same year, Peter Wagner invited Wimber back to Fuller for one of the boldest stunts of Wagner's academic career.

Wagner had spent the better part of a decade arguing to evangelicals that they needed to be open to charismatic and Pentecostal practices if they wanted their churches to grow, but now he seized the bull by the horns. Together, Wimber and Wagner created a Fuller course titled "MC510: Signs, Wonders, and Church Growth," which was explicitly about promoting these charismatic practices. It would become legendary, even notorious.

On paper, the Signs and Wonders course was being taught by Wagner, but John Wimber did most of the instructing. Every one of the eighty-five seats in the class filled, based on the course title and Wagner and Wimber's reputations. It was a three-hour class, and Wimber would teach for the first two hours. A gifted storyteller, he would often draw illustrations from miracles he had performed or witnessed. Then for the last part of the session, they would segue into "the clinic," where Wimber would invite the presence of the Holy Spirit and begin offering "words of knowledge"—personalized divine revelations—to members of the class. After that, he'd invite students or others present who needed prayer to come forward, and he'd instruct the other students, using these live subjects, on how to pray for healing, how to cast out demons, and how to hear God's direction for that person.[11]

The students were spellbound, many of them having never seen anything like this. When it was repeated in future terms, the course broke every enrollment record in Fuller's history. Wimber's clinic portion of the session began attracting overflow crowds, including many who were not even Fuller students.[12] According to reports, students were healed of physical and emotional maladies, and soon hundreds of students were trying to audit the course.

The course surfaced a profound hunger in wider evangelicalism for these types of experiential and miraculous stories. *Christian Life* magazine, a national evangelical publication, devoted an entire issue to the Signs and Wonders course, and it sold better than any issue they'd ever published. I have interviewed people who were Fuller students at the time, and so memorable and controversial was Wagner and Wimber's Signs and Wonders course that Fuller alumni still sometimes speak reverently of "MC510," a simple class code rendered into something momentous, revelatory.

Wagner and Wimber's course proved as suspect among the Fuller faculty as it was popular among their students. Most Fuller professors were cessationists, and on top of that, Fuller was trying to be a respectable, centrist evangelical seminary. Here Wagner was bringing in an avant-garde pastor to teach students how to heal people in a for-credit course. Evangelicals were talking, and Wagner even overheard whispers that "Fuller Seminary is going charismatic."[13] The academic credibility of the seminary was on the line, other faculty worried, recognizing that, given the fervor around Wimber and his experiential teaching, the course's "goals and methods [are] not open to normal academic critique."[14]

After four years of this—as the course enrollment was hitting 250 students each quarter, and Fuller staff were being posted at the doors to keep out unregistered students—the rest of the Fuller faculty intervened. With the rationale of preserving Fuller's reputation among its constituents, they forced the cancellation of the course.

These experiences—teaching MC510 and having it canceled—led to two paradigm shifts for Wagner. The first corroborated his early instinct, as a seminary student, that most theological learning was uselessly abstract and irrelevant. By this point, he was a tenured professor and a missiologist with a solid reputation. But Wagner determined that he didn't care what his fellow professors thought or did. He was going to push the boundaries of evangelicalism, come what may.

I interviewed Kay Hiramine, an entrepreneurial Fuller student who became a teaching assistant and right-hand administrator for Wagner through most of the 1990s. One day, after receiving what he characterized as a "blistering letter" critiquing something Wagner had written, Kay asked him, "Pete, does it wear on you that you're like a lightning rod?"

Wagner responded, "I really like to push the limits when it comes to what God is doing. I'm highlighting things that are pretty radical to really challenge the status quo." He went on, "You know what? We'll let the theologians and the historical writers and the biographers deal with it after I'm dead."[15]

Wagner's second paradigm shift was more global. Through his friendship with Wimber and four years of watching miracles unfold in class after class, Wagner had become a convinced charismatic. All the other major transitions and paradigm shifts of Wagner's remaining career flowed out of this transformation.

Scouting the Fourth Quadrant

By the late 1980s, Wagner had become a top-tier leader in global evangelicalism. He was a respected, albeit controversial, professor at Fuller Seminary, one of the premier global evangelical seminaries. He was a preeminent expert in church growth, an exciting field for many evangelical pastors and leaders. Rick Warren, the soon-to-be-renowned Baptist pastor of Saddleback Church, did his doctorate in ministry degree in church growth under Wagner, and Warren's 1993 dissertation would become part of the foundation for his mega-bestselling books, *The Purpose Driven Life* and *The Purpose Driven Church*.[16] Wagner was also serving on the Lausanne Committee for World Evangelization (LCWE), a major force in global evangelicalism. Originally conceived by the evangelist Billy Graham, LCWE linked together multiple mission movements and denominations.

Wagner, however, was always looking for a grander arena into which the evangelical church could increase. He had been a semi-successful missionary, but then he was drawn to church growth as a strategy for pushing forward missionary endeavors abroad and evangelism efforts at home. He was attracted to Pentecostalism's growth potential, but then Wimber gave him up-close access to a supernatural register.

Now, however, he struggled to translate Wimber's tactile, charismatic-gifting, Spirit-powered ethos into a broader framework. After all, not every church or group was going to join up with Wimber's Vineyard movement. Where was the larger arena into which this could expand?

Wagner was also growing increasingly discontented with what he called "mainstream evangelicalism": its denominational structures and its evident incapacity to expeditiously accomplish the goal of world evangelization.[17] "I felt that things were becoming a bit routinized and that the earlier cutting-edge zeal had been diminishing," he would later write. "I didn't have the language for it then, but now I know that I was detecting that LCWE was becoming an old wineskin. I could not yet imagine what the new wineskin might be; nevertheless, I started pulling back from LCWE so that I would be as available as possible to move into the new when it did come."[18]

In Wagner's vocabulary—alluding to Jesus's parable in Mark 2:21–22—"old wineskins" are ways of doing Christianity that might have had their time but are now outmoded and inflexible. New wineskins represent the new ways—often antagonistic and contentious—in which God is leading the church.

Wagner had spent his early career firmly planted in the first quadrant (denominational, noncharismatic), where most evangelicals were. Through his exposure to Pentecostalism, his church growth passions, and then his partnership with Wimber, Wagner became a leading voice within 1970s and 1980s first-quadrant evangelicalism, making the case for learning from third-quadrant Pentecostalism and other charismatic expressions.

In 1989, at nearly sixty years old, Wagner would meet another charismatic leader, a prophet who would precipitate another major shift in his life by welcoming him into the utterly un-"routinized" and unstructured environment of the fourth quadrant. Her name was Cindy Jacobs. We'll look at this transformative encounter in more depth in the next chapter. If John Wimber and the Vineyard represented a mild-mannered, mainstream-evangelical-friendly form of charismaticism, Cindy Jacobs was at the other end of the spectrum.

In their first meeting, Jacobs cracked open an entirely different understanding of Christianity for Wagner. She talked to him about prophecy, about styles and strategies of prayer that could heal nations, and about grand-scale spiritual warfare—concepts that were both exciting and foreign to someone like Wagner. To Wagner's eyes, these were the "new wineskins" he had been waiting for.

That first conversation with Cindy Jacobs gave Wagner a peek into an Independent Charismatic world that was still being born. At that time, the number of nondenominational megachurches were beginning to increase, and exponentially so, often built on Wagner and others' church growth theories. The present-day Independent Charismatic leadership culture was in its infancy; recall that Paula White herself migrated from Pentecostalism into the Independent Charismatic space in the early 1990s. You could think of this nascent Independent Charismatic environment of the 1980s as similar to a first-generation Silicon Valley: tons of innovative new ideas floating around, experimentation with new practices, not a lot of clear boundaries or brands, and many startup organizations and startup careers.

Jacobs became Wagner's tour guide into this world brimming with possibilities. She showed him around the existing Latter Rain–descended networks of leaders, making relational connections between Wagner and other charismatic pastors, prophets, and apostles. These Latter Rain-influenced beliefs were a huge leap beyond what he had encountered before, and much of Wagner's energy in the early 1990s was devoted to exploring and translating ideas among the quadrants, taking the new "technologies" from this cutting-edge Independent Charismatic region and making them palatable for mainstream (first- and second-quadrant) evangelicals. Wagner would write a letter to Jacobs in 2000 saying that two people—Cindy herself and John Wimber—had most impacted the trajectory of his life.[19]

Through Jacobs and other leading-edge charismatic figures she introduced him to, Wagner became convinced that these nondenominational charismatics were the primary growth edge of global Christianity. And he wasn't wrong: in 1970, there were roughly 44 million of these Independent Charismatics in the world. By 2020, it was 312 million. This segment of Christianity has increased more than sevenfold in the space of fifty years, making this diffuse nondenominational charismatic trend one of the fastest-growing religious movements in history.[20]

Strategic Spiritual Warfare and the 10/40 Window

Some of the major new "technologies" that Wagner would adopt and popularize were in the area of "spiritual warfare." Spiritual warfare is a common belief and practice among evangelicals across the four quadrants, premised on the theological idea that demons are bent on attacking Christians, who must resist these malign spiritual forces through prayer and other spiritual disciplines. This concept emerges out of passages in the New Testament, especially the book of Ephesians, where martial imagery describes Christians taking up their faith as armor because Christians "do not wrestle against flesh and blood, but against principalities, against powers, against the rulers of the darkness of this age, against spiritual hosts of wickedness in the heavenly places" (6:12).

Most Christians who practice spiritual warfare think of it as an individual or a communal struggle: battling one's own personal demons or, perhaps, exorcising demons from someone else. This was John Wimber's understanding of spiritual warfare, and Wagner was mostly in sync with Wimber through the 1980s.

But in 1988, Wagner would speculate, "Could it be possible that Satan, frequently referred to in Scripture as 'the god of this age,' assigns certain demonic spirits under him to promote the kingdom of darkness in given nations, cities, regions, cultural groups, or other segments of the world's population? . . . I am very much interested in learning more about possible territorial hierarchies of demons."[21] In essence, Wagner was seeking a grander vision of spiritual warfare that could dovetail with his church growth ideas. What if the trick to expanding the church lay in decoding the demonic hierarchies and territorial boundaries of the spiritual realm? A year later, he would meet Cindy Jacobs, who had been speculating and thinking along the same lines.

Jacobs's theology, which Wagner adopted and adapted, held that behind the low-level, personally harassing demons that most believers battled through spiritual warfare were high-level demon commanders and generals—the mysterious "principalities" and "powers" mentioned in that Ephesians passage. As he had already hinted at in 1988, Wagner would ultimately label these overseer demonic entities "territorial spirits": demons who controlled literal geographical territories or human institutions. And together Wagner and Jacobs would develop a framework called "strategic-level spiritual warfare" that was meant to overpower and displace these territorial spirits.

Jacobs and Wagner would bring these ideas to bear in the 1990s through a mission's prayer campaign dedicated to praying for something called the 10/40 Window: a geographical region between ten degrees and forty degrees north latitude, which encompasses most of North Africa, the Middle East, and a huge swath of Asia. The concept was coined by a colleague and friend of Wagner's, the evangelist Luis Bush. In Bush's formulation, accomplishing the evangelization of the entire world meant that the 10/40 Window needed to be the primary focus of Christian prayer and missionary activity.

Wagner leveraged his Fuller and Lausanne Committee connections to circulate these strategic-level spiritual warfare concepts into mainstream evangelicalism using the 10/40 Window campaign. If you were an evangelical in the United States in the 1990s, chances are that you at least heard about—and perhaps participated in—the annual prayer and fasting cycles for the 10/40 Window. There were 10/40 prayer guides, coordinated fasting sessions for the 10/40 Window, and whole curricula designed for Sunday school use. My family attended a noncharismatic, denominational evangelical church in the 1990s, and I remember constant appeals for prayer that the gospel would reach those living in the 10/40 Window. By 1997, at the height of the 10/40 Window campaign, Wagner and Jacobs estimated that fifty million evangelical Christians around the world were concertedly praying, using guides and frameworks that they helped create.[22]

Along the way, Wagner, Jacobs, and their friend Dutch Sheets also built a massive, networked prayer and information-sharing infrastructure, called the Strategic Prayer Network, with thousands of prayer activists spread around the United States and the world. Though Wagner's strategic spiritual warfare ideas predated his NAR ideas, if we picture the ideology of the NAR as a three-legged stool, strategic-level spiritual warfare is the first of those legs.[23]

John Wimber, who remained close to Wagner after their MC510 course was disbanded, grew quite concerned about these strategic-level spiritual warfare ideas. While certainly a practitioner of garden-variety spiritual warfare, Wimber spoke out against the strategic spiritual warfare frameworks, arguing that Wagner and his new charismatic colleagues were being too hubristic and even endangering people in their machinations about overthrowing demonic hierarchies. Wimber was one of several of Wagner's friends who threw up a red flag and warned that his theology was becoming extreme, all to no avail. This disagreement induced a falling out between Wagner and Wimber that would not be resolved before Wimber died in 1997.

The Postdenominational Church

Beliefs about modern apostles and prophets who would emerge to lead the church had been circulating in eddies around the small fourth-quadrant world since at least the 1950s, when the Latter Rain revival first proposed the apocalyptic return of apostles and prophets. By the 1980s, some Independent Charismatic leaders had begun calling themselves "apostles," and there were already clusters of Independent Charismatic leaders, including Cindy Jacobs, who were identifying themselves as "prophets."

Excited about these new ideas and the promise of a de-institutionalized, agile, modern church, Wagner developed a theory about what he was calling the postdenominational church. In 1996, he convened a National Symposium on the Postdenominational Church in Pasadena, sponsored by Fuller, gathering a group of approximately five hundred respected leaders from around the world to think about these incipient phenomena. Jacobs was tapped to lead seminars at the symposium. As Wagner wrote to the participants in his welcome letter, "In this symposium, you will get a penetrating insight into what many believe will be the cutting-edge of world Christianity as we move into the Twenty First Century."[24]

A few weeks prior to the symposium, Wagner devoted his column in *Ministries Today* magazine to laying out his working definition of what made a church cutting edge and postdenominational:

- They "often appear to be independent, yet they tend to network with each other in loose affiliations."
- "They are wary of being encumbered by organizational structures commonly associated with denominationalism."
- They are usually "Pentecostal or charismatic, yet the churches themselves eschew such labels."
- "Their form of church governance typically is based more on relationships than on official documents or rigid structures."
- "Many of them are megachurches," but they often divide into "small groups or 'cells' in which practical ministry can occur."
- They generally "speak openly of God restoring apostles and prophets to the church," though not all leaders apply those titles to themselves.
- And while most of these are nondenominational already, "a denominational church can be postdenominational in the way it conducts its church life."[25]

This was, more or less, Wagner's theory leading into the symposium. These churches and ministries, he believed, would shape the future growth of Christianity.

On the day that the symposium was supposed to begin, however—May 20, 1996—Wagner and a group of the planners drove to nearby Los Angeles to have lunch with Pastor Jack Hayford, one of the elder statesmen of Pentecostalism and a top leader in Aimee Semple McPherson's Foursquare denomination. Kay Hiramine, who was running point on organizing the symposium, narrated the story to me.

Wagner and Hayford were friends, but as soon as he saw Wagner that day, Hayford said, "Oh, Peter, I am *grieved* to see you."

Wagner was taken aback. Hayford proceeded to lay out his argument against this "postdenominational" language. He himself, as a pastor deeply committed to his denomination, was excited about the things Wagner was working on. "I love you, but you are hurting so many people with this term 'postdenominational.' You have made me into a dinosaur," Hayford told Wagner.

Peter Wagner, ever ready to make an intellectual pivot, immediately proposed that they change the name. Over the course of their lunch, the group tossed out different titles and options until one of the people there threw out the phrase "New Apostolic Reformation." Hiramine, who was present, does not recall whose idea it was, but he's confident it wasn't Wagner's. The whole group seized on this, and, Hiramine quips, "we banged that name out—the New Apostolic Reformation—in less than a lunch."[26]

At the conclusion of the National Symposium on the Postdenominational Church a few days later, Wagner got up to announce that even the title of the symposium was now irrelevant because they had landed on a different title: the New Apostolic Reformation. The crowd of five hundred premier leaders in charismatic Christianity erupted in applause for, as Hiramine puts it, an "Amen-hallelujah time." From that point forward, the NAR became the driving impulse of Wagner's life.

In May 1996, at this lunch meeting, and in the entire Postdenominational Church symposium, the NAR was born. No one in attendance—including Wagner—could have fully known at the time what it would become. This is where, I believe, we can see the first glint of the religiosity that would fuel January 6.

That gathering was not wild-eyed or frenetic or even political, and it did not happen in some obscure, ultra-right-wing, white nationalist Christian gathering. No, it happened among some of the most influential and promising leaders of American evangelicalism, under the auspices of one of the foremost evangelical seminaries in America.

Building the New Apostolic Reformation

As Peter Wagner began hanging around with Jacobs and other prophets and proto-apostles, he began receiving personalized prophecies from them that he was one of God's new apostles, with a key role to play in advancing the new reformation. He deeply believed that God was calling him to organize and oversee leadership networks to further this transformation of the church.

One might assume that a professor with a PhD in the social sciences would be skeptical of such mystical proclamations. But Wagner had become a firm believer in the reality of these prophetic words, and from the mid-1990s until his death, he would make every effort to follow the guidance of these prophets. As had already occurred in his Signs and Wonders classes with Wimber, Wagner's own identity had gotten entwined with his research subjects.

Starting after the Postdenominational Church symposium, Wagner threw himself into creating a scaffolding for this NAR. By 1996, a cluster of these leaders and networks, including both Sheets and Jacobs, had relocated to Colorado Springs, and Peter and Doris Wagner decided that they should move there too—again, in response to prophecies. They moved in June 1996, just a month after the National Symposium on the Postdenominational Church concluded. Fuller Seminary had a satellite campus in Colorado Springs, so Wagner became a resident faculty member there.

Another key player in building out this NAR model was a prophet-apostle named Chuck Pierce. Pierce had been mentored by Cindy Jacobs in Texas in the 1980s, and through Jacobs, he encountered the Wagners. In 1998, Peter and Doris would persuade Pierce to come work for them and help orchestrate their institution-building. So from 1998 to 2000, Pierce lived in Colorado Springs to work closely alongside the Wagners, before returning to Texas.[27] Pierce would go on to become Peter Wagner's closest deputy and a virtual adopted son to the Wagners.

Peter also molded his Fuller courses around these new ideas, developing classes like Discerning Spiritual Strongholds, Confronting the Powers, and Churches in the New Apostolic Paradigm. For years, Wagner imparted the ideas and frameworks of the NAR to hundreds of Fuller students integrated into their seminary education. But as the twentieth century drew to a close, Wagner became convinced that Fuller was no longer an adequate platform for him. In 1999, he left Fuller earlier than he had originally planned to pursue the NAR project full time.

What Wagner managed to accomplish in this final stage of his life—between 1999 and 2010, when he retired—is nothing short of remarkable. Wagner was a prolific author but not, in my view, a gifted theologian. His primary training, after all, was as a missionary and a social scientist. Most of his theological ideas were borrowed, rebranded, or repackaged from the work of others.

But Peter Wagner was an organizational genius, and he excelled at gathering highly talented, like-minded leaders into shared projects. By this time, Wagner had spent thirty years researching what worked well for facilitating movement growth, so he brought a finely honed set of instincts to sketching out an infrastructure for what he called *the most radical change in the way of doing church since the Protestant Reformation!*[28]

Charismatic believers, downstream from the Latter Rain movement, had been talking about these apostolic and prophetic governance concepts for decades, but Wagner was the first to build an architecture that could hold together networks and leaders while maintaining their independence. He brought coherence and superstructure to what had previously been fragmentary and disordered.

In this third career, Wagner would build and administer eight overlapping institutions that he believed could serve as a replicable model to advance the NAR. All of these NAR institutions were developed, centrally, around what we could call the second ideological leg of the NAR stool: the idea that churches and ministries should be governed primarily through apostles and prophets. We'll look at what that means practically in chapter 4. Doris Wagner, Peter's steadfast partner, was directly involved in leading and directing most of these institutions, though Peter remained the public face. These linked institutions had a sort of hub-and-spoke design so that they all were tied to the Wagners but could each operate separately. These institutions, their acronyms, and their functions can get a little wonky, so let me just profile a few of the most important ones that will come up repeatedly in this book.

First, Wagner created the Wagner Leadership Institute (WLI), a sort of alternative seminary. In many ways, WLI was Wagner's anti-Fuller seminary, where he intentionally structured the curriculum and course topics for maximum practical impact. He sometimes joked to his colleagues that he had spent thirty years of his life teaching at Fuller *Cemetery*, where faith and godly ambition went to die.[29] Thousands of adept charismatic church leaders would take classes at WLI, taught by Wagner and his mentees, on topics like what it means to be an apostle, how to build networks, how to conduct strategic-level spiritual warfare, and so on. Eventually, WLI would have dozens of extension campuses spread around the globe, all explicitly "designed . . . to meet the needs of leaders who have become a part of the New Apostolic Reformation."[30]

Second, Wagner helped establish the International Coalition of Apostles (ICA) in 1999, and he served as the convening apostle. Many people were experimenting with these Latter Rain-fivefold-apostolic-prophetic ideas at the time, and not all of them linked up with Wagner's networks, but many did. Wagner determined who could join the ICA, what the criteria for membership should be, and what the content of their annual meetings would be. His hope was that the ICA could be a sort of professional society for apostles. Wagner designed the ICA as a horizontal networking space where apostles could prioritize "meeting and connecting with peer-level apostles."[31] He did not have any direct spiritual authority over the more than five hundred apostles who eventually joined the ICA, per se, but their choice to affiliate signaled their interest in and alignment with his emerging NAR paradigms. He hoped, through the ICA, "to introduce as many other leaders as possible to the New Apostolic Reformation and its implications for the Kingdom of God."[32]

Third, together with Cindy Jacobs, Wagner also created a roundtable of the most prominent charismatic prophets in the country that they titled the Apostolic Council of Prophetic Elders (ACPE), made up of a group of about twenty-five personally invited prophets. The ACPE was a cohort of seasoned prophets, who would gather annually, compare notes on what they felt they were hearing from God, issue collective declarations, and hold each other accountable.

The final NAR institution that I'd like to highlight is the most mysterious and the most important. Starting around 2002, Wagner decided to formalize his large group of mentees and disciples into something called the Eagles' Vision Apostolic Team (EVAT), which included twenty-five of his closest apostles and prophets. These EVAT members were, customarily, also members of the other NAR institutions and often helped Wagner lead them. The roster of EVAT members was never public, but Wagner did keep lists in his files, and the group membership stayed pretty consistent over the years.

EVAT was unique among the NAR structures because, in Wagner's vocabulary, the EVAT members had a "Covenant Relationship" with him.[33] For the select group of EVAT members, Peter Wagner was their own apostle. In fact, even though some of them were his contemporaries in terms of age, the EVAT members called Wagner their "spiritual father," and he called them

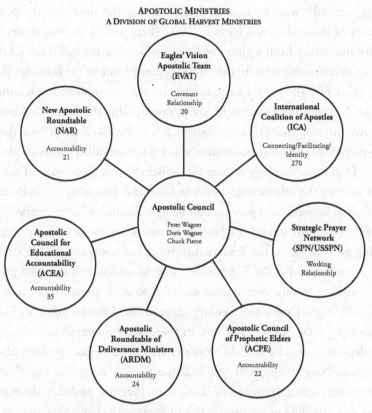

Fig. 2.1 Recreated from a 2002 diagram in Peter Wagner's files demonstrating the networked nature of the early NAR institutions. Courtesy of Fuller Theological Seminary archives.

"spiritual sons and daughters." Also, unlike the members of any other NAR institution, EVAT members contributed directly to Peter Wagner's modest salary, a tithe of sorts to their mentor, apostle, and spiritual father. EVAT was the true ideological and relational inner core of the NAR.

Dominion! and Seven Mountains

You might sensibly wonder how a group of supernaturally fixated apostles and prophets, bent on restructuring the church, became a hyper-politicized movement. In truth, radical political theologies had been circulating in these nondenominational charismatic networks since at least the 1980s, though these networks were so scant and dispersed at the time that the practical impact of these ideas was fairly limited. These radical theologies were generally emanating from a group of Calvinist theologians called the Christian Reconstructionists, who, in the 1970s, became some of the theological leading lights of right-wing Christianity.[34] There's a complicated backstory, to which I cannot do justice here, about cross-pollination occurring between the Reconstructionists and the charismatics in the 1980s and 1990s. And the key marker of this cross-pollination was a doctrine called *dominion theology*.

Dominion theology is rooted in a distinctive interpretation of the Bible that centers the relationship between God and humanity on authority. It holds that because God gave human beings "dominion" over creation (Gen. 1:28), God must intend for human beings today to be active partners in ruling over the earth. The Reconstructionists and many charismatics, including the televangelist Pat Robertson, came to understand this as a present-day mandate to take over human societies so as to govern them according to God's reign. Dominion theology aims to build the kingdom of God on earth right now. So in the 1980s, as these ideas migrated into the diffuse nondenominational networks, some charismatics began speaking about a Kingdom Now theology. If you hear the phrase "Kingdom Now" or find charismatics using language of dominion, they are probably downstream from this mingling of Reconstructionist ideas with charismatic ones.

Some of the people who came into Wagner's inner circle were already immersed in these Reconstructionist ideas, but others were not. One of the leading Kingdom Now proponents among Wagner's mentees was Dutch Sheets, who would serve as the Wagners' pastor in Colorado Springs. Wagner was not interested in running the NAR like a hierarchical, centralized structure where he set and dictated the theology. Instead, he learned from his mentees and helped amplify their ideas. So in the early NAR, you can see these dominion ideas seeping into Wagner's circles and becoming major topics of discussion and debate.

As a latecomer to charismatic identity, Wagner had not deeply bought into, nor was even well informed about, these dominion ideas, so they had a limited impact on the early NAR. But then in the mid-2000s, Wagner—always eager to find a grander scale—became fascinated with these dominion teachings, especially when he encountered a younger pastor-apostle named Lance Wallnau. In chapter 5, I tell the story of how Wallnau's version of dominion theology—structured around what he calls the Seven Mountains of Culture—recast the NAR networks with a broader ambition to change whole societies. Throughout 2007 and 2008, Wagner and Wallnau used the infrastructure and relational connections of the NAR networks to systematically publicize these Seven Mountains / dominion theology ideas that had already been simmering inside NAR circles for years. In a December 2007 address to his ICA, Wagner said, "I am more certain than ever that God is calling his people to experience the most radical paradigm shift at least since I have been in Christian ministry which is well over half a century."[35] And that "paradigm shift" was the Seven Mountains concept and dominion theology. This aggressive political theology became the third and final leg—along with strategic spiritual warfare and the leadership of apostles and prophets—of the NAR stool.

In early 2008, Wagner published his most in-your-face book titled *Dominion! How Kingdom Action Can Change the World*, in which he braided together his own style of dominion theology, the Seven Mountains, and his strategic spiritual warfare concepts from the 1990s. Knowing the power of the written word, Wagner also encouraged all of his disciples to write books. So dozens of books pushing this paradigm for societal takeover were published in the charismatic devotional and media space in this era.

In *Dominion!*, we can see the fully developed Wagnerian vision: the church should be governed primarily by charismatic apostles and prophets, who will lead it into concerted and orchestrated campaigns of strategic-level spiritual warfare, through which the church can transform societies. In the book, he quoted one of his favorite verses: "Our battles are no longer physical [as they had been for the people of God in the Old Testament]; they are spiritual. Jesus said, 'From the days of John the Baptist until now the kingdom of heaven suffers violence, and the violent take it by force' (Matthew 11:12). We will not take dominion by remaining passive. We will only take dominion if the Body of Christ becomes violent and declares war on the enemy!"[36] Indeed, that verse, Matthew 11:12, was one of Wagner's most potent biblical citations because he read it as a directive, straight from the mouth of Jesus, for Christians to engage in spiritual violence to advance the kingdom of God on the earth.

From this point on, a marked shift becomes visible in NAR identity, ambition, and method—toward focusing on politics and conquering positions of influence in society. NAR apostles and prophets began building ties with right-wing political campaigns and insinuating themselves into activist circles on the right. Wagner and the NAR started out with a vision to revolutionize the governance of the Christian church. During the 2000s, they began scheming for the full-scale re-formation of society.

The Lakeland Debacle

One more episode from this era of the NAR bears mentioning because it spotlights a temperamental divide within the NAR that is still present today. As we've seen, one of the core unifying and motivating passions of the Independent Charismatic world is the desire for revival. I cannot overstate how deep-seated this hope is for charismatics—the hope that God could suddenly break into the workaday world with an overwhelming outpouring of Holy Spirit power. By the time these dominion theology beliefs had been layered into the NAR, Wagner and many others were rhetorically pairing "revival" and "reformation," imagining that a mass charismatic revival would help to trigger a wholesale transformation of society.

In April 2008, an apostle named Stephen Strader, a member of Wagner's ICA, invited an idiosyncratic young evangelist, Todd Bentley, to his church in Lakeland, Florida, to lead a short-term series of revival meetings. A major revival broke out, and the planned one-week series of nightly meetings became four months of seven-days-a-week healing and revival services. Tens of thousands of charismatic Christians began converging on Lakeland to see and experience the revival. The internet had evolved enough by that point that they could live stream services, so tens of thousands more could follow along remotely. Soon GOD TV, a charismatic televangelism channel with an international reach and an audience of millions, began preempting its own planned programming to air the nightly services, drawing the eyes of charismatics around the world to what they began calling the Lakeland Outpouring.

The Lakeland revival was marked by evident miracles of faith healing at the hands of Bentley, and charismatics with a deep knowledge of revival history even hoped that it might signal the rebirth of the healing revivals of the 1940s and 1950s. They saw many parallels between Bentley and William Branham, the similarly controversial revivalist who inaugurated that heyday of charismaticism.

Todd Bentley was a caustic character, tattooed and burly, thirty-two years old at the time, who had come from a hardscrabble background in British Columbia. By the age of seventeen, he had racked up a sexual assault conviction, committed at the age of thirteen against a younger boy, and four drug overdoses.[37] After Bentley, proverbially, found Jesus, his delinquent youth became part of his redemption story. Bentley had an exaggerated and even violent flare on stage in Lakeland, sometimes punching or kicking people in front of the frenzied crowds as a means of "healing" them. He was also preaching some ideas that were, even in the wild and woolly prophetic world, seen as aberrant and perhaps heretical.

Stephen Strader, the apostle who hosted Bentley, recognized that this revival—with a combustible revivalist, thousands in attendance daily, and hundreds of thousands watching on GOD TV or online—was more than he could handle. At the end of May, he appealed to Wagner and the leadership of the ICA, asking, "Where are the apostles? You have taught me that apostles need to rise up and take their place. For the past ten years, we've been talking about the restoration of apostles. This is day sixty of the Outpouring and I have not heard from the apostles."[38]

This request divided Wagner's inner circle. Ché Ahn, a Fuller student who had studied under Wagner and become a top-flight apostle and EVAT member, had some previous relationship with Bentley and was all in with Lakeland. Ahn wrote to his followers, "THIS IS THAT for which we have all waited."[39] Ahn even appeared on stage with Bentley at Lakeland and helped to facilitate some of the healings. Likewise, Chuck Pierce, one of Wagner's most trusted prophetic advisers, was excitedly endorsing the revival.

But others of Wagner's disciples were more skeptical. They worried that this Lakeland business was so high-profile and so volatile that, as one of them wrote to Wagner, "we will all be painted by the brush of what happens in Lakeland."[40]

Eager for the possibility that this could be the early stages of a global revival and maybe trigger the anticipated transformation of American society, but also cognizant of Bentley's instability, Wagner decided to institute a two-step process. He would gather a group of leading apostles to do a public commissioning and alignment ceremony for Bentley, and then he would assign some apostles, led by Ché Ahn, to help Bentley, privately, clean up his act and be held accountable. "Alignment" was a very important word for Wagner, signaling that a person or ministry was connected and submissive to an apostle's authority.

So on June 23, 2008, more than a dozen NAR apostles descended on Lakeland for an internationally televised "apostolic alignment" ceremony.[41] In his remarks during the ceremony, Wagner did not betray his own reservations, but instead, broadcasting live to hundreds of thousands, he effused, "Prophets have been telling us for years that God is about to launch an extraordinary spiritual awakening with signs and wonders, and for over two months Todd Bentley has been leading one of the obvious fulfillments of those prophecies."[42]

By June 30, one week after the ceremony, more than 400,000 people from more than 100 countries had attended the Lakeland Outpouring in person, and millions more had live streamed or watched the revival online.[43] It appeared that Wagner and the NAR had threaded the needle and that they were now, behind the scenes, guiding a noteworthy, media-catapulted, global revival.

Then it all fell apart. On July 9, ABC's *Nightline* news magazine show aired an exposé on Bentley's criminal history and his questionable revival practices. ABC's reporters could not confirm a single case of healing, despite the dozens of healings that were being televised nightly and despite Bentley's promises that he could provide documentation. *Nightline* also cast suspicion on Bentley's finances. A few weeks later, it came out that Bentley had been drinking during the revival, and he was divorcing his wife because he'd fallen in love with their nanny.

Throughout these weeks, as news report after news report dropped about Bentley, Peter Wagner was trying to maintain equilibrium among his cohort of opinionated apostles who all now felt publicly bound up with the scandal. On the day that Bentley's separation from his wife became public, Wagner received 1,700 emails from apostles and other leaders, and Wagner would complain to his supporters, "I have become a lightening [*sic*] rod for a number of severe criticisms."[44] Bentley eventually left the scene, the revival sputtered out, and Peter Wagner was left holding the mess. Wagner tried for some weeks to keep the revival going on a more scaled-down level without Bentley, but all the public scandals had discredited everyone involved.

In the wake of this fiasco, a number of apostles resigned from the ICA. At one point, Doris Wagner, answering Peter's email while he traveled, would write to a friend of his, "[Peter] is probably one of the most misunderstood men on planet earth, who is either loved or hated, with not much middle ground. He is truly a holy person whom many are either jealous or envious of. . . . We have lost friends over this."[45]

The Lakeland debacle cast a pall over Wagner's impending retirement, and it also raised searching questions about his whole NAR paradigm. If Wagner and others had concerns about Bentley all along, why did they make their endorsement ceremony so public? If so many prophets were hearing straight from God, how come none of them heard from God about Bentley's secret vices? If apostolic governance gave leaders more flexibility, did it also incentivize flashiness over depth?

Lakeland also revealed a subtle rift within Wagner's mentoring circles and networks. Some NAR leaders were aspiring to slow and steady growth of a church movement, not wanting to get caught up in politics or controversy. Others wanted to see, at any cost, dramatic and even apocalyptic revival and reformation break out suddenly and miraculously. It was largely this second group who would put their shoulders into Donald Trump's presidency and January 6.

A Wavemaker

Peter Wagner retired in 2010 at the age of eighty. He did not choose a single successor but instead divvied up the many NAR institutions among his closest EVAT members. Chuck Pierce took over Wagner's more personal networks. Ché Ahn became the international chancellor for WLI. John Kelly, an EVAT member who helped create the ICA, assumed leadership of that professional body. Cindy Jacobs took the lead with the ACPE and also inherited much of Wagner's prayer and spiritual warfare infrastructure.

Though many of these institutions still exist, this partitioning of leadership brought a pronounced and formal end to the founding era of the NAR. EVAT was the one structure that Wagner did not hand off to anyone because it was his own circle of mentees, which no one of them could reasonably assume. He continued gathering the EVAT members annually up until his death in 2016.

As Wagner anticipated years earlier, his career of courting controversy and pushing the envelope has generated continued debate about his legacy and impact. Among the Independent Charismatics, Wagner is widely revered. Yet while some first- and second-quadrant evangelicals still celebrate Wagner's church growth concepts, many others have been extremely critical of his NAR ideas. In fact, in some noncharismatic evangelical circles, the NAR (they often pronounce it "the *nahr*") has become a byword, castigated as unbiblical, a form of heresy, and even a cult. This critique has very little to do with the NAR's politics or extremism, but instead these noncharismatic evangelicals have especially latched on to this idea of modern-day apostles and prophets—which was in no way original to Wagner—as the centerpiece of their theological censure.

Wagner briefly came out of retirement in 2011 to defend himself. Countering his critics, he wrote an article with the very acute title "The New Apostolic Reformation Is Not a Cult."[46] A couple of months later, he even went on the NPR interview program *Fresh Air* with Terry Gross to try to buttress the movement's reputation.[47] Neither of these attempts did much to quell the criticism.

As we've seen, Independent Charismatic culture is fast-paced, entrepreneurial, and faddish. This is the nature of nondenominational and deinstitutionalized spaces: parlance and terminology are ephemeral, with few abiding institutions to hold memory or create traditions. Leaders are constantly reinventing themselves, polishing their brands, and looking for a receptive audience.

While it had many dimensions, within the Independent Charismatic ecosystem, the NAR concept was primarily an organizational project and a branding exercise. Few of the core NAR ideas—indeed, even the NAR title itself—were original to Peter Wagner, but he bundled them together under the NAR heading. In the face of the Lakeland Outpouring scandal, mounting theological criticisms from first- and second-quadrant evangelicals, and Wagner's decision not to hand the empire over to one single heir, the NAR brand has not fared well. You won't find many people who positively identify with the NAR anymore, even among the people who populated Wagner's networks. The NAR brand was tarnished, so it was mostly abandoned.

The irony is that Peter Wagner's ideas have found incredible traction, and the leaders he mentored have flourished beyond anything he could have expected. But the label that Wagner preferred and promoted has died the death of a thousand cuts. Thinking back to his lunch with Jack Hayford and others in 1996, you can almost imagine Wagner embracing the irony and pivoting again, dropping the NAR title just as he did the postdenominational church. Because, after all, who cares about a title?

As the 2016 election cycle and primary campaigns began, Peter Wagner's health had begun to decline. He developed a heart arrhythmia, and he retreated from his endless speaking requests. But in February 2016, as the Republican primaries were beginning and conservative evangelicals were divided over whether to line up behind Ted Cruz, Marco Rubio, Ben Carson, or Donald Trump, Peter Wagner decided to publicly weigh in on a presidential race for the first time in his life.

Taking to his little-used Facebook page, Wagner wrote:

> For public distribution
>
> From C. Peter Wagner (This is a personal statement only—not representing any church or organization)
>
> I like Donald Trump
>
> Although I've never done this before, I am ready to come clean on this year's politics. In my entire life I've never witnessed such an interesting presidential campaign. I favor Donald Trump for our next president. . . .
>
> I have logged 85 years as a citizen of the USA, and I have never been so discouraged about our nation. We are in dire straights [*sic*]. I believe that much of America's malady has been caused

over the years by the establishment politics of both parties in
Washington, DC . . .

I believe that Trump has the qualities necessary to "make
America great once again," as he would say. . . . Nothing will
change if we vote for the status quo. Let's step out. Let's put
someone different in the White House.[48]

This was certainly not the most high-profile evangelical endorsement
that Donald Trump would receive in 2016. But from the perspective of history, it was one of the most consequential. Wagner was not a frequent Facebook user, but his friends and followers were watching. From the point of
Wagner's endorsement up until the present, the NAR leaders became the
trailblazing Christians championing the political career of Donald Trump.

On October 21, 2016, Peter Wagner died. He was eulogized by his
many fans and followers as one of the most nonconformist and trailblazing
charismatic leaders of his generation. To his critics, he died as one of the
arch-heretics of the twenty-first century. One of Wagner's final conscious
acts, in hospice care, was to fill out his absentee ballot for Donald Trump, a
choice his followers hailed as prophetic when, two weeks later, Trump won
the election.

One of the frequent exhortations that Peter Wagner had for his EVAT
sons and daughters was "I want you to go further and farther than I ever
have."[49] And they did. Five of the members of EVAT were present at the
January 6 insurrection, with one of them joining the riot by speakerphone.
Another seven or eight EVAT members contributed directly to the mobilization of Christian support for Trump's "Stop the Steal" campaign.

This means that half of Wagner's closest spiritual sons and daughters,
the inner core of the NAR, were directly involved in guiding the Christian
side of the post-2020 election pro-Trump campaign. That is the story we'll
explore in the remaining chapters of this book.

The most befitting description I've found of C. Peter Wagner's legacy
and impact came during an interview I had with an NAR leader named
James Nesbit. He was a loyal Peter Wagner supporter and a member of the
ICA. Nesbit is a minor celebrity in Independent Charismatic circles because

of his digital prophecy art. He's part of an entire market of artwork created by charismatic Christians based on their own or others' prophecies. Nesbit makes dramatic renderings of prophecies from major NAR figures, often mixed with biblical imagery, frequently depicting violence or spiritual warfare. James Nesbit's artwork was posted on numerous social media profiles of people who were either at the Capitol on January 6 or egging on the rioters.

On January 6, James Nesbit himself was with a group of about thirty NAR intercessors, apostles, and prophets who were stationed next to the US Capitol, leading worship and spiritual warfare against territorial spirits during the riot. I asked Nesbit about that day, and I asked him about the legacy of Peter Wagner in relation to American politics. How would Peter Wagner think about his legacy and what the people he mentored have done?

"What Peter Wagner saw way in the distance, what he lived for, is happening now and will happen," Nesbit replied. "It's waves that are coming. And every prayer that's been prayed, the waves are coming again and again and again. Peter Wagner was a wavemaker, and he started making waves, and the waves have not gotten any less since he passed away. They've grown more and more intense."[50]

3

GENERALS OF SPIRITUAL WARFARE

CINDY JACOBS ALWAYS knew she was special. Born in San Antonio, Texas, in 1951, to a father who was a former Hell's Kitchen gang member turned Southern Baptist pastor, little Cindy presciently predicted the birth of her younger sister. As a four-year-old, alone with her mother in their ramshackle house, she said, "I'm going to have a baby sister." Her mother, who had had a miscarriage before having Cindy, responded, saying, "Actually, Cindy, you're our last child," not knowing at the time that she really was pregnant with another girl.[1] Most people would chalk this up to either a mystical premonition or a kids-say-the-darnedest-things coincidence. But for Cindy Jacobs, it's the first stepping stone in her spiritual biography.

As noncharismatic Baptists, her parents didn't have any grid for understanding her seemingly supernatural insights, and they wondered if little Cindy had extrasensory perception (ESP) or some other paranormal abilities. "I just knew things, but I didn't know anyone who knew how to help me. I didn't know why I knew things. I didn't know what to do with what I knew," Cindy reminisces.[2] At the age of nine, she recalls, she felt strongly that God was calling her to preach, but there were no female preachers in her provincial Baptist surroundings.

Describing her rough and tumble teenage years, Jacobs says, "I knew things about people. I mean, I could actually scare people . . . I was kind of a hothead . . . [if] people crossed me . . . I would use that gift to cut them down. I'd tell them, 'This is your weakness.' Oh, I'd just start naming their problems, and God had to redeem me of that."[3]

Heavy lies the prophetic calling on a young person's head, particularly if she has been raised among high-strung first-quadrant evangelicals. "We were told everything was the devil," Jacobs says of her Baptist roots. "The Assemblies [of God] or the Pentecostal churches: they were just heretics in our thinking."[4]

She started college at Grand Canyon University, a Baptist school in Phoenix. This was the late 1960s and early 1970s, the era of the Jesus People, and ideas about deliverance from demons and prophecy were spreading outside of the Pentecostal denominations into other evangelical and Catholic circles. Music and singing proved an outlet for Jacobs, and she began experimenting with speaking in tongues while singing, privately exploring the boundaries of what her mysterious powers were: "I was so changed that people started coming up to me on campus at Grand Canyon to say, 'You got Spirit-filled, didn't you?' And I'd be like, 'Who told you? I haven't told anybody.' I thought I'd be excommunicated from the campus."[5]

At one point during her time at Grand Canyon, a radical commune of Christians became aware of Cindy's purported powers and spent five hours trying to cast the demons out of her because they thought her ability to know people's secrets must be coming from some wicked supernatural source.[6] Eventually, Jacobs would transfer to Pepperdine University in Los Angeles to pursue her passion for music, majoring in singing and classical piano and also earning a master's degree. That separation from her Baptist roots would prove another major step in Jacob's spiritual adventures.

Cindy Jacobs, like Aimee Semple McPherson and Paula White, has experienced a profound empowerment through Pentecostal-charismatic Christianity. Built around interior experiences and exterior manifestations of Holy Spirit power, charismatic spirituality has often been an equalizing force, elevating the voices of women and people of color in ways that bypass traditional Christian hierarchies. Women have found ways to claim religious authority not through traditional learning, which has often been barred to them, but through the more difficult-to-refute personal accounts of experiences and insights direct from God.

I would contend that no Christian woman living today has capitalized more on this experiential point of access to authority or attained greater spiritual renown than Cindy Jacobs. Seventy years after her first sibling's premonition of prophecy and fifty years since her awkward and unsuccessful exorcism experience in college, Cindy Jacobs today is one of the most respected charismatic prophets in the world. She is easily the most honored prophet in the United States. An energetic and emphatic septuagenarian with a penchant for red shoes, Jacobs still travels the globe leading prophecy conferences, mentoring younger prophets, meeting with world leaders, and adroitly utilizing the evidently supernatural fits of knowledge that made her an oddball teenager.

One of Cindy Jacobs's sayings is "The controversy of today is the commonplace of tomorrow."[7] This maxim offers a sort of heuristic for understanding her life and journey. She has spent the past four decades ferrying ideas and practices from the realm of controversy on the charismatic margins into the mainstream of American Christianity and American politics.

Jacobs was also Peter Wagner's first spiritual daughter, his sometimes-mentor and sometimes-mentee whose connections and prophecies spurred him along at several pivotal stages in the construction of his NAR networks and frameworks. If Peter Wagner was the theorizer, scholarly popularizer, and network-builder of the NAR, Cindy Jacobs was the mystical goad, the spur who pushed Wagner along many stages of his own development, from spiritual warfare to envisioning Christian conquest of whole societies. Indeed, the set of ideas and theologies she developed with Peter Wagner steered her to within steps of the US Capitol on January 6.

No Prophet Is Accepted in Her Own Country

Cindy's father died in 1973, the same year that she married Mike Jacobs, an airline executive. She was reluctant to marry Mike when he proposed because she'd imagined that, given her sense of special calling, she would probably become a missionary or a pastor's wife—some supportive, secondary female ministry role. Instead, it is Mike who has wound up playing second fiddle to Cindy's globally famous ministry life. Cindy sometimes laughingly recounts how Mike says, "I knew Cindy before she was *Cindy Jacobs*." The young newlyweds, living in Los Angeles while Cindy finished her master's degree at Pepperdine, were searching for a church that fit them.

Mike's secretary told Mike and Cindy about her church, Crenshaw Christian Center, which is a major fixture of the Black community in Los Angeles today but at the time had just recently been founded. Unbeknownst to Jacobs, the pastor of that church, Fred Price, was a notable figure in the Independent Charismatic Word of Faith movement, which, as we saw in chapter 1, is part of what is colloquially called the prosperity gospel. Mike and Cindy didn't even know what a *charismatic* was at the time, but the first time they visited, someone there spoke in tongues and then translated it for them as a message from God telling them to stay. So the next week they officially joined the church. Cindy recollects, "We didn't care. We were full of the Holy Spirit, and we were the token whites, pretty much, at the time in Fred's church. . . . We learned so much. He was a magnificent teacher!"[8]

It's not difficult to imagine someone with the self-confidence and seemingly preternatural insights of Cindy Jacobs finding a noncharismatic evangelical church that embraced women's equality in leadership—those do exist—and becoming a rip-roaring female preacher. Or she might have, conceivably, landed somewhere in the third quadrant, a charismatic denominational setting, that would have celebrated her gifting as prophecy but with some guardrails. Nearly all charismatics agree that prophecy is a spiritual gift endowed by the Holy Spirit to reveal the mind and the will of God. But that's about where the agreement ends.

The charismatic denominational spaces—what we're calling the third quadrant—value the supernatural spiritual gifts, but they also keep them relatively constrained within the horizons of the congregation. This is particularly true in the case of a potent gift like prophecy, which, unbridled, can wreak all kinds of havoc. Just imagine a rogue prophet going community to community, telling people whom they're supposed to marry, making wild predictions, or demanding money in exchange for prophecies. These are the sorts of challenges that inevitably surface with charismatic leaders, so denominations have developed clear guidance on topics like prophecy to keep them within some bounds.

But Cindy Jacobs didn't land in some egalitarian evangelical church or some structured Pentecostal environment. Instead, she entered into an Independent Charismatic space where her intuitions and sense that God was speaking through her were fostered by very powerful existing theological frames.

Consider, for example, this passage from George Warnock's *Feast of Tabernacles*, one of the prime mystical Latter Rain texts from the 1950s, describing the advent of the fivefold leadership gifts: "Ministries of apostles, prophets, evangelists, pastors and teachers are being established in the church, established moreover by God Himself, and their Trumpet-call shall not go unheeded. Their word shall be with authority. . . . And their authority shall not be by self-appointment, nor by human-appointment, but rather by the appointment of the Holy Spirit, and the ordination of Christ. Soon there will be a 'language' uttered in the congregation of the saints which men shall understand; for it shall be the Trumpet-call of power and authority, even as the very oracles of God."[9]

This was the conceptual universe that Cindy Jacobs found herself in, and it's easy to see how she embraced an identity as one of "the very oracles of God." There was room in the Independent Charismatic environment, oxygenated as it was by these Latter Rain ideas, for people to really pull out the stops on prophecy.

Still, the first decade of Cindy's married life centered on being a mother to their two young children. She was involved at the churches their family attended, leading worship and teaching Bible studies, but nothing dramatic. Mike was laid off from his airline job in 1979, and the young family moved back to Cindy's native Texas, to the small town of Weatherford outside Dallas. It just so happened that Texas was a noteworthy hub of this Latter Rain thinking.

At the age of thirty, Cindy began feeling God inviting her to embrace the calling to preach that she'd sensed in her childhood. Once she began, she was a sensation, and invitations to preach or to prophesy or to pray for healings suddenly bowled her over. Navigating through leadership circles heavily influenced by the Latter Rain visions, Cindy came to believe that she was one of these latter-day prophets, a self-understanding that integrated all the strange insights and anti-charismatic experiences of her youth. As Jesus had said, "No prophet is accepted in his [or her!] own country" (Luke 4:24).

Likewise, Cindy's continued pursuit of her calling was not without opposition. When her five-year-old daughter was enrolled in a local Baptist Christian school with strong anti-charismatic and male-leadership-only sensibilities, teachers and administrators at the school told her that her mother was surely a witch because she was traveling around praying for healing for the sick. Later they would even tell her younger son that his mother must not love him because she was traveling so often to preach.[10] These slings and arrows from her fellow Christians only seemed to fuel Cindy's sense of unique destiny.

Generals of Intercession

Cindy Jacobs was by no means the only charismatic Christian claiming an identity as a prophet in the early 1980s. As she explored her own charismatic capacities and learned from the Independent Charismatic world, Jacobs met many other leaders who were hearkening back to the Latter Rain ideas and believing God was commissioning them as prophets or apostles.[11] A whole collective of these modern-day prophets had gathered in Kansas City—aptly called the Kansas City Prophets—and there were inklings of the start of an entire prophetic movement, complete with mentoring for young prophets and theorization of how prophets should operate.

It is worth highlighting a couple of these like-minded charismatic prophets. The respected Latter Rain-influenced prophets of the 1980s included people like Bill Hamon, a leading enthusiast and experimenter with the fivefold ministry concept. Cindy Jacobs tells the story of being with Mike at a charismatic conference in Phoenix in 1984 when Hamon approached them, introduced himself, and said, "God has a word for you." That "word" described developing a prayer and intercession campaign with a group of five major Christian leaders, a prophecy that Jacobs claims later came to pass.[12] Cindy would also become famous for offering these types of out of the blue, "thus saith the Lord" proclamations, but it's clear that she first personally experienced these styles of direct revelation through people like Hamon.

Another ambitious leader in the Dallas charismatic world was a pastor and prophetic figure named Dutch Sheets. Sheets was, in the 1980s, an instructor at the Dallas-based charismatic school, Christ for the Nations Institute (CFNI), and a pastor at a local nondenominational church. Jacobs was a frequent speaker at and collaborator with CFNI and was clearly influenced by the people and ideas there.[13] After they met in the 1980s, Sheets and Jacobs would become lifelong collaborators all the way to January 6 and beyond.

Cindy's seizing on these Independent Charismatic paradigms proceeded to the point that, in 1985, she and Mike founded a new organization called Generals of Intercession, "a missionary organization devoted to training in the area of prayer and spiritual warfare."[14] Cindy narrates the inspiration for the organization in a vision she had one day during a private prayer time. She asked God, "Father, since Satan is not omnipresent or omniscient, how is he so effective in his war over the nations?" and God's reply came to her: *strategy*. God told her, she said, that "the enemy has a strategy for every nation and ministry." She felt a strong sense that God was calling her to gather together Christian "generals" who could develop prayer battle plans and strategies to counter the devil's strategies.[15]

Cindy's idea of healing or prophesying to nations also embraced a radical reinterpretation of Jesus's Great Commission, which he gave to his disciples in Matthew: "Go therefore and make disciples of all the nations, baptizing them in the name of the Father and of the Son and of the Holy Spirit, teaching them to observe all things that I have commanded you" (28:19–20).

Prior to this point, Jacobs, like most Christian interpreters throughout history, had read these as instructions to bring the message of the gospel to the people of the nations—that is, to share the message of Jesus with individuals and communities. But in 1985, Jacobs was awakening to a different interpretation: "We are called to disciple whole nations and teach them to observe everything God commanded," she would later write.[16] She believed that just as individuals could be plagued by sin and possessed by demons, so, too, could whole nations be mired in sin and oppressed by hierarchies of demons and need prophetic divine intervention. Adapting the Latter Rain ideas, Jacobs began teaching that prophets and other Christian leaders could mobilize massive intercession campaigns to tactically defeat Satan and bring whole nations under the kingdom of God.

Mike and Cindy Jacobs's Generals of Intercession ministry would have limited reach through the remainder of the 1980s. Only when Cindy happened to share a car ride with C. Peter Wagner would the organization really take off.

Spiritual Fathers and Daughters

In 1989, Peter and Doris Wagner were attending a gathering of prayer leaders in Washington, DC, for the US National Day of Prayer. During the lunch break, the Wagners rode in the same car as Mike and Cindy Jacobs. After hearing about their organization, Generals of Intercession, Wagner asked curiously, "What do Generals of Intercession do?"

Cindy Jacobs replied, "We pray for the healing of nations." This answer provoked Wagner's curiosity even further. This was, as far as I can tell, one of Wagner's first exposures to the Latter Rain blueprint for global revival through fivefold leaders. As their conversation unfolded, Wagner recognized that Jacobs was describing a captivating vision of Christianity.

As I outlined in the previous chapter, many Christians believe that an active cosmic war—a battle between angels and demons—is going on all around us and that people are affected by these skirmishes. Spiritual warfare entails Christians getting involved in this spiritual combat through practices like personal devotional prayer, worshipping God, fasting, and, on the more intense part of the spiritual-warfare spectrum, exorcisms of demons. It's tempting for outsiders to think that any use of spiritual warfare language signals extremism, but what I've just laid out is fairly widespread and even mainstream throughout the evangelical and Pentecostal confessions and even in parts of Roman Catholicism. The late 1980s was the heyday for a pair of Christian novels by Frank Peretti, *This Present Darkness* (1986) and *Piercing the Darkness* (1989), which together sold more than 3.5 million copies and that dramatically and violently depict an immediate interface between human actions and angelic and demonic combat.

Most of the people who believe in spiritual warfare practices consider them to be individually—or, at the widest aperture, communally—centered. In other words, spiritual warfare is about casting off one's own personal demons or protecting one's community from malign spiritual influences. The paradigm shift that Cindy Jacobs was initiating for Peter Wagner was, in many ways, the same one that she had undergone just a few years earlier: broadening the arena of spiritual warfare from delivering individuals from evil forces to mobilizing spiritual warfare campaigns to target whole nations for deliverance and salvation.

In Jacobs, Peter Wagner found a fellow traveler, another longtime first-quadrant evangelical turned charismatic. Jacobs ushered Wagner into a whole new theological universe, one populated by modern-day prophets and apostles, prophecies and expectations of global revival, and charismatic strategies for healing and discipling whole nations. Though she did not have a seminary education and was a full generation younger than him, Jacobs walked in a level of authority and gifting that amazed Wagner.

By 1989, Wagner had published nearly thirty books, and before the day of their car-ride meeting was over, Peter had already introduced Cindy to one of his favorite editors, who was at the same gathering. By the end of the day, negotiations had begun for what would be Jacobs's own first book, *Possessing the Gates of the Enemy: A Training Manual for Militant Intercession.*[17]

Cindy became almost an adopted daughter in the Wagner household. She wrote in 1995, "I missed my dad so much after he died and then the Lord sent Peter to be my spiritual dad."[18] Until his death in 2016, Peter Wagner would serve as a surrogate father for Cindy, supporting her and upholding her in ministry in a way that her deceased, noncharismatic Baptist father never could.

The Prayer and Spiritual Warfare Movement

Through the course of the 1990s, Cindy Jacobs and Peter Wagner would become pioneers of a burgeoning prayer and spiritual warfare movement that electrified not only the Independent Charismatic sector but huge swaths of the wider evangelical world. Wagner would later write, "I believe that the decade of the 1990s is characterized, more than any other decade in recent Christian history, as the decade of launching large-scale, high-level spiritual warfare on behalf of world evangelization."[19] Starting in 1991, he had Cindy guest lecture in his Fuller courses, bringing her ideas into contact with more conventional evangelical cohorts. Through Fuller, the Lausanne Committee, and his publishing, Peter Wagner had credibility among and deep access to influential networks of evangelical leaders. By inviting Cindy into such gatherings and spaces, he helped to introduce her "high-level spiritual warfare" concepts into mainstream evangelical venues.

Cindy also used her credibility in her networks to begin introducing Peter to her colleagues, fellow up-and-coming Independent Charismatic leaders. She brought people like Dutch Sheets and Bill Hamon into Wagner's orbit. Jacobs would later hire her prophetic mentee Chuck Pierce to help run Generals of Intercession, and after she introduced him to the Wagners, he would go to work for them, administering several of Wagner's nascent NAR institutions. Like Jacobs, Pierce became a right-hand prophet to Peter Wagner and virtually an adopted son.

You can see a marked shift in Peter Wagner's activity and in his writing after the initial meeting with Jacobs. The dozens of books he published prior to 1989 had mostly centered on church growth theories and strategies. After meeting Jacobs, he began publishing works with titles like *Engaging the Enemy* (sometimes published as *Territorial Spirits*, 1991), *Warfare Prayer* (1992), *Breaking Strongholds in Your City* (1993), and *Confronting the Powers* (1996).

Across these books and through his co-teaching with Jacobs, Peter Wagner developed elaborate theoretical systems for understanding how prayer and spiritual warfare could affect whole regions and nations. He would ultimately argue that there are three levels of spiritual warfare:

1. *Ground-level spiritual warfare*: Praying for and casting demons out of individual people. This level also may include praying for the "unsaved," that God would win the battle for their souls.
2. *Occult-level spiritual warfare*: Discerning where demonic forces have found footholds in individuals and localities through occult objects and human collaborators, such as Ouija boards, witchcraft, and—in what became a near obsession with the prayer warriors—Masonic temples and communities.
3. *Strategic-level spiritual warfare*: Wagner, Jacobs, and their collaborators came to believe that the phrases from Ephesians about "powers," "principalities," "the rulers of the darkness of this age," and "spiritual hosts of wickedness in the heavenly places" were actually descriptions of complicated hierarchies of demons with different tiers of influence. Wagner would call these commander demons, in his own phrasing, "territorial spirits."

The first two levels of spiritual warfare would be cognizable and mostly unremarkable to many evangelicals. But this third type, strategic-level spiritual warfare, was something quite new, and, subsequently, it would serve as the first ideological leg of the NAR stool.

Central to Wagner's emerging theory of spiritual warfare was the belief that the supernatural realm ("the spiritual") interfaces with the physical ("the natural") realm in real time and space. As he put it, the target of strategic-level spiritual warfare was "higher ranking powers of darkness assigned to geographical territories or significant human social networks."[20] A central outworking of Wagner's theories was that *you could not cast out territorial spirits at a distance*. If territorial spirits are entrenched in real geographical regions and real-world communities, displacing them from those regions would require on-site ("boots on the ground") prayer and concentrated warfare. This simple shift in the theology of prayer—from something that can be done anywhere into a tactical, on-site battle for authority over territory—would become a critical factor shaping the Christian presence on January 6.

Jacobs invited Wagner and her prophet friend Dutch Sheets to serve on the board of Generals of Intercession, and together these three leaders formulated plans for wholesale spiritual warfare to take back spiritual territory from the territorial spirits. They developed strategies of "spiritual mapping": a practice in which prophetic intercessors walk around cities and neighborhoods to discern and name the territorial spirits and occult footholds that buttress those invisible demonic forces. Spiritual warfare, as a concept, already invokes violence, and this group of strategic-level spiritual warriors around Wagner and Jacobs vigorously leaned into that military jargon. They would talk about spiritual warfare battle plans, weapons of spiritual warfare—Wagner called his online bookshop The Arsenal—and methods of spiritual violence to "take it by force," as Matthew 11:12 means in their interpretation. Prayer teams who were physically present became "boots on the ground" to enact these strategies.

This strategic-level spiritual warfare framework proved to be very controversial, but neither Wagner nor Jacobs was a stranger to conflict. Wagner had started teaching about these ideas in his Fuller classes, training up mainstream evangelical pastors and missionaries in his elaborate cosmic warfare conceptions. Moreover, in 1990, Wagner and Jacobs convened a group in Pasadena composed of respected leaders from their networks of friends and colleagues to try to find ways of implementing these new strategies. Out of this group was born a structure called the Strategic Prayer Network. Wagner was the international coordinator of the group, but, for a time, it was institutionally housed under Jacobs's Generals of Intercession.

The 1990 gathering that birthed the Strategic Prayer Network was written about by the religion editor for the *Los Angeles Times*, who happened to be an acquaintance of Peter Wagner's. It triggered a heated internal dispute among the Fuller Seminary faculty, who, especially since the

Signs, Wonders, and Church Growth course crack-up a few years earlier, were primed to be concerned about Wagner's activities. Now they worried that Fuller's public reputation would be linked to Wagner's wild theories about demonic hierarchies. The ferment around these concerns became so great that Wagner was asked to attend a special faculty meeting to discuss his views. He would later jest that the only thing that prevented the meeting from "becoming an outright heresy trial was the comforting fact that the official Fuller statement of faith had nothing to say about the demonic," so they had no formal grounds to censure him.[21] The faculty did write a letter of concern, which became part of Wagner's employee record.

The American branch of this global warfare network was called the United States Strategic Prayer Network (USSPN). While it predated Wagner's NAR organizations, the USSPN was a foundational layer for Wagner's leadership networks. It had strategic prayer warfare coordinators in all fifty states, many of them friends of Cindy's, and it was overseen successively by Peter Wagner, Cindy Jacobs, Dutch Sheets, and Chuck Pierce. These prayer coordinators became central hubs of contact for NAR networks in each of the fifty states, and they would organize strategic prayer warfare campaigns, including sending spiritual warfare "strike teams" to specific locations to confront territorial spirits.

Operation Ice Castle

By about this point in the book, you may be wondering why you are reading about people you've never heard of organizing 1990s prayer networks you've never heard of and what any of them have to do with the Capitol Riot. But stay with me for a moment.

The 10/40 Window effort had become the beating heart of the global evangelical missions focus of the 1990s. Tens of millions of Christians in the United States and around the world were praying for the 10/40 Window, donating to mission agencies to send missionaries there, and doing spiritual warfare against the demons in control of that territory. Peter Wagner was the central person coordinating prayer mobilization for this global campaign, and he used the opportunity to implant his newfound strategic-level spiritual warfare ideas into broader prayer organizations and networks.

This interweaving of prayer, prophecy, the 10/40 Window, and strategic-level spiritual warfare culminated in what has to be one of the strangest episodes of 1990s evangelical history. One of the prophets and coordinators in the Strategic Prayer Network, Ana Mendez, who served as the regional coordinator for Southern Mexico, became convinced while praying for the 10/40 Window that there was a territorial spirit named the Queen of Heaven who had established a spiritual stronghold on "the highest of high places, Mt. Everest."[22] She consulted with Wagner, Jacobs, and other prayer coordinators, and they decided to initiate a strategic-level spiritual warfare expedition to dethrone the Queen of Heaven and dislodge her from her perch over the 10/40 Window. They called it Operation Ice Castle.

So in September 1997, Wagner helped organize a team of twenty-six prophetic intercessors and spiritual warriors from Mexico, Costa Rica, Colombia, the United States, and Vietnam to travel to Nepal to be boots on the ground confronting the Queen of Heaven. Doris Wagner, who is very respected in these spiritual warfare circles, even traveled with the group. Accompanying her was a promising young American spiritual warrior named Rebecca (Becca) Greenwood, who was only thirty years old at the time. Doris was suffering from severe arthritis, so she and Greenwood stayed at a hotel at thirteen thousand feet up the slopes, while the rest of the team ascended to twenty thousand feet to locate the spiritual castle of the Queen of Heaven.

They spent three weeks in Nepal, blowing shofars, prophesying, and interceding against the territorial spirits. Wagner, Mendez, Jacobs, and others would later claim that this secretive operation—a sort of special-forces adjunct to the 10/40 Window campaign—was one of the keys to unlocking the 10/40 Window to further evangelization. Peter Wagner published an entire booklet about it titled "Confronting the Queen of Heaven," and Ana Mendez made a documentary with footage from the trip.

When I interviewed Becca Greenwood, she brought up this Operation Ice Castle experience not with a sense of embarrassment or chagrin about one's youthful misadventures. No, she was proud of her participation, counting it among her greatest achievements in a career of skirmishing with Satan's forces.

This bizarre episode illustrates just what a profound commitment Wagner's circle had to these strategic-level spiritual warfare ideas. They were willing to be boots on the ground for three weeks on the side of Mt. Everest to do battle against one of these territorial spirits. And it also enables you to draw a straight line from what Wagner's followers were doing with the 10/40 Window and Operation Ice Castle in 1997 to how they responded in the aftermath of the 2020 election.

"The Anointing of Apostle of Prayer"

The primary focus of the NAR early on, as the title implies, was with the new functions and gathering of apostles. But Cindy Jacobs would be instrumental in centering the role of latter-day *prophets* within the movement. As Wagner's thinking developed, he came to imagine prophets and apostles working hand in hand to bring about global revival, with prophets receiving guidance directly from God and apostles serving as the implementers, putting God's direction into action. Particularly early on, Jacobs was *the* prophetic voice, speaking direct words from God to Wagner and modeling the importance of prophets for apostles.

It is difficult to overestimate the importance of Cindy Jacobs for the remainder of Wagner's life. She was at times his co-builder of the NAR, at other times his right-hand prophetic adviser, and at times the networker giving Wagner entré into Independent Charismatic circles he'd never encountered. At every stage in the development of Wagner's thinking about the NAR, there was Cindy Jacobs, advising her spiritual father and offering prophecies to nudge and bolster him.

In contrast with more megalomaniacal personalities, Wagner originally resisted the idea that he could be an apostle. A major hang-up for him was that he originally thought of apostles as a singular class of church-network-building entrepreneurial leaders. At that stage, Wagner personally wasn't interested in building such a network. He had never even pastored a single congregation. So he decided he would be the theorist and teacher of the burgeoning apostolic trend.

But in 1995, Cindy Jacobs approached Peter at a conference with this message: "The Lord would say today, 'My son, Peter, today I put the anointing of apostle of prayer upon you. I put the mantle upon you of an Abraham, a patriarch, and I'm calling you forth into the land of promise.'"[23] Wagner was very amenable to such personal prophecies, and from their first meeting with Cindy Jacobs until Peter's death in 2016, Peter and Doris Wagner kept a journal of every prophecy they received from the prophets. By Wagner's retirement in 2010, this prophecy journal was 159 single-spaced pages.[24]

This 1995 prophecy of Jacobs's is the first time the term *apostle* shows up in the journal in reference to Wagner. He was also actively organizing and orchestrating global prayer campaigns, so the title "apostle of prayer" tied into a strong sense of existing identity and calling.

Jacobs's prophecy and ensuing conversations opened up the possibility to Wagner that there might be different kinds of apostles. He would ulti-mately distinguish between "vertical apostles" (those overseeing networks of churches and ministries) and "horizontal apostles" (those whose pri-mary ministry was networking together with different apostles). Thinking of himself as a horizontal apostle, or an "apostle of prayer" as Jacobs had prophesied, allowed room for Wagner to embrace this new self-conception and envisage himself not merely as a theorist but also as an anointed leader within this reformation.

It was through this initial prophecy from Jacobs—and a couple of oth-ers that he would receive from other prophets in the 1990s—that he became convinced he actually was one of these new apostles. Wagner came to per-ceive himself as a networker of networks, gathering the leaders of the NAR for cross-pollination and mutual mentorship. Once Wagner acceded to the idea that he was an apostle, things began to move rapidly in the building of the real-world NAR.

One attribute of Peter Wagner's distinctive and migratory career was that he did not so much "move on" from old ideas as backfill them into his new frameworks. His 1970s church growth theories segued into his 1980s signs and wonders phase with John Wimber, and then both of those became central underlying frameworks for his 1990s spiritual war-fare strategies. Likewise, as he absorbed and adopted the fivefold ministries frameworks about apostles and prophets and began building the NAR in the 2000s, following Jacobs's lead, those very apostles and prophets became the anointed "Generals of Intercession," commanders of coordinated spiritual warfare. Apostles and prophets, Wagner believed, carry a special divine commissioning and a special authority to cast out high-level demons. So an apostolic council, alongside more placid functions like church-building, could function as a "War Council" with strategies coming from "the Apostolic Generals."[25]

How Peter Wagner Finally Left Fuller Seminary

Cindy and Mike Jacobs moved to Colorado Springs in 1993, where their friend Dutch Sheets had recently relocated. While in Colorado, they hired a young couple, Jonathan (Jon) and Jolene Hamill, to help run Generals of Intercession. The Hamills would eventually prove very significant in interfacing between the NAR and the Trump administration. In 1996, Peter and Doris Wagner decided to move to Colorado Springs, too, a first step toward Peter's planned retirement from Fuller in 2000 at the age of seventy.

Peter had long been dissatisfied at Fuller, bucking against his faculty colleagues' criticisms and the "mainstream" (noncharismatic) sensibilities of the seminary. In June 1998, Cindy prophesied over Peter Wagner, "For the Lord would say, 'I am going to build a seminary here in Colorado Springs. I am going to gather leaders from around the world. . . . It is going to happen quickly. The Wagner Institute is so big that you cannot imagine how big it is.'"[26] This prophecy was striking and appealing to Wagner at the time, but he couldn't see any feasible way to leave Fuller early. He had never truly monetized his spiritual warfare, publishing, or other ministry side projects, so the Wagners were still practically dependent on their Fuller income.

A month later, Wagner was having dinner with a dozen of his apostolic mentees, and one of them asked him, "Peter, why are you at Fuller?" Slightly flustered, Wagner responded, "Well, I need the money." The group of apostles in the room began to exhort Peter, "We're your biggest supporters. We need time with you. We need you to mentor us and father us." Kay Hiramine, who was running Wagner's non-Fuller projects, eventually turned to Peter and asked, "Well, Pete, how much are you making?"

Wagner detailed his academic salary for them. The assembled apostles—who were accustomed to frank conversations about money and managing big budgets—began discussing, and by the end of the dinner, all of the apostles in the room had agreed to each chip in ten thousand dollars a year to replace Wagner's salary and free him up to pursue the NAR projects.[27] This was, in many respects, the inception of EVAT, Wagner's inner circle of financially supportive mentees.

So it was Jacobs's prophecy, paired with this blunt, brass-tacks conversation in 1998, that precipitated Wagner's early retirement from Fuller. Within less than a year of Jacobs's prophecy, he had already begun building a new seminary, Wagner Leadership Institute, to fulfill her foretelling.

One of the top students who came through WLI was Becca Greenwood, the young intercessor who had accompanied Doris to Mt. Everest. She moved to Colorado Springs when Peter hired her husband, Greg, to be the registrar at WLI, and Wagner later hired Becca to be his personal assistant. Along the way, she gained a bachelor's degree and then a doctorate in practical ministry from WLI, with special mentorship from Jacobs. Though she was a generation younger than Jacobs and two generations younger than Wagner, Becca Greenwood grew into one of Wagner's most adept spiritual warriors.

As all this institution-building was going on in the late 1990s, Cindy Jacobs approached Peter with a request: She and a group of her peers were creating a roundtable of respected and seasoned prophets to gather annually, compare notes on what they felt they were hearing from God, issue collective prophecies, and mentor each other. Jacobs felt that having a group of prophets meet without apostolic oversight was not fitting since apostles were the essential governors of the church. So she asked Peter to be the convening apostle of the group that they titled the Apostolic Council of Prophetic Elders. Peter and Doris Wagner attended and convened every ACPE meeting until 2008.

The membership of the ACPE was by invitation only, making it a prestigious group for aspiring fivefold prophets to belong to. Jacobs's sterling reputation combined with Wagner's organizational genius has made the ACPE a crucial credentialing association for top-tier fourth-quadrant prophets in the United States, and many of the highest-profile charismatic prophets have been part of the group, if only for a season. It still exists, now led directly by Jacobs. They gather in November or December each year to discuss their prophetic insights and issue a declaration in January called "The Word of the Lord." These "Word of the Lord" certified prophecies are published in charismatic media, and they are often seen as more reliable than idiosyncratic words from individual prophets.

So by the year 2005, when Wagner was seventy-five years old, he was presiding over a burgeoning network of networks that he called the NAR. The ICA had more than 430 members, influential charismatic leaders and pastors who were all trying their hands at being apostles. Wagner Leadership Institute, with courses taught by many of Wagner's inner-circle mentees, was serving hundreds, maybe even thousands, of students per year and expanding the WLI footprint through international franchises—Indonesia, Korea, and Canada—and five additional regional campuses in the United States. The ACPE, which he oversaw with Cindy Jacobs, was gaining increasing prominence and anchoring the American prophetic movement. And his EVAT mentees were becoming some of the leading luminaries of the Independent Charismatic world.

None of these institutions had existed a decade earlier, when Wagner first embraced the NAR concept. When you add them together with the USSPN's state-by-state coordinators, there were between five hundred and one thousand leaders in Wagner's networks at their high point. By the mid-2000s, the NAR was a known quantity and a real leadership force in the Independent Charismatic sector, with a battalion of leaders and networks all aiming to revolutionize the church. And through it all, by Wagner's side, was his prophetic counselor, mentee, charismatic tour guide, and spiritual daughter Cindy Jacobs.

Cindy Jacobs and 2016

Let's fast-forward through the next decade. Peter Wagner retired in 2010, handing off the reins of his many institutions and networks to various spiritual sons and daughters. Logically, he asked Cindy Jacobs to take over convening the ACPE, a role she has held since 2009. In 2008, Peter also handed off leadership of the fifty-state USSPN to Cindy. She rebranded this elite strategic-level spiritual warfare network as the Reformation Prayer Network, which remains to this day as the title.

Over that time span leading to 2015, Cindy Jacobs's prophetic celebrity star continued to rise. In 2015, on its fortieth anniversary, *Charisma Magazine*, the leading media organ of the Pentecostal-charismatic movements, published a list of "40 People Who Radically Changed Our World." All the people on the list were—predictably—Christian leaders, most of them Pentecostal or charismatic, and they were predominantly American. The list included many Christian leaders who would be familiar to most Americans: Billy Graham, Joel Osteen, Pat Robertson. It also included two members of Wagner's EVAT: Bill Hamon, an important old-guard prophet in the ACPE by then, and Cindy Jacobs. The magazine also featured Jacobs on their cover that year with the headline "A Prophetic Army Rising Up— Cindy Jacobs: God is raising up prophetic people worldwide to release an awakening marked by signs, wonders and miracles."[28]

It is not a stretch to say that by 2015, and very much continuing today, Cindy Jacobs was perhaps the most recognizable and respected modern-day charismatic prophet in the world. She has been a bellwether of the growing popularization of modern-day prophecy. While charismatics have long cherished prophecy as a practice, through her own prophecies and her leadership of the ACPE, Cindy Jacobs has mainstreamed the Latter Rain-inspired phenomena of individuals claiming the church-governing office of prophet— they *are* prophets; they don't just *practice* prophecy. Or as *Charisma* wrote in 2015, "Over the last 30 years, Cindy has come to exemplify the prophetic movement as it has grown in acceptance."[29] James Goll, another key member of the ACPE, said to me in an interview, "Cindy Jacobs walks in an authority, whether it's a man or a woman, unlike few people on the planet today."[30]

When the ACPE released their "Word of the Lord" for the coming year in January 2016, given the atmospherics around the Republican primary and Donald Trump, Jacobs's summary was cautious: "We sought the Lord about the upcoming U.S. elections, and the Lord did not speak to us about who would be the next president. He did indicate that He was preparing a patriot, but we would have to pray earnestly."[31] It wasn't until Peter Wagner endorsed Trump one month later that Jacobs really threw in with the Trump campaign.

In June 2016, as the presidential primary was wrapping up and Donald Trump had all but consolidated the nomination, there was a real reckoning among evangelical leaders across all the quadrants. Could they truly get in line to support a reprobate real-estate mogul and playboy? A noteworthy and underreported gathering that seemed to turn the tide toward Trump occurred that month in New York City, with a gathering of more than one thousand evangelical pastors and prominent leaders. This meeting, at which Trump spoke and reportedly won over a large segment of the evangelical leadership echelon, was convened by a star-studded list of more than thirty-five respected leaders of the religious right. These leaders included James Dobson, Ralph Reed, Tony Perkins, and, yes, Cindy Jacobs.[32]

Even as these behind-the-scenes maneuvers to get evangelical leaders aboard the Trump train were occurring, Peter Wagner was dying. In his final months, Cindy took on the role of spokesperson for the Wagner family, conveying health updates and prayer requests to the watching charismatic world. When Peter died in October, she wrote in tribute, "Peter Wagner was one of God's great generals. Today, I have been on the phone with those he considered to be his sons and daughters. All of us have a story, whether it is . . . Lance Wallnau, Ché Ahn, Chuck Pierce, Rebecca Greenwood. . . . None of us would be where we are now without his wisdom, guidance and promotion."[33]

Not to be deterred by grief from her prophetic political agenda, Cindy directed her energies into the Trump 2016 spiritual warfare campaign. Along with other NAR leaders, she mobilized the Reformation Prayer Network and all the other linked spiritual warfare networks to pray for the election and for Trump's victory. The vehicle for this mobilization was called the As One coalition, which brought together prayer and spiritual warfare organizations. Many of these were NAR-led—Dutch Sheets Ministries, Generals of Intercession, and Lou Engle's The Call—but others were more broadly evangelical.[34] This unity prayer movement had a nonpartisan veneer. But scratch a little below the surface, and you can see that every leader and organization in the coalition was Trump-supporting.

Reflecting back on this campaign, Cindy Jacobs would comment that it was "an urgent Pentecostal type of prayer" that, in effect, got Trump into office: "There is no way he could have been elected if it weren't supernatural."[35] Whether or not that is true, what we see in the 2016 election cycle is a prodigious mobilization of prayer and spiritual warfare networks on behalf of Donald Trump, with NAR leaders, especially Jacobs, serving as generals of spiritual warfare at the heart of that mobilization, all built on the foundational spiritual warfare paradigms that Sheets, Jacobs, and Wagner had pioneered in the 1990s. These efforts at galvanizing strategic-level spiritual warfare on Trump's behalf would continue unabated during the Trump presidency.

"A Spiritual Warfare Presidency"

Lance Wallnau, another EVAT member and main character of chapter 5, once labeled the Trump administration "a spiritual warfare presidency."[36] This is a good summary of how the NAR leaders regarded the period from 2017 to 2021. With the ever-growing legion of prophecies about Trump and a handful of influential NAR and Independent Charismatic leaders advising Trump, they believed that God had ordained and anointed Donald Trump for office and opened doors for their influence to spread.

Just as the 2016 Trump campaign brought about an unprecedented alignment of NAR networks and spiritual warfare campaigns, once he was elected, these same networks solicitously positioned themselves as some of the foremost Christian supporters of Trump. These ongoing spiritual warfare efforts kicked off publicly a week before Trump's inauguration when a group of NAR prophets—including EVAT members Cindy Jacobs, Becca Greenwood, Dutch Sheets, and Lance Wallnau, as well as ACPE members Harry Jackson and Lou Engle—helped lead a spiritual war council in Washington, DC, entitled POTUS Shield; *POTUS* is shorthand for *president of the United States*. The NAR leaders and dozens of other charismatic celebrities and prayer warriors gathered at the National Press Club "to surround the new president and the government with prayer" and "to discern, declare and decree the strategies of God for America."[37]

It is difficult to capture just how much optimism and jubilation accompanied this crew of apostles and prophets during this period. They believed that, thanks to their spiritual warfare campaigns, God's anointed leader had taken power, and they were going to push as far and as hard as they could to see their agenda enacted through Trump.

In fact, the night of the inauguration, as galas and celebrations occurred across Washington, DC, these same leaders and hundreds of other prominent Christians reveled at a dedicated Christian Inaugural Gala. Apropos of their newfound cache in broader right-wing Christian circles, the speakers roster at the Christian gala was dominated by NAR figures: Cindy Jacobs, Dutch Sheets, Lance Wallnau. Paula White spoke, and her husband performed a couple of Christian anthems. In the drama surrounding Trump's inauguration, few analysts noticed how the speakers list at the Christian Inaugural Gala elevated a new species of Independent Charismatic evangelicals, a trend that would very much continue in the ensuing years.

Perhaps even more striking than the NAR leaders eagerly positioning themselves in close proximity to the White House were the reciprocal efforts by the Trump administration to enlist and engage these groups. In June 2018, when Donald Trump was in Singapore leading a delicate set of negotiations with Kim Jong Un about North Korean nuclear weapons, Vice President Mike Pence helped to facilitate an intercession conference call convened by Dutch Sheets, Cindy Jacobs, Lance Wallnau, and Bill Hamon (all EVAT members) as well as Harry Jackson, Mario Bramnick, and Ramiro Peña (key Trump evangelical advisers with deep NAR ties).[38] These prayer calls were sponsored by Jacobs's Reformation Prayer Network and other networked spiritual warfare groups that Wagner and Jacobs yoked together in the 1990s and early 2000s.

Through POTUS Shield, Trump's Evangelical Advisory Board, and Paula White's advocacy, NAR leaders had multiple inroads to White House access and influence. But a crucial hinge around which much of the NAR-Trump administration activity turned was that same couple, Jon and Jolene Hamill, who had worked with Cindy Jacobs and Peter Wagner in Colorado Springs.

By 2016, the Hamills were running an organization called Lamplighter Ministries, headquartered in Arlington, Virginia. Cindy had brought the Hamills and Becca Greenwood and several other younger generation leaders into the ACPE, and they became integral to this new alliance between NAR spiritual warfare networks and the Trump administration. The Hamills were part of the POTUS Shield gatherings. They attended the Christian

Inaugural Gala. They were helping to convene the prayer calls with Mike Pence and the NAR prayer leaders.

"President Trump—in all of his complexity—has been uniquely commissioned by God to lead America in this time. And the results have been astounding!" the Hamills would write in their 2020 book, *White House Watchmen*. "Perhaps more than any time in recent American history, prayer has helped to fuel this governmental turnaround . . . prayer that has produced documented results that many times were spoken into existence beforehand through God's mysterious, sometimes unsettling, gift of prophecy."[39] Indeed, in the midst of the 2020 election cycle, hundreds of charismatic prophets (many of them attached to the NAR, but also from other Independent Charismatic streams) were prophesying in chorus that it was God's will for Trump to win the 2020 election.

The One Voice Prayer Movement

In the summer of 2019, it was rumored among people in the know that Paula White was going to get an official office in the White House. That summer, White was visiting the church of Apostle Guillermo Maldonado. Maldonado, one of Trump's preeminent evangelical advisers, was a Honduran-American apostle and pastor of a bilingual megachurch called El Rey Jesús with more than twenty-five thousand members in Miami. Maldonado was also part of Wagner's ICA and served as an assistant dean at WLI's Florida extension.[40]

There, at Maldonado's church, the longtime ACPE member James Goll approached White and Maldonado about a dream he'd had. Based on the dream, Goll prophesied to White that she was being called to start a new "governmental" prayer movement that would be a "network of networks."[41] Planning began that summer in the background for this very thing, primarily driven by NAR leaders.

A few months later, in November 2019, when Paula White got the White House job, one of the first things she did was announce what she called the One Voice Prayer Movement. She asked Jon and Jolene Hamill to manage and launch this new prayer initiative, and so, in early November 2019, a whole contingent of NAR leaders—including Dutch Sheets,

James Goll, Cindy Jacobs, Becca Greenwood, and Jon and Jolene Hamill—gathered in DC at the White House to plan. In the persistent chaos of the Trump administration, few news media outlets or political pundits took notice, but this new prayer initiative was historically significant for two reasons.

First of note was the very existence of a prayer campaign being launched from the White House by a White House staffer. Here a government employee—an ordained minister, in White's case, evidently as part of her official role—was coordinating an overtly religious and overtly charismatic Christian prayer movement. While the One Voice Prayer Movement maintained the facade of an apolitical "unified voice of prayer as we seek God's direction and calling for our nation," underneath the surface it was bristling with partisan proclivities.[42] Moreover, all the gathered leaders were prominent Trump political and theological allies, turning this prayer campaign, functionally, into a spiritual accessory of the 2020 Trump presidential campaign, which was gearing up around the same time. To my knowledge, the constitutional permissibility of the One Voice Prayer Movement was never adjudicated in court, but a White House employee spearheading a patently Christian prayer movement mocks the idea of a separation between church and state, and it would seem to potentially violate the Disestablishment Clause of the First Amendment.

Second, and perhaps even more historically consequential, was what the One Voice Prayer Movement would morph into after the 2020 election. Throughout the remainder of 2019 and the election season of 2020, these prayer leaders would gather several times to lead prayer conference calls or nationwide Zoom meetings. But after the voting, and after the election was called for Joe Biden in early November 2020, the One Voice Prayer Movement leaders would initiate a series of online mass prayer meetings they titled the Global Prayer for Election Integrity calls.

Almost all the Global Prayer for Election Integrity Zoom meetings were facilitated by NAR leaders, and they were a central organizing space for Christians who wanted to oppose the results of the 2020 election and see Donald Trump reinstated to another term. There were at least eighteen of these Zoom meetings between November 5, 2020, and January 6, 2021, and more than 1.1 million viewers either joined the calls live or viewed the video recordings of them during that same period.[43] The calls, some recordings of which were posted online, trafficked in conspiracy theories about faulty or corrupted voting machines. They were also full of strategic-level spiritual warfare language and inculcated the belief among Christians that the "stealing" of the election from Donald Trump was a demonically orchestrated plot against America.[44]

On the Election Integrity calls, NAR apostles and prophets mingled with like-minded Trump evangelical advisers but also with right-wing leaders such as Pennsylvania state senator Doug Mastriano, provocateur and strategist Steve Bannon, Trump's former National Security Advisor Michael Flynn, and evangelical heavy hitters like James Dobson. The little-noticed prayer movement that Paula White started in 2019 transformed into one of the most important vectors for gathering Christians to oppose the legitimacy of the 2020 election. One of these prayer calls occurred at the exact time that the Capitol was being breached on January 6, 2021, with leaders from Paula White's prayer movement sending video and text updates from onsite at the Capitol Riot to the 1,500 "prayer warriors" who were live on the call.[45]

The One Voice Prayer Movement and the Global Prayer for Election Integrity calls were not solo NAR affairs, and people from other intercessory organizations and networks joined. But both of these initiatives were led by the highest levels of NAR leadership and bolstered by the prayer and spiritual warfare infrastructure that Peter Wagner, Dutch Sheets, and Cindy Jacobs built in the 1990s. Cindy Jacobs helped lead some of the Global Prayer for Election Integrity calls, as did Becca Greenwood and Jon and Jolene Hamill. This was what Wagner and Jacobs had always wanted: NAR apostles and prophets acting as generals of spiritual warfare and orchestrating massive networks of prayer activists.

Jericho Marches

When the 2020 election was called for Joe Biden in early November and Trump refused to accept those results, all of the prayer and spiritual warfare systems that the NAR had built around Trump—POTUS Shield, the One Voice Prayer Movement, and the myriad charismatic prophets and prophecies assuring Trump's reelection—became the machinery of a spiritual warfare blitzkrieg. These NAR networks furiously and rapidly flexed, enlisting thousands and even millions of intercessors to join the unprecedented spiritual warfare campaign to see Trump reinstated.

In tandem with the national Global Prayer for Election Integrity calls, a series of spiritual warfare marches—frequently led by local NAR leaders, especially the state coordinators from the USSPN—began in the various swing-state capitals, the same cities and government buildings where legal challenges to voting and elector-certification processes were being brought by Trump's legal team and local legislator allies. These marches were called Jericho Marches, after the famous biblical Battle of Jericho, where the people of Israel were instructed to lay siege to the Canaanite walled city of Jericho by marching around the city, blowing trumpets, and crying out to God until God miraculously intervened and the walls crumbled. In imitation, the pro-Trump Jericho Marches involved ecstatic prayers, words of prophecy, people blowing shofars, and marching around government buildings. The shofars, rams horns originally used in Jewish liturgy, puzzled many noncharismatic observers, but these had long been deemed a weapon of spiritual warfare in NAR and other Independent Charismatic circles. In some of the swing-state capitals, particularly Harrisburg, Pennsylvania, these Jericho Marches became an almost daily occurrence.

The main event Jericho March happened in Washington, DC, on December 12, 2020. It was purposefully timed to happen concurrently with several of Trump's legal appeals landing before the Supreme Court, an arbitration many Trump supporters anticipated might be the means by which the election would swing back Trump's way. That wintry December day, thousands of people gathered on the National Mall to pray, worship, and hear rousing speakers, including conspiracy theorist Alex Jones, former Trump National Security Advisor Michael Flynn, and Oath Keepers leader Stewart Rhodes.

Two EVAT members also spoke that day: Lance Wallnau was there in person, and Cindy Jacobs delivered a video exhortation to the crowds. Cindy quoted Ephesians about spiritual warfare and said, "Let's believe that we are anointed to deal with corruption, that we are anointed to bring change."[46] At the end of the December 12 Jericho March, participants took up their shofars and marched around the US Supreme Court building, petitioning God for a Trump victory. That evening, pro-Trump protesters violently clashed with pro-democracy counterprotesters in DC; four people were stabbed, and the Proud Boys vandalized two African American churches, setting fire to their Black Lives Matter banners.[47]

"This Will Not Turn Violent!"

A lot of converging forces, campaigns, coalitions, and marketing efforts drew Trump supporters into the crowd on January 6. But to charismatic Christians, January 6 was pitched as another Jericho March—the ultimate Jericho March, in fact. Jacobs decided, just a few days before the January 6 riot, that she needed to be there, to be boots on the ground.[48] It was surely not lost on any of her attentive supporters that General Cindy Jacobs was going into battle.

Jacobs arrived in Washington, DC, early, and Jon and Jolene Hamill had finagled a White House tour on the afternoon of Tuesday, January 5. So the day before the Capitol Riot unfolded, the Hamills, Jacobs, and some other intercessors and leaders from the One Voice Prayer Movement meandered through the East Wing of the White House. Together they prayed, decreed, and did strategic spiritual warfare. Jon Hamill would later describe how, after the tour, Jacobs and the group stayed in the White House to pray with a "senior [Trump administration] official who had requested prayer."[49]

That senior official who requested a blessing from Cindy Jacobs on the eve of the Capitol Riot has never been identified. White House visitor log records released by the congressional January 6th Committee reveal that Jacobs was at the White House for nearly three hours that day.[50]

On January 6 itself, the same NAR-aligned Christian group that had sponsored the 2017 Christian Inaugural Gala (Women for a Great America) requested a permit for a protest outside the Capitol. Six protest permits were requested and cleared by the Capitol Police for events on the Capitol Grounds on the day of January 6. Such requests take weeks to process, so they were not merely fly-by-the-seat-of-your-pants petitions but required real forethought.

A striking fact lies buried in plain sight in the story of these permits. Of those six permits for protests outside the Capitol on January 6, two were granted to official Stop the Steal organizers and one to an anti-COVID-19 conspiracy group associated with the Oath Keepers. The other three permits went to Independent Charismatic groups. Of the permits requested for protests that day, half were awarded to Christian groups.

The particular permit pertaining to Cindy Jacobs's group requested a small stage, a microphone, and a speaker system.[51] So there on the southeast corner of the Capitol on a stage, during the riot, were Cindy Jacobs, Becca Greenwood, and about thirty other NAR apostles, prophets, and prayer warriors, including James Nesbit, the prophetic artist who told me about Peter Wagner being "a wavemaker." They posted videos on Facebook, so it's very clear what was going on.[52] Members of the group were kneeling, and some were wrapped in Appeal to Heaven flags. Others were blowing shofars. Using their speaker system, they were broadcasting prayers, offering apostolic declarations, speaking in tongues, and performing live worship music.

When I interviewed Becca Greenwood and asked her about that day, she told me that they were there to pray "for protection for our nation and our nation's capital. . . . We were praying for peace."[53] They were praying, yes, that there would not be violence—but also that the counting of the electoral votes would be deferred via "an audit" in Congress. That was the scheme Trump's allies in Congress were pushing for, and it was a miracle the NAR leaders had come to do strategic-level spiritual warfare for on Trump's behalf.

Cindy Jacobs prayed into the microphone,

Lord, send your angels, send your angels all around the Capitol,
Father . . . not one person is going to get killed here today,
not one person is going to get taken out. And we pray that the
message will go into the Senate and the House that there are
citizens outside saying that they want an audit.

I do pray calm. I do pray peace. We thank you for this in the name
of Jesus. *This will not turn violent, in the name of Jesus.* We declare
no violence. We take control of the atmosphere of this protest.

Becca Greenwood prayed, "Lord, we thank you voices can be heard without violence. . . . Release your angels. Release your peace into this situation. Lord, we thank you, Father God, every person will be protected."

Another intercessor in the group took the microphone and prayed,

> Lord Jesus, we pray right now against the territorial spirits
> right over this place. . . . And though we see this violence over
> these protests, I pray a prayer of peaceful protest going on right
> now. Lord, we will not be distracted from what the real issue is,
> and that is the territorial spirits that have been controlling the
> chambers of our Congress. . . . Lord, we ask you, God of the
> heavens, Lord of the armies of heaven, dispatch your warriors
> today in order to take care of those territorial spirits and in
> order to see your destiny for this nation released.

It is difficult to imagine that a more direct line could be drawn between the NAR and the theology of Peter Wagner and the Capitol Riot. Here two of Wagner's spiritual daughters are praying and doing strategic-level spiritual warfare against "territorial spirits," just steps away from the intensifying violence of the insurrection.

I have spent a lot of time researching Cindy Jacobs, reading her books, watching her videos, and tracing out her journey from gifted daughter of a poor Southern Baptist preacher to one of the most empowered female religious leaders in the world. But at the end of the day, the image of Cindy Jacobs that I cannot shake is this one: Cindy Jacobs—right-hand prophet and co-builder of the NAR with Peter Wagner—standing with her red boots on the ground at the Capitol Riot, praying and decreeing and declaring yards away from an assault on American democracy.

Spiritual Warfare Everywhere

Today, if you listen closely, you can hear the rhetoric of spiritual warfare insinuating itself into the jargon of American right-wing politics, even among people who are not charismatic.

Florida governor Ron DeSantis, a Roman Catholic, has taken to quoting that Ephesians 6 passage about the armor of God, but he'll swap out the phrase *the devil* for *the Left*: "Our state is worth fighting for. This country is worth fighting for. So put on the full armor of God, and take a stand against the Left's schemes."[54]

Trump strategist Steve Bannon has called Democratic candidates "satanic," "pure evil," and "someone who hangs with Satanic Groomers."[55]

And perhaps most chilling, just a few months before an attacker broke into Nancy Pelosi's house and brutally beat her husband with a hammer, Michael Flynn, Trump's former National Security Advisor, while campaigning for a Midwestern charismatic pastor running for Senate, said, "This is a war that we're in, this is a big-time spiritual war. I mean people like Nancy Pelosi, she's a demon."[56]

You could multiply these examples by the hundreds. Right-wing activists, pundits, and politicians have adopted a robust good versus evil, angels versus demons, cosmic combat framing of American politics. And of course there is that indelible image of Paula White, a White House employee, petitioning for "angels from Africa" to come over and assist President Trump in overthrowing the 2020 election results.

How did we get here? How did the most banal of policy disputes and disagreements come to be depicted in terms of Manichaean, militant vocabulary? Obviously, the polarization within American politics is not mono-causal, and a multitude of forces is driving the wedge into this ever-widening epistemic gap in how different Americans even know what they know. But this pugnacious application of spiritual warfare language and imagery to American politics came from somewhere.

At their fateful 1989 meeting in a car on the way to lunch, Peter Wagner and Cindy Jacobs hazily recognized that each of them was holding a piece of the future they both wanted. Wagner had evangelical credibility and respect and a curiosity about seeing prayer and spiritual warfare expand on a global scale. Jacobs held prophetic authority and charismatic ideas of mobilizing spiritual warfare on behalf of nations. Together they made the controversial, fringe ideas of the 1990s the commonplaces of today.

The Trump era pushed the accelerator pedal to the floor on this already escalating trend of spiritual warfare politics. By the 2016 presidential campaign, Wagner, Jacobs, and the NAR networks had created spiritual warfare strategies, practices, and a networked intercession infrastructure that they used to buoy the cause of Donald Trump. His four years in office were, to them, a "spiritual warfare presidency," and these orchestrated spiritual warfare offensives became so interwoven with Trump's cause that when he lost the 2020 election, Wagner and Jacobs's strategic spiritual warfare networks kicked into high gear. Together, the NAR leaders executed one of the greatest prayer campaigns in human history, all to upend the 2020 election.

If one was immersed in charismatic media or social media in the period from November 2020 to January 2021, the markers and themes of this mustering of spiritual warfare to see Trump reinstated were inescapable. To everyone outside of that ecosystem, these efforts looked like quirky, one-off Jericho Marches and idiosyncratic conference calls led by self-proclaimed "prophets." But on January 6, 2021, this massive spiritual warfare whisper campaign exploded into view around the US Capitol.

In the trajectory of Cindy Jacobs, we can see the direct line from charismatic evangelical prayer mobilization in the late twentieth century to the charismatic optimism and fury on display around the Capitol on January 6.

When I think of Wagner's three types of spiritual warfare—ground-level spiritual warfare (personal prayer and exorcisms), occult-level spiritual warfare (discerning where malign spiritual forces were gaining power through arcane or occult practices), and strategic-level spiritual warfare—the first two, honestly, do not cause me to lose any sleep. As much as performing exorcisms or labeling Masonic temples as occult strongholds could possibly harm individuals or even lead to intercommunal conflict, both of these sets of spiritual practices and assumptions are widespread in evangelical and Pentecostal circles. Neither presents society-wide threats to American civic life.

But strategic-level spiritual warfare? Layered into already roiling partisan politics? Where conservative and right-wing Christians envisage their fellow citizens, and often their fellow Christians, as literally driven by demons? In a theological milieu where Christians believe they need to "disciple whole nations" as though any society is a simple, monolithic whole? That is an escalating force in political polarization, one it is difficult to imagine ratcheting down.

If your political opponents are, literally, inspired by demons, then there's no negotiating with them. Demons are not meant to be negotiated with; they are meant to be battled, exorcised, and expelled. As we saw on January 6, this rhetoric of spiritual violence stokes real-world violence. You can only proclaim that a group of people or a political party is filled with demons for so long before someone decides that those demonic vessels must actually be physically attacked.

❦ 4 ❧

THE SECOND APOSTOLIC AGE

WHILE CINDY JACOBS and other NAR leaders were doing a prayer tour of the White House on the eve of the insurrection, the planners of the Stop the Steal campaign were holding a pump-up rally in Freedom Plaza just a few blocks away. This event was the largest pro-Trump gathering in Washington, DC, on January 5, setting the stage for Trump's infamous rally on the Ellipse the next morning and the riot that would ensue. The Freedom Plaza event was officially titled the Rally to Revival, a conspicuous attempt to cater to Christian Trump supporters.

This rally, like many pro-Trump events building toward the Capitol Riot, was part prayer meeting, part wild-eyed airing of conspiracy theories, and part campaign speechifying. On that cold and sometimes rainy afternoon, praise bands led the crowd in evangelical-style worship; pastors took the stage to exhort the raucous audience. Ali Alexander and other orchestrators of January 6 pushed election lies and Trump slogans, and name-brand Trump backers—like conspiracy theorist Alex Jones, former National Security Advisor Michael Flynn, and convicted felon Roger Stone—encouraged the seething crowd to not back down the next day.

Among the dozens of speakers who took the stage over the course of the seven-hour rally was a California pastor of a suburban evangelical church called Harvest Rock Church. In his brief remarks, this pastor told the story of his church's legal fight against California governor Gavin Newsom's 2020 COVID-19 restrictions, a fight he took all the way to the US Supreme Court. This pastor fervently declared that America was on the verge of being taken over by communism in the form of Joe Biden and Kamala Harris. He told the crowd:

> How many of you know that this is the most important week in America's history? . . .

I believe this week we are going to throw Jezebel out and Jehu
is going to rise up, and we're going to rule and reign through
President Trump and under the lordship of Jesus Christ,
because I'm telling you the consequences are severe if Biden [or]
Harris becomes president . . .

We are here to change history. I believe we are going to shift
this nation and this election that's been stolen from Donald
Trump and from the United States of America. This is why
it's so important that we gather tomorrow and pray and show
up and just take the stand to show the world that this is the
most egregious fraud—the most scandalous [thing]—that has
happened in U.S. history. . . .

We are going to take a stand until justice prevails because the
foundation of God's throne is justice and righteousness. And
we're going to say yes to justice this week, and we are going to see
President Trump be our president for the next four years. . . .[1]

On the surface, this scene is a textbook example of white Christian
nationalism. This pastor's short speech conflates the advance of the kingdom
of God with the interests of Christians in the United States: "We [Chris-
tians] are going to rule and reign through President Trump and under the
lordship of Jesus Christ." Threaded through the speech are Bible references
to bolster a sense of right-wing biblical patriotism, affirming the righteousness of Donald Trump and his allies, the "justice" of overturning a democratic election because it's God's will, all against the backdrop of the looming
threats of evil and communism.

The few news sources that took any notice of this particular pastor,
by and large, wrote it up that way: right-wing, Christian nationalist, pro-
Trump pastor says extreme things about God and Trump. But this pastor
was not a white nativist Christian nationalist. His name is Ché Ahn, and
he is a Korean American pastor of a multiethnic megachurch in Pasadena,
California, who immigrated to the United States as a child.

Nor was this speech merely a rehearsal of generic, conservative
Christian-nationalist talking points. Ché Ahn is a globally recognizable

charismatic apostle and among the most visible and vocal proponents alive today of the NAR. And while it is unlikely that most of the people in that January crowd had ever heard of Ché Ahn before, he is one of the most respected and revered charismatic Christian leaders in the world.

In the previous chapters, I introduced the NAR as having an ideological three-legged stool, and we saw how Wagner's framework of strategic-level spiritual warfare was the first of those legs. In this chapter, we'll look at the stool's second leg: apostolic and prophetic governance. We can understand this through three lenses on Ché Ahn's life: through his fascinating forty-year journey through the heart of some of the most dramatic and controversial developments in global evangelical Christianity, through his close friendship with and entanglement in the vision of C. Peter Wagner, and through the many forces that brought him to that stage on the day before the storming of the Capitol.

But first let's consider a question that has structured the entire trajectory of Ché Ahn's career: how do you govern Independent Charismatic churches? This question might seem mundane and tangential relative to the drama of the Capitol Riot. But in their revolutionary approach to Independent Charismatic church governance, Ché Ahn and his mentor Peter Wagner set up—in a roundabout way—a powerful contributing factor to the Capitol Riot.

How to Govern Charismatic Churches

To be charismatic is to seek fulfillment of two deep and driving desires. The first desire is mostly individual: charismatics want to feel supernatural power flowing through them. This personal desire usually gets discussed under the rubric of the biblical "spiritual gifts." Charismatics want to be filled with the Holy Spirit on a deep, existential level so that they can participate in a world of miracles, ongoing revelations, and a personal sense of closeness to God.

The second desire is more communal and global: charismatics want to be part of an extraordinary work of God in the world. This is usually framed in terms of seeking "revival": a fresh, unpredictable, collective outpouring of God's Spirit in such a way that thousands or millions of people are rejuvenated in their faith. Many Christians in many traditions hope for revival and talk about it in different ways. But I have never encountered any section of Christianity so singularly preoccupied with revival as Independent Charismatics. They pray for revival, prophesy about revival, strategize for revival, study revival history, and hanker for a bracing new work of God.

The steadfast pursuit of these two desires is what gives charismaticism its remarkable energy and even gravitational pull. For many Christians, the promise of having Holy Ghost power flow through you and seeing the extraordinary outpouring of God's energy into the world is irresistible. But these two entwined charismatic desires also create a great deal of instability. If everyone in a religious community is seeking to be filled with power—if everyone thinks they can hear directly from God and quest after revival—then charismatic churches tend to have a "too many cooks in the kitchen" problem. How do you keep a community of charismatics all rowing, or praying, in the same direction? This is the question that has structured Ché Ahn's life and the spur for the revolution he would help trailblaze.

Conventionally, there are three answers to the challenge of governing and channeling the energy of charismaticism. Option 1 is *denominations*. Denominations are bureaucratic and broadly democratic organizations that carry traditions and hold geographically dispersed churches in coalition. Denominations offer churches administrative and executive oversight— training and ordaining pastors, auditing budgets, and uniting disparate churches in a cooperative vision. As we've already seen, many charismatics of various stripes, especially Pentecostals and Catholic charismatics, fit quite comfortably within denominations, and the denominational policies and leadership hierarchies manage to keep all the charismatic energy in bounds. This blending of charismatic spirituality and denominational governance is what defines the third quadrant in our model.

But for more hardline or institutionally suspicious charismatics, this curbing and hemming in of the *charismata* by human institutions is misbegotten and invalid. After all, shouldn't the Holy Spirit guide the church, unfettered and uncircumscribed by human bureaucracies? Peter Wagner and his cohort came to view denominations with contempt. They saw them as nitpicking, managerial structures that always keep a lid on revival, squelching the volatile and assertive work of the Holy Spirit.

The same is true for most Independent Charismatics, who are, by definition, nondenominational: they gravitate to and congregate around diffuse
churches and ministries—nondenominational megachurches, televangelist
ministries, itinerant evangelists and prophets—where they can partake of
supernatural spiritual gifts and where the fires of revival can burn unchecked.
So for occupants of the fourth quadrant, Option 1 is out from the start.

Option 2 is what I call the *charismatic pastoral dictatorship*. This model
of church governance elevates a single person—a man or a woman but
usually a man—as the iconic pastor. In this model, the charismatic pastor has near autocratic power, and the rest of the community wraps itself
around that person's giftedness and insight. You can find churches like this
in nearly every branch of Christianity as charismatic pastors certainly have
no monopoly on Christian-leadership narcissism. But it's an especially
acute phenomenon among Independent Charismatics, where institutional
constraints are few.

The charismatic pastoral dictatorship can be a very effective model if a
community is seeking fast growth. Depending on how gifted the pastor in
question is, they can make things feel quite extraordinary for a good while; a
blossoming megachurch can quickly ramp up and even grow exponentially.
It can feel a lot like revival. But the pastoral dictatorship rarely ends well
because there's a finite cap on how expansive and extraordinary a single-
person-dependent church or ministry can become. Pastors who are invested
with that amount of power tend to flame out or become despotic. Autocratic
expectations breed autocrats.

Option 3 for an Independent Charismatic church is to adopt a
more boring *congregation-based democratic model* of governance. As with
all democracies, this is a give-and-take, and there are different systems for
working this out. A congregation can elect a representative board to keep the
pastor's power in check, or the pastor can be directly regulated and directly
removed by congregational vote. This can be much more sustainable than
the charismatic pastoral autocracy, but democracy is also tedious and contentious. Democracy depends on balancing competing power sources and
half-measure compromises. Very few charismatic communities can maintain
that sense of revival momentum amid banal congregational budget meetings
and slow-moving consensus building.

C. Peter Wagner, Ché Ahn, and their whole NAR circle offered a new solution to this troublesome question of church governance. What would distinguish them and set them on a revolutionary path is their embrace of option 4, what I call the *spiritual oligarchy* model: a style of church governance that Peter Wagner championed and Ché Ahn would perfect. Wagner believed that the twenty-first century had inaugurated a Second Apostolic Age, a new era akin to the era of the early church, in which the apostles and prophets reigned supreme. Now let's return to Ché Ahn's journey to see how this idea would play out.

From Korea to Pasadena

In his short speech on January 5, Ché Ahn points directly to his family's immigrant experience as a motivating force for his Trump support. He succinctly tells the story of how his father, B. Young Ahn, a pastor in Pyongyang, was arrested and imprisoned by communist forces in 1950. Only after American forces entered North Korea during the Korean War was Ché's father freed and able to flee to South Korea. There his father met his mother, they had baby Ché and his brother, and then the family emigrated to the United States, with Ché arriving in 1960 at the age of four.

B. Young Ahn was the first Korean Southern Baptist pastor in North America. The experience of persecution and communism in Korea haunted the young immigrant family. As Ché put it to me in an interview, "The horrors of communism [were] in my parents' DNA, and, of course, I grew up with that. . . . We have relatives and family members who are stuck in North Korea and who were sent to prison camps and concentration camps."[2]

Growing up in suburban Maryland, Ché Ahn, like many pastors' kids, went through a rebellious phase, becoming addicted to drugs at the age of fifteen. He began experimenting with Zen Buddhism and questioning his own religious identity. Then one night at a party when he was seventeen, he desperately asked his parents' God to reveal himself. "The presence of God came all over me. I didn't know what was happening at that time," Ché told one interviewer. "The Holy Spirit came over me. And I began to weep uncontrollably."[3] He cried intermittently for three days, basking in the love of God.

Ché attended the University of Maryland and got involved in a local Independent Charismatic church named Covenant Life Church, whose leadership had all converted or become charismatic through the Jesus People movement. It was there that Ché Ahn met and married his wife, Sue, and began raising their family. As we saw in the previous chapter, this Independent Charismatic sector, even in the early 1980s, was dynamic and experimental and exciting. Ché became an apprentice pastor at Covenant Life, and other church leaders recognized that he was "extremely gifted," if also a bit unformed.[4]

Even as Ché joined Covenant Life Church, that community was in the midst of a great experiment. The leadership was very influenced by the ideas of the 1950s Latter Rain revival, and they were one of the first groups in the United States to actually try out this apostolic governance model. Under the leadership of Ché Ahn's mentor, Larry Tomczak, the church proposed that they form an apostolic association of churches with Larry serving as the apostolic leader. So it was in 1982 that Covenant Life Church created an apostolic umbrella organization called People of Destiny International (PDI).

It was also in that transitional moment in 1982 that Ché, in his late twenties, awakened to a new sense of calling from God. He had a dream in which a Black man came to him and said, "Come to Los Angeles; there's going to be a great revival." As he awoke from the dream, Ché concluded that God was calling him to move to California.

It took two years, but Ché finally convinced the leadership at People of Destiny to allow him to start a new church under their apostolic auspices in Southern California. In 1984, Ché moved to Pasadena to set up a new PDI franchise on the West Coast. He persuaded a friend from Maryland, another PDI member named Lou Engle, to make the cross-country move with him and help seek revival and pioneer the new church. At the time, Engle was aimlessly mowing lawns, experimenting with the gift of prophecy, and leading Bible studies for People of Destiny.[5] Engle and Ahn would become fast friends and, eventually, global celebrities in Independent Charismaticism.

Wagner, Wimber, and "the Eighties from Hades"

As he was in the process of moving to California, Ché's father prevailed on him to not merely follow the Independent Charismatic convention of gaining ministry training on the job but to actually get an accredited ministry degree. So Ché enrolled at Fuller Seminary, and the first person he looked up was Professor C. Peter Wagner, whom he'd heard of and knew to be a conventional evangelical who was an ally to charismatics and Pentecostals. Peter and Doris Wagner were happy to meet this eager, charismatic young seminarian, and Peter counseled Ché on what Fuller courses to take and which "liberal" professors he should avoid. Thus began one of the most important relationships of Ché's life. He would eventually come to call Peter Wagner his spiritual father and spend most of the rest of his life enacting the NAR program that Wagner had yet to formulate.

Ché Ahn arrived at Fuller Seminary while the seminary was still in the throes of the MC510 controversy. He enrolled in Peter Wagner and John Wimber's standing-room-only course, and buoyed by his own Holy Spirit dreams, Ché saw the seeds of revival in Wagner and Wimber and the buzz they were causing at Fuller. He was immediately impressed with both men and came to see them both as mentors. After finishing his basic master's in divinity (a standard pastor's degree), he enrolled in a doctorate in ministry (an advanced pastor's degree) program at Fuller to spend more time around Wagner and other faculty mentors.

Yet even as he was flourishing in seminary, the People of Destiny outpost church that Ché Ahn and Lou Engle had moved across the country to establish was struggling. To be sure, in just a few years they had gathered around five hundred members for the new congregation, a perfectly respectable, mid-to-large church—by no means a failure. But Ahn and Engle didn't want a middling suburban church; they had come to California chasing something extraordinary. They wanted the revival that had been promised.

Even as Ché was entering Wagner's orbit, things were shifting back home at People of Destiny headquarters. The apostolic network effort was foundering and the leadership team was pivoting away from the charismatic, ex-hippie, Jesus People culture that Ahn and Engle knew toward becoming a very prominent network of Calvinist churches. A power struggle emerged between Ahn's mentor Larry Tomczak and the People of Destiny cofounder, C. J. Mahaney. Mahaney took over as primary leader of the network in 1991 and began guiding it in a more Calvinist and less freewheeling charismatic direction. Eventually, they would change the name of the network from People of Destiny to Sovereign Grace Ministries, and shortly thereafter, Tomczak was forced out.

As these changes occurred, this nondenominational community of churches slipped into the very "pastoral dictatorship" model I've mentioned. By the 2010s, Sovereign Grace Ministries would gain its own infamy as scandal after scandal broke in local DC and Maryland news about child abuse cover-ups, authoritarian leadership patterns, and Mahaney's megalomania.[6]

Amid these changes in the umbrella organization and the mediocrity of their own Pasadena church, Ché Ahn and Lou Engle were deeply frustrated. As Engle would later put it, their dreams had become nightmares. In 1993, Cindy Jacobs approached her friend Ché Ahn with a prophecy: 1993 will be the hardest year of your life, and you'll have to leave the church you founded, but you'll stay until 1994. So began the inglorious end of Ahn's People of Destiny career. His California revival endeavor had run aground, and he was dispiritedly leaving the church he'd founded with such high hopes. Ché was aimless and depressed.

The decade of relatively fruitless work in Southern California had taken its toll on Ahn and Engle. They would later joke about how they had experienced "the eighties from Hades." Then, in 1994—right on cue, per Cindy Jacobs's message—revival arrived: in Toronto, Ontario, of all places.

Revival, Toronto-Style

Depending on your religious background and what you were doing in the mid-1990s, the phrase *Toronto Blessing* may mean absolutely nothing. Or it may conjure images of people rolling on the ground laughing in spiritual rapture. It started at a Vineyard church, one in John Wimber's by-then-burgeoning quasi-denomination. John and Carol Arnott, the pastors of the Toronto Airport Vineyard, invited a little-known Vineyard pastor from St. Louis, Randy Clark, to preach in January 1994. What happened next was one of the most remarkable religious phenomena of the late twentieth century.

Clark was not the most animated or humorous preacher, but by the end of the first meeting, the majority of people present in the church were ecstatically laughing and rolling on the ground. This exuberant experience would come to be called *holy laughter*, and it was the signature spiritual expression of the revival that came to be called the *Toronto Blessing*. Over the next two years, hundreds of thousands of charismatics from all over the world would flock to the Toronto Airport Vineyard to see and experience the extraordinary outpouring firsthand.

The Toronto experience was, for those who embraced it, an encounter of joyous liberation and catharsis. They believed that the Holy Spirit was unleashing these new rapturous manifestations, which not only included holy laughter but also what people described as being "drunk in the Spirit," jumping up and down ("pogo-ing"), and occasionally even barking like dogs, roaring like lions, or squawking like chickens. In Toronto, the revival-driven charismatic energy was off the chain. Randy Clark and the Arnotts became charismatic heroes at the heart of the new outpouring. But the practices of the Toronto Blessing—the holy laughter and other manifestations—also rapidly spread to thousands of other North American churches as charismatic pilgrims brought testimonies and infectious excitement back with them.

Stuck in their malaise, Ché Ahn and Lou Engle heard about what had happened in Toronto. A few weeks after the revival began, they attended a conference at the Anaheim Vineyard, John Wimber's flagship church in Southern California, and the holy laughter began to break out there too. The two heavy-hearted pastors sat in the auditorium and watched as the elated laughter swept through the crowd like a wave. Here is Ché Ahn's telling of the story: "Lou poked me with his elbow and excitedly yelled, 'It's coming towards us! It's coming towards us!' I remember saying, 'Well, I'm not going to laugh.' But when the Holy Spirit hit our section, I felt myself getting inebriated. I could not stop laughing. It lasted at least twenty minutes. Everything was funny—even though no one was saying anything funny. It was a wonderful, refreshing experience that seemed to invigorate every part of my being. I didn't even notice until later that my depression was gone! I was excited about ministry again."[7]

This was the revival and personal renewal that Lou and Ché had been waiting for, what they'd moved cross-country to find. A few months later, they would travel to Toronto to drink from the revival's source.

Inspired by their new Toronto Blessing experience and eager to not see the revival pass them by, Ché Ahn and Lou Engle determined to start a new church of their own in April 1994. They named the new church Harvest Rock. Ché Ahn had taken classes with John Wimber at Fuller and respected him deeply. Now it seemed like the Vineyard was the place to be—the upstart charismatic denomination where revival had emerged—so Ahn and Engle chose to affiliate Harvest Rock Church with the Vineyard. Just a few months after its birth, Harvest Rock Church was renamed the Vineyard Christian Fellowship of Greater Pasadena.

Along the way, as they entered the Vineyard movement, Ahn and Engle met and befriended the Arnotts, Randy Clark, and other figures at the center of the Toronto phenomenon. They invited the Arnotts and other Toronto leaders to come to their newly founded church in Pasadena. When the same experiences broke out there, their embryonic little church became known for a time as "the Toronto of Southern California."[8] They began meeting in a local auditorium, holding euphoric nightly revival meetings. From their perspective, the prophesied and long-awaited revival in Los Angeles had arrived, and now they were at the center of it.

The Spiritual Oligarchy

If my earlier claim is correct—that charismatics yearn to both be filled personally with Holy Spirit power and to be part of something extraordinary— then we can begin to understand why the Toronto Blessing exercised such magnetism and uplift for people like Ché Ahn and Lou Engle. But just like Wimber's Signs and Wonders class at Fuller, the energy and eccentricities of the Toronto spectacle also attracted unwanted attention.

John Wimber wanted the Vineyard to span the gap between mainstream evangelical sensibilities and Pentecostal spirituality. Yet the Toronto Blessing threatened to tip that balance, linking the Vineyard movement with people being inebriated with the Holy Spirit, barking like dogs, and rolling ecstatically on the floor. The remarkable verve and vitality of revival were counterpoised against the institutional and governance needs of the Vineyard.

So within months of Ché Ahn and Lou Engle joining the Vineyard movement *because* of the Toronto Blessing, John Wimber decided to amputate the Toronto revival from the Vineyard churches. It wasn't a hostile separation per se, but Wimber made it clear that the churches insisting on continuing to propagate Toronto-style manifestations needed to disaffiliate from the Vineyard. Jack Hayford, Peter Wagner, and others tried to intervene and see if there was some way to prevent this fissure, but Wimber was adamant.[9] After only nine months of existing as a Vineyard church, Ahn and Engle joined the other Toronto outcasts. Their church became an independent Harvest Rock Church once more.

It is no coincidence that around this same time Peter Wagner began working on the postdenominational church theory that morphed into the NAR. Independent Charismatic church governance was stuck in the mud. Many charismatics, Wagner included, had revered Wimber and seen the Vineyard as the leading edge of a new, balanced movement of charismatic churches. But from the hardliner perspective, Wimber missed his moment when he closed off the Toronto Blessing churches. Charismatic people are ambitious and eager Christians, believers who want revival and fireworks and power, but charismatic associations and denominations are more cautious and institutionally wary of the bedlam that can ensue. The NAR was an idea ready-made for that moment.

With his NAR proposal, Wagner was saying: what if we could govern churches through a *spiritual oligarchy* made up of apostles and prophets? An oligarchy is a form of government that features a select caste or echelon of elites who develop power-sharing agreements to split up their domain. An oligarchy, unlike an autocracy or a dictatorship, is not built around a single person, nor is it bound up in bureaucratic processes. And it does not democratically or systematically draw authority from the consent of the governed. Oligarchies are more flexible than dictatorships. The dictatorship rises or falls with the singular leader, but in an oligarchy, the group of oligarchs can support each other, and the oligarch caste can grow or contract as needed.

Wagner was suggesting a *spiritual* oligarchy, one in which the newly commissioned apostles and prophets take over huge chunks of the Independent Charismatic landscape. He built on the foundation of Latter Rain ideas about the rebirth of the apostolic and prophetic roles (fivefold ministries) that had been kicking around for decades. Wagner was interested not only in the concept of new apostles and new prophets but also in finding a way to have it all hang together organizationally. Remember, Peter Wagner was not a scholarly theologian. He was a social scientist who dabbled in Christian theology. So while his NAR ideas have a theological dimension, and Wagner found his rationale in his interpretation of the Bible, the schema of the NAR is also organizational and pragmatic.

When powerful oligarchs compete directly, it can degenerate into civil war. So central to Wagner's NAR concept is the principle that apostles do not publicly fight with other apostles. In Wagner's mind, if you could just get the apostles and prophets—these supernaturally ordained oligarchs—to work together noncompetitively, they could unite in seeking revival and also take over the whole landscape of churches, and the whole system would be stable and cooperative. Indeed, at a sociological level, this is what all those seemingly obscure and low-profile institutions that Wagner built after he retired from Fuller were about. Wagner was trying to create relationships and power-sharing agreements among the most talented leaders of the Independent Charismatic world so that they wouldn't fight with each other over which church belongs to whom. Instead, they would work as partners. Wagner was building an ideology and an infrastructure for this charismatic spiritual oligarchy.

Let me be clear that *spiritual oligarchy* is my phrase, not Wagner's. But Wagner was very explicit in his rejection of the other church governance models: he argued that democracy and denominations (options 1 and 3) moved too slowly to perpetuate the required revival. He said, "One of the biggest changes from traditional churches to the New Apostolic Reformation is the amount of spiritual authority delegated by the Holy Spirit to individuals."[10] He also strongly rejected the idea that apostles were "autocratic, self-centered, [or] egotistical."[11] For Wagner, the authority of the apostles, including his own, was rooted, yes, in their charismatic gifting but also in their willingness to come together as God's chosen elites to work in concert.

And through all the building of the NAR, all the theologizing of apostles and prophets, all the selection of new spiritual oligarchs, there next to Peter Wagner, through thick and thin, were Ché Ahn and Lou Engle. In Wagner's theory, apostles are network-building entrepreneurs, but they usually need the guidance of prophets to know God's will. So just as Apostle Peter Wagner had his prophet advisers (Cindy Jacobs and Chuck Pierce), likewise Apostle Ché Ahn invited Engle to be his right-hand prophet. Engle would become a core member of Cindy Jacobs's ACPE.

When Wagner founded the Wagner Leadership Institute in 1998, Ché Ahn joined the faculty, and when WLI created regional franchises around the world, Ché Ahn became chancellor of the Pasadena campus and later the South Korea one as well. When Wagner took on leadership of the ICA, he appointed Ché Ahn to his apostolic council of advisers. When Wagner created his EVAT group of personal mentees, there, of course, was Ché Ahn. And as the fledgling apostles around Wagner started trying to actually implement this oligarchic model of doing church, Ché Ahn was at the front of the pack.

The Call DC and Charismatic Revival Fury

Part of what put Ché Ahn and Lou Engle on the map in the broader Independent Charismatic world was a spectacle: a mass event titled The Call DC. Arguably, Ché Ahn, Lou Engle, and their NAR cohort helped *create* the very mass-gathering, prayer-and-warfare styles that were on display on January 6. You see, twenty years before the Capitol Riot—during the presidential election that ultimately elevated (via US Supreme Court decision) George W. Bush—Lou Engle received a prophetic vision that he was supposed to lead a massive gathering of young people for a day of prayer and fasting on the National Mall in Washington, DC. This event would counter what Engle and Ahn viewed as a creeping cultural tendency toward apostasy, particularly through the liberalizing US courts and the toleration of abortion. This gathering would make Ché Ahn and Lou Engle international celebrities in the charismatic world.

True to their typical division of roles, Ché Ahn agreed to be the president and "apostolic architect" who would oversee the logistics of The Call DC, while Lou Engle provided the prophetic vision and direction.[12] What came together in September 2000 was a pivotal and impressive event, with, according to various estimates, between 300,000 and half a million teenagers and twentysomethings fervently worshipping Jesus on the National Mall with the Capitol Building silhouetted behind the stage. Ché Ahn, Lou Engle, and other Independent Charismatic leaders preached extensively to the crowds that day, interspersed with furious and fervent sets of worship songs. Michael W. Smith, one of the best-known Christian music artists in the world at the time, helped to lead worship. Dutch Sheets, James Goll, Cindy Jacobs, Larry Tomczak, and others exhorted and prophesied over the crowds.

If you watch videos of The Call DC now, the event eerily foreshadows the demeanor of January 6. People are worshipping and weeping and blowing shofars, with the Capitol Building behind them. There is apocalyptic preaching about the fate of America. Engle had asked that all participants fast from food to prepare their hearts for the day, so there's even a bedraggled, on-edge, desperate quality to the massive crowd.

The rhetoric that surrounded The Call DC had many of the same political and Manichean spiritual warfare markers that stoked January 6. Before the event, Engle gave an interview to Cindy Jacob's Generals of Intercession newsletter. "I just feel like there's a holy violence in the air," he said. "Even now, to start the year [2000], there are a couple thousand kids in California fasting, seizing the Kingdom through prayer."[13] In case you didn't catch it, that is a subtle invocation of Matthew 11:12, "The kingdom of heaven suffers violence, and the violent take [or, in some translations 'seize'] it by force."

In fact, one of the prayers offered from the stage during The Call DC was, "Lord, we turn our hearts to the Capitol building. . . . Lord, would your fire just flood through the Capitol, your fire of revival just flood through the Capitol building."[14] After the event, Engle opined, "I believe The Call DC was part of a shift in the heavens and that God has thrown a window open. . . . We have entered a season of time in a massive [spiritual] war. It's Pearl Harbor. It's Nazirites [the biblical sect of ascetic adherents to strict Judaism that included John the Baptist] or Nazism. We are in a war, and if we don't win, we lose everything."[15]

If I had to boil the spiritual genre of the Capitol Riot down to one phrase, I would call it charismatic revival fury. It was a potent mix: charismatic supernaturalism, the craving for revival, and militant fury at an American culture gone morally and spiritually awry. While there are many forebodings of this charismatic revival fury energy in American Christian history, The Call DC is the first place I've found where you see this charismatic revival fury operating openly, publicly, and politically: there on the National Mall, at the height of an American presidential election.

After the hugely successful first event, The Call became a roadshow, with Engle leading similar gatherings in other major US cities, guiding hundreds of thousands of charismatic evangelicals to fast and petition and pray for America. After a couple of years at the apostolic helm, Ché turned the whole thing over to Lou, and The Call became Engle's signature prophetic platform, further saturating the charismatic evangelical atmosphere with NAR spiritual warfare and revival practices.

Apostolic Networks Gone Global

The notion of worldwide, dispersed networks of churches and ministries, superintended by an elite caste of apostles and prophets: for those new to these ideas, it might all sound infeasible or just strange. But this model of doing church has exploded in growth since Wagner started writing about it in the 1990s. Whether it was through prophecy or his own expertise in church growth, Wagner was among the first major Christian leaders, and certainly the preeminent scholar, to recognize and embrace this burgeoning trend. Today you have thousands of churches in the United States and hundreds of thousands around the globe embracing this fivefold or apostolic-and-prophetic governance model.

Ché Ahn is a perfect case study of how an apostle-to-be goes about forging a network of aligned churches and ministries. Having sat under Wagner's tutelage at Fuller for a decade and grappling with his own disappointment at the crack up in the Vineyard over the Toronto Blessing, Ché Ahn jumped on board with Wagner's NAR program from the get-go.

In 1995, Cindy Jacobs gave Ché Ahn another prophetic word: "You're not to join another network; I have called you to be an apostle. You will be like Abraham, a father of many. And you'll have churches on every single continent."[16] After that, Harvest Rock Church began calling itself a "new apostolic church," and, in October 1996, less than a year after taking Harvest Rock Church out of the Vineyard, Ahn created Harvest International Ministry (HIM), his own apostolic network. It started with fourteen churches, most of them local to California and having connected with

Ché Ahn through the Toronto-style revival meetings in Pasadena. The Call DC gave Ché Ahn and Lou Engle's careers rocket fuel, and it gave them charismatic-celebrity spiritual capital to spend as they set out to build a global apostolic network.

By 2004, HIM was up to 120 churches, most of them in the United States or South Korea. By 2008, there were 8,000 churches and ministries, spread over six continents, under Ahn's apostolic leadership. By 2015, it was 20,000 ministries all over the world. And today, Ché Ahn's HIM has over 25,000 churches and ministries in more than 65 countries. Just to put these numbers in context, today the Vineyard Association of Churches has around 2,500 churches globally. Ahn's apostolic network is now more than ten times the size of the denomination he was cast out of.

Here's the crazy thing: most American evangelicals are familiar with the Vineyard, but few evangelicals outside of the fourth quadrant have even heard of Harvest International Ministry. HIM is probably the largest apostolic network governed by an American apostle, and it might well be the largest apostolic network in the world, but because it doesn't fit most people's categories, it operates off the books of official evangelicalism.

And Ahn's network is just one global apostolic network. There are thousands more being led by apostles like Ché Ahn, other Peter Wagner acolytes, and other fivefold leaders around the world. This apostolic network model—which was virtually unknown thirty years ago, when Peter Wagner started fiddling around with some NAR ideas—has become a covert but massive force within global Christianity.

So the question you might rightfully ask is: Why? Why do churches voluntarily join up to sit under Ché Ahn's or someone else's apostleship? What's in it for them?

I believe this apostolic network model of organizing churches has taken off in the Independent Charismatic world for at least three reasons. First, apostolic and prophetic governance is *charismatic*. It is facilitated through supernaturally gifted leaders, not bureaucrats or administrators. It's a personality-and-spiritual-gifting driven form of leadership. Apostles and prophets don't go around saying, "So after much deliberation, many meetings, and a long budgeting process, here's what we came up with." They say, "I prayed about it, and God revealed to me that we should move forward with this budget." In everything they do, the apostles and prophets point to a divine hand that is inspiring and leading them.

Second, apostolic and prophetic governance *is cooperative*. It's outward-facing. Apostles aren't fighting with each other or bickering over individual congregations. Instead, each apostle is focused on building out their own network. Networks can expand either through apostles and others starting new churches or by existing churches joining up with an apostolic network, sometimes through ditching their denominational ties. In fact, churches can belong to multiple apostolic networks. That happens fairly frequently, with churches or ministries claiming alignment with multiple apostles. The model is multiplicative.

Third, and maybe most importantly, apostolic and prophetic governance *feels extraordinary to everyone involved*. With prophets like Cindy Jacobs or Lou Engle saying, "Thus saith the Lord," people feel like God is speaking directly to them. You have apostles casting grand visions, making apostolic decrees, and building massive, globe-spanning revival networks. At the congregational level, pastors and church members don't feel like they are merely a generic, autonomous, local nondenominational church. No, they are part of an ambitious, expansive revival network! And sometimes their apostle or one of their apostle's friends or a prophet will even come speak at their church. This underlying experience—being a part of a global movement in which apostles and prophets are hearing words from God—hits all the charismatic dopamine-release triggers. Put simply, the apostolic and prophetic governance model scratches where charismatic churches and ministries itch.

HIM has many of the trappings of a denomination. It offers pastor-training conferences, leadership mentoring, equipping and funding for new church plants, and oversight to congregations. It trains and sends missionaries around the world. It has its own university. But what makes HIM and other apostolic networks distinct from denominations is that the heart of the network is not a democratic decision-making process or bureaucratic bylaws or committees. At the center of HIM is one man, Ché Ahn, who identifies and understands himself as an apostle, commissioned directly by Jesus, in partnership with other apostles.

To be sure, the HIM website lists a board of directors, an apostolic council of advisers to Ché Ahn, and regional apostolic teams. You might be forgiven for thinking its governance is similar to other nonprofits or denominations. But as Ché Ahn makes clear in his 2019 book *Modern-day Apostles*, those governance boards are appointed by Ahn himself and are made up of other apostles and prophets—his fellow oligarchs. They have little independent accountability or oversight.[17] This is the practical outworking of Wagner's idea that, in the NAR, God is increasing the "amount of spiritual authority delegated by the Holy Spirit to individuals." The leaders of apostolic networks are not elevated by the grassroots or governed through some bylaw structure. No, "from the top down" is a good summary of how power and authority flow in Wagner's oligarchic model of apostolic networks.

The Most Loyal Disciple and Successor

One of Peter Wagner's repeated exhortations to his EVAT mentees was "I want you to go further and farther than I ever have." When we examine the life of Ché Ahn, we can see Wagner's hope become reality. Ché has taken the vision of the NAR, the revivalist networks of churches led by apostles and prophets, and he has implemented it to the nth degree. Yet through it all, Ché Ahn has stayed loyal to Wagner. Since Wagner's death in 2016, many people in his networks and even former EVAT members have subtly downplayed some of Wagner's ideas and signature phrasings, particularly as the "NAR" title has become controversial. But Ché Ahn still boldly proclaims the vision of the NAR, and Ahn writes books that mirror, sometimes section by section, books that Peter Wagner wrote and concepts that he published. Ché Ahn is Peter Wagner's most loyal disciple, one who has far surpassed his mentor.

Indeed, to the degree that any one person is a successor to Peter Wagner, I would argue that it is Ché Ahn. In addition to creating HIM, the premier US-centered apostolic network in the world, Ché Ahn has been at the heart of the expansion of the platform for NAR ideas and frameworks. In truth, while popular, Peter Wagner was a disruptive figure who inspired great affection from those around him, but Wagner also always wanted to brand everything with his own signature concepts and phrases. Many Independent Charismatic leaders were already primed by the midcentury Latter Rain revival to be excited about apostolic and prophetic church leadership in the 1980s and 1990s, but not all of them attached themselves to Wagner's

NAR brand. Some preferred to maintain their formal independence while utilizing similar apostolic and prophetic leadership paradigms.

In 2008, Ché Ahn created a collaborative group called Revival Alliance to bring together HIM and five of the most important non-NAR five-fold ministry networks. All of the six apostolic power-hitter couples in the alliance had had personally transformative experiences through the Toronto Blessing. They include:

- Ché and Sue Ahn
- Randy and Deanne Clark (Randy was the original preacher who instigated the Toronto Blessing and now leads the Global Awakening apostolic network.)
- John and Carol Arnott, the pastors of the then-Toronto Airport Vineyard Fellowship who now run the Catch the Fire network
- Bill and Beni Johnson, leaders of the charismatic empire that is Bethel Church in Redding, California, which includes Bethel Music—a leading evangelical worship-music brand with immense reach—and the Bethel School of Supernatural Ministry (Bethel and the Johnsons will feature significantly in chapter 6.)[18]
- Heidi and Rolland Baker, whose international missions agency, Iris Global, is seen by many Independent Charismatics as an exemplary, miracle-driven missionary endeavor
- Georgian and Winnie Banov (Georgian leads Global Celebration, an apostolic missions agency, and Global Celebration School of Supernatural Ministry.)

I would not count the Revival Alliance partners, beyond the Ahns, as properly within Wagner's NAR as none of the others formally aligned with Wagner or sought his mentorship, preferring to develop their own brands. Yet the alliance members are vital hubs for carrying and propagating the new way of doing church that Wagner articulated. In fact, Ahn and his Revival Alliance partners were some of the leaders who pushed Peter Wagner into the whole Lakeland Outpouring debacle in 2008 by vouching for the erratic evangelist Todd Bentley.

When Peter Wagner announced and began preparing for his retirement in 2010, he entrusted to Ché Ahn one of the crown jewels of the Wagner realm: Wagner Leadership Institute. This was somewhat fitting in that, among Wagner's EVAT members, Ahn was the only one who held a doctorate from an accredited and respected evangelical school (Fuller).

So in 2010, Ché Ahn became the international chancellor of WLI, with its thousands of students, scores of faculty, and dozens of extension campuses spread across the United States and around the world.[19] In a surprising turn, Ché Ahn has gone from a man reluctant to even get a seminary degree to overseeing a global Christian-leadership training institution. Under Ahn's guidance, WLI would become Wagner University.

Accurate information about enrollment or student demographics at Wagner University is difficult to come by, but it continues to be a training academy of the NAR. The university carries on propagating Wagner's ideas, though now the courses are taught by a mix of old-school NAR leaders, up-and-coming young apostles and prophets from their networks, and Ahn's Revival Alliance colleagues.

Harvest Rock Church and the Supreme Court

So how did a Pasadena-based, Toronto-blessed global leader in the NAR—an apostle with tens of thousands of churches and ministries taking their cues from him, the international chancellor of Wagner University—end up on that stage on January 5, 2021, spiritually stumping for the election-denying Donald Trump? The answer to this question draws together everything we've already seen about Ché Ahn but adds in Harvest Rock Church's legal battles before the US Supreme Court.

In the spring of 2020, as the public health crisis of the COVID-19 pandemic wrapped around the globe, states and localities urged everyone to lock down and stay home. Harvest Rock, like nearly all American churches, closed its doors briefly and moved to offering virtual services. A few months later, though, many Americans, and many Christians, resented what they perceived as government overreach into their private and communal lives. Ché Ahn and the leadership of Harvest Rock felt that, by July 2020, it was time to cautiously reopen the church to in-person worship. At the same time, California governor Gavin Newsom was instituting an even more severe COVID-19 lockdown order, barring in-person congregational gatherings. Fueled by their own charismatic sense of rightness and divine sanction, Ahn and the Harvest Rock leadership chose to defy the governor's new order and sue Newsom to get the order reversed.

This combative step instigated a multi-month battle between Ché Ahn and the local Pasadena prosecutor. The prosecutor, seeking to enforce the governor's order, threatened Ché Ahn with jail time and said he would fine Harvest Rock members for every infraction, that is, every time they attended a worship service. Ché Ahn hired a high-power evangelical law firm to try to create a precedent for other COVID-ban-defying churches.

Through the summer and into the fall of 2020, Harvest Rock Church's case was meandering its way through the appeals process to ultimately end up before the US Supreme Court. Leading into that fall, the COVID-related cases that had come before the Supreme Court were generally decided in favor of the local authorities—mayors, governors, health boards—prioritizing the grave threat posed by the pandemic. Then on September 18, 2020, Ruth Bader Ginsburg, the revered heroine of the liberal bloc of the Supreme Court, died.

So less than two months before the 2020 presidential election, suddenly the decisive coalition of the Supreme Court was hanging in the balance. The NAR networks, in general, and Ahn and Engle, in particular, had long been vehement antiabortion activists, dedicated to seeing the Supreme Court reverse its *Roe v. Wade* decision. Now, on top of that general ambition to transform the high court, Ahn and Engle's own cofounded church was literally on the Supreme Court docket.

It just so happened that another major charismatic Christian gathering was slated to be held on the National Mall in late September 2020. While this event was not branded as The Call, it was an organizational and spiritual descendant of Ahn and Engle's original event. The Return boasted an even larger cast of charismatic Christian celebrities on the stage than the earlier events. Ché Ahn was there to offer a prayer before the live crowd of seventy-five thousand, and millions more watching the live stream, once again with the Capitol Building silhouetted behind him:

Father, we know everything rises and falls with leadership, and as leaders, as pastors, as apostles, prophets, evangelists, pastors, and teachers, we repent for our sins. . . .

I pray, Lord God, that we would see revival begin right here in the United States, this state that you have given us as an apostolic nation.

Have mercy upon us. Lord, I want to pray that you would overturn *Roe v. Wade*. Lord, I thank you with Ginsburg being, ah . . . who passed away. Lord, I believe that [Amy Coney] Barrett will be the judge that will help us to overturn *Roe v. Wade*. That we would see a moral reformation, we would see revival and transformation take place.

Lord, you've asked us to disciple nations as your leaders, we're to equip the saints for the work of ministry, help us to empower and encourage and be a great healer to the next generation of leaders.[20]

Ché Ahn prayed this prayer at The Return on the morning of September 26, 2020. A few hours later and a few blocks away, Donald Trump spoke from the White House Rose Garden to formally nominate Amy Coney Barrett to replace Ginsburg. She would be confirmed to the high court mere days before the presidential election.

Amy Coney Barrett proved to be exactly the kind of Supreme Court justice that Ché Ahn hoped for. As soon as she joined the Court, COVID-ban decisions regarding houses of worship began swinging in the other direction, favoring religious freedom arguments over public health. In December, she helped issue a "shadow docket" (expedited) ruling in the Harvest Rock Church COVID-19 case, deciding in Ché Ahn's favor.[21] Indeed, in early 2021, California governor Gavin Newsom was forced to pay $1.35 million to cover Ché Ahn and Harvest Rock's legal fees over the matter. And less than two years later, Amy Coney Barrett would be the deciding vote on the coup de grâce: overturning *Roe v. Wade* and the court-mandated federal right to an abortion.

"Whatever We Bind on Earth"

All this brings us back to Ché Ahn's enigmatic speech delivered at the Rally for Revival on the eve of the Capitol Riot. To those unfamiliar with Independent Charismatic or NAR discourse, Ahn's speech might sound like a random or even unintelligible string of Bible references. To those in the know, his speech sounded coherent, logical, and pointed.

In his January 5 speech, Ahn narrates the story of his legal battle with Gavin Newsom, connecting it to his father's immigrant experience: "They want to arrest law-abiding citizens who simply want to worship Jesus? And I'm saying to myself: I'm not in Communist North Korea. I'm not in Communist China. I'm in the United States of America. How dare they try to arrest people who want to experience and worship God! This is our first constitutional right."

He describes the Harvest Rock case coming before the Supreme Court and applies lessons from his choice to stand against the oppressive California government to the effort to protest the counting of electoral votes the next day:

> So we appealed to the Supreme Court. . . . and they said it is
> our constitutional right to worship, you will not be arrested,
> you will not be fined. It set a precedent for the church and all of
> a sudden L[os] A[ngeles] County said, "Churches, OK, you can
> meet."

> Here's the point: We have to stand in boldness. The righteous
> are bold as lions [Prov. 28:1]. We have to be courageous, and I
> want to say: pastors, you have to lead the way. We are to be the
> head and not the tail [Deut. 28:13]. Can I hear an Amen?

> And so we are here to change history. . . .

But the most important part of Ché Ahn's speech that day comes when he invokes Matthew 16 and Jesus's instructions to the original apostles: "I want us to pray. I believe one will put a thousand to flight, two ten thousand [Deut. 32:30]. I believe that he's given us 'the keys of the kingdom,' Matthew

16:19. Whatever we 'bind on earth will be bound in heaven. Whatever we loose on earth will be loosed in heaven.' Would you join me in binding the spirit of Jezebel off of this election?"

This passage in Matthew 16 is a central locus for ecclesiology, or Christian reflection and theology about the church. Jesus, speaking to Peter and the other apostles, promises his authority will accompany them and they will have the "keys to the kingdom of heaven" so as to bind and loose in heaven and on earth. From Ché Ahn's perspective, a demonic "spirit of Jezebel"—a major territorial spirit and frequent charismatic image for a malign power of chaos and debauchery—had taken over the country. With these words, he was using all of his spiritual warfare authority as an apostle to bind that spirit so that Trump could have another term.

I have interviewed Ché Ahn. I've read his books, and I've listened to hours of his preaching. I am convinced that Ché Ahn showed up on January 5 not to give a little speech nor stir up a crowd. He came to Washington, DC, that day as an apostle—the most devoted disciple of C. Peter Wagner, a general of spiritual warfare, an oligarch wielding immense spiritual authority—to decree and declare, to bind and to loose, and to spiritually push Donald Trump across the finish line.

It is tempting for many to write off Ché Ahn—along with other participants in the events of January 6—as a crackpot. But Ché Ahn is not a lunatic or an imbecile. He is an extremely sophisticated and influential leader, the sort of leader with whom tens of thousands of churches globally have aligned themselves. And on January 5, Ché Ahn was acting and speaking in a way that was perfectly consistent with the worldview of those followers.

Ahn believed that God had ordained Donald Trump to have another term. He believed that literal demons had hijacked the 2020 election, robbing Trump of his rightful win. And he believed that his presence and his words that day could change spiritual realities.

The next day, on the morning of January 6, Ché Ahn left his DC hotel room to attend Trump's notorious rally at the Ellipse. This time, Ahn wasn't leading the DC throng, but instead he was a part of it. As the rally ended and participants began marching across the Mall to the Capitol Building, by his own account, Ahn went back to his hotel room to use the bathroom. He decided to take a short nap and ended up sleeping through the riot. Then again, perhaps Ché Ahn felt that he'd already done his part.

Christian Supremacy

What are we to make of Ché Ahn? His is a remarkable American story: an immigrant child who came to the United States fleeing oppressive North Korean communism to become one of the most influential religious luminaries of our era. Objectively, Ché Ahn's life and ministry have influenced well into the millions of believers, both in the United States and globally. He has taken the ideas and the program of C. Peter Wagner and proven just how potent they can be.

When I interviewed him, I pointed out that many of his fellow evangelicals—indeed, many of his fellow Fuller Seminary alumni—believe that all this apostles-and-prophets business is heresy and that it is fundamentally unbiblical. He replied:

> Every move has criticized the next move; so, you know, the
> Catholic church criticized Martin Luther in 1517 with his
> teaching on justification by grace through faith and *sola
> scriptura*. . . . But then Martin Luther criticized the Anabaptists;
> he thought they were heretics for believing in baptism after
> conversion. And the list goes on: [Church of England leaders]
> criticized John Wesley, and then John Wesley's Methodists
> criticized the Pentecostals. . . . So, throughout church history,
> we've had this. Just being criticized by other church leaders
> doesn't bother me. . . . That's just the same [pattern] as in 2,000
> years of church history.[22]

Ahn is not wrong about the sequence of Christian movements giving way to new ones. The stalwarts of the old paradigm do tend to chastise the leaders of the new. And it's true that in the past quarter century, these ideas of apostolic and prophetic governance, what I've called the spiritual oligarchy model, have become the organizing structure for a huge segment of the Independent Charismatic world, which itself encompassed more than 300 million people globally in 2020. Maybe Ché Ahn really does represent the next historic movement in global Christianity.

Yet what accompanied the progressing movements that Ahn name checks was a widening circle of inclusion in the leadership of the church. Lutherans wanted everyone to be able to interpret the Bible, not just the Roman Catholic hierarchy. Anabaptists wanted every believer to have the chance to choose faith. Methodists fought for more rights for lay preachers and lay leaders in the church. And Pentecostals not only brought women into leadership but believed anyone could be filled with the Holy Spirit.

Through these different iterations of Protestantism, we have witnessed an increasing enfranchisement of Christianity, a move toward inclusion that paralleled the expanding democratization in the modern world. What are the denominations if not a governance structure for churches rooted in democratic checks and balances and the just inclusion of more voices?

In contrast, while Ché Ahn speaks the language of democracy and justice and constitutional rights, his ultimate vision is a retrenchment from democracy in the church and society. The spiritual oligarchy, while it may have the vocabulary of populism and empowerment, is creating a new entrenched charismatic church celebrity elite. And when Ché Ahn declared on January 5 that "we are going to rule and reign through Donald Trump and under the lordship of Jesus Christ," he was imagining a future in which Christians operate all the levers of power in America. He was hoping, as were many that day, for a miraculous intervention on behalf of Donald Trump, a divine coronation that would bring about the height of Christian privilege and power in the United States.

Many people today would call Ché Ahn a Christian nationalist, and there's definitely truth in that. He clearly hopes to see the United States operating as a Christian nation. Yet that descriptor is not quite adequate to the task of explaining Ahn's worldview. The set of movements and inclinations that get called Christian nationalism today is usually quite preoccupied with the boundaries and borders of modern nations. Christian nationalism is a vision committed to making a particular nation—the United States or Brazil or Hungary or Russia—a Christian one. But nationalism also tends to carry a certain xenophobic connotation; that is, Christian nationalistic fervor tends to include a wariness of outsiders, a preoccupation with Christianizing one's own nation, even if that's at the expense of caring about other nations.

In that sense, the term *Christian nationalism* doesn't fittingly describe Ché Ahn or the NAR movement, which is very international and global in its orientation. Ché Ahn and many of the apostles and prophets and adherents of the movement can more helpfully be understood as *Christian supremacists*. A Christian supremacist, by my definition, occupies the most extreme end of the Christian nationalist spectrum. Survey data show that many Christian nationalists in the United States are muddled and sentimental in their aims: nostalgic for recovering an idealized past but also, perhaps surprisingly, frequently in favor of religious equality and the separation of church and state.[23]

Christian supremacy is much more organized and ideological than Christian nationalism, and it's more comprehensive in scope too. Christian supremacists aren't just venting their feelings about the United States needing to be more Christian; they have a plan and a program. And they have a global vision that transcends parochial US concerns.

Christian supremacy emerges out of various strands of Christian theology, and it amounts to a theological habit of mind that parallels white supremacy in upholding one type of person as more trustworthy, fit to lead, and inherently virtuous than others. A Christian supremacist is someone who thinks that Christians should occupy authoritative and privileged positions in culture, politics, and other domains of public life. In other words, Christian supremacists believe that Christians—by dint of being Christians—are morally elevated above the rest of humanity and are empowered by God to govern civil society. Christian supremacists divide the world into stark binaries: the kingdom of God versus the kingdom of Satan, Christians versus the rest of demon-plagued humanity, those enlightened by the gospel versus those driven by base and carnal desires.

Certainly, not all evangelicals and not all charismatics are Christian supremacists. I would even say that not all apostles and prophets are Christian supremacists. Yet a sizable faction on the margins of those worlds is.

Christian supremacy is a movement whose ambition is a realignment of the global order. If you look at Ché Ahn's life, you'll find a huge segment of his calendar is filled with international travel, visiting the vast apostolic network he's setting up around the world. He wants to see those Christians in those countries empowered by the Holy Spirit take possession of the political, cultural, and social domains of their societies too. Christian supremacists may jubilantly declare Jesus is king over all creation, but as long as we're waiting for Jesus to return, they're keen to govern in his stead.

When Ché Ahn says, "We are to be the head and not the tail," this is charismatic-speak for *Christians should be supernaturally empowered by God to lead society*. When Ché Ahn says, "We are going to rule and reign through Donald Trump and under the lordship of Jesus Christ," he evokes a future in which Christians have coercive power to order society according to their agenda.

Since January 6, Ché Ahn's celebrity and clout have increased. Now, like many other frontline charismatic leaders who stood with Trump's effort to overthrow the election, Ché Ahn has become an inside player in the religious right. In fact, if you want to know which pastors have real juice with Christian voters, watch where politicians congregate and which leaders they seek out. Harvest Rock now occupies that tier of must-visit churches for ambitious Republican politicians on the hunt for supporters. Sarah Palin recorded a congratulatory video celebrating Ahn and Harvest Rock's victory over Gavin Newsom. Palin, along with Trump's former secretary of state, Mike Pompeo, joined Ché Ahn on stage at Harvest Rock for a conference in July 2021, signaling their desire to be seen with him.[24] Senator Josh Hawley, another ambitious hardline Christian politician, recorded a long-form interview with Ahn at Harvest Rock that fall.[25] Kari Lake, the losing Arizona governor candidate in 2022, has given the keynote address at one of HIM's leadership conferences.[26]

Ché Ahn is an accomplished, forward-thinking church leader, ushering in Wagner's Second Apostolic Age. If he has his druthers, the apostles and prophets' spiritual oligarchy will continue to expand, and one day all of America—indeed, all of the world—will submit to Christians, under the lordship of Jesus Christ.

But the NAR agenda goes far beyond apostolic declarations or imagined futures. Part of what Wagner and his cohort have constructed is a dedicated, charismatic program and plan for Christian supremacy, undergirded by prophecy. That program is called the Seven Mountain Mandate.

SEVEN MOUNTAINS

THE ENDURING PUZZLE of why so many evangelicals support Donald Trump has occasioned dozens of books, hundreds of academic papers, thousands of op-eds, and millions of social media posts. Eighty-one percent of white evangelicals voted for Trump in 2016 and in similar numbers in 2020. That's a higher percentage of white evangelicals than voted for Ronald Reagan (1980, 1984), George H. W. Bush (1988, 1992), George W. Bush (2000, 2004), John McCain (2008), or Mitt Romney (2012).[1] A 2018 survey that included nonwhite evangelicals showed a more muddled picture but one nonetheless firmly in Trump's camp, with 58 percent of all evangelicals voting for Trump (77 percent of white evangelicals, 9 percent of Black, 41 percent of Latino/a, and 48 percent of other ethnicities).[2] Moreover, across these two presidential elections, evangelicals—particularly, but not exclusively, white evangelicals—have proved to be one of Donald Trump's most loyal constituencies, perpetually expressing their approval of the job he did in office and intensely backing him against any rivals, including politicians who were more outwardly evangelical and more overtly upstanding.

So how did Trump elicit and secure such ardent evangelical support? Or as the question has been posed to me by liberal Christians, Jews, Muslims, and nonreligious people, how could anyone who claims to be moral and religious support that man?

No simple explanation can account for the complex behavior of tens of millions of American voters, but this chapter puts in place one big piece of the puzzle as to how this evangelical-Trump alliance came about. We've already examined the way that Paula White used her position of influence advising Trump to integrate her fellow Independent Charismatic (fourth-quadrant) leaders into the highest echelons of the religious right. Now we'll look at the broader structures of power in American evangelicalism and the theological ideas that were used to vindicate Christian Trumpism.

What are the actual biblical citations or theological frames that evangelicals have used to articulate their Trump support? Where did those frames come from? And how have those ideas interacted with the powerful evangelical establishment and its elites? We will consider these questions through the prism of a man who has been, inarguably, one of Donald Trump's most prominent evangelical champions: Lance Wallnau. While Wallnau is not a household name in broader American evangelicalism, and you may have never heard of him, we cannot fathom evangelical support for Trump without understanding the pivotal role that Wallnau's theology and prophecies have played in creating an evangelical rationale for making Trump king of the mountain.

A former charismatic pastor who's now a mottled blend of motivational speaker, business consultant, prophet, theologian, and political pundit, Wallnau was, in 2015, a fringe Independent Charismatic character, an unlikely spiritual guide for the movement of Christian Trumpism. But no evangelical leader has done more to theologically backstop the presidency of Donald Trump than Lance Wallnau.

Like Ché Ahn and Cindy Jacobs, Lance Wallnau was a mentee of Peter Wagner's, and he contributed significantly to the NAR ideology and movement growth. Along the path of understanding Wallnau—having grasped the strategic-level spiritual warfare and apostolic governance dimensions of the movement—we'll also come to understand the third and final leg of our NAR stool: its political theology, which has been shaped around Wallnau's concept of the Seven Mountain Mandate. But before we get to Wallnau and his ideas, we need to think about the evangelical establishment that Wagner, Wallnau, and Trump were so successful in disrupting.

Establishment Evangelicalism, Evangelical Elites, and Donald Trump

Evangelicalism, as a modern movement, emerged in the United States in the 1940s. To be sure, many people were using the adjective *evangelical* (as in "evangelical Christians") in the nineteenth and early twentieth centuries, but the term was then roughly a synonym for Protestant, representing a wide spectrum of liberal and conservative Christian denominations and identities.

Early twentieth-century conservative American Protestantism was dominated by a theologically reactionary movement of churches and leaders who called themselves "the Fundamentalists." The Fundamentalists were frustrated with how loosey-goosey many of their fellow Protestants had become. They worried about the creeping influence of biblical criticism that was increasingly popular in American seminaries and universities and undermined many conventional assumptions about the Bible. They worried about the lax morality of the Progressive Era. They worried about the growing integration of Darwin's theory of evolution into science. The Fundamentalists were also deeply pessimistic and antagonistic toward American culture and, really, anyone who disagreed with them.

So in the 1940s, a still-conservative but more congenial and erudite group of Fundamentalist leaders decided that they were tired of the gloomy separatism and internal bickering of Fundamentalism, and they invested in identifying with a different term: *evangelical.* This group of ex-Fundamentalists, which centered on the evangelist Billy Graham, would go on to found a raft of institutions: *Christianity Today* magazine, the flagship journal of American evangelicalism; Fuller Theological Seminary, the foremost seminary of the young movement; and the National Association of Evangelicals (NAE), an umbrella organization for various Protestant denominations who wanted to adopt this more affirmative *evangelical* as their moniker.

Over the decades, more organizations—missions agencies, seminaries, Bible colleges, universities, publishing houses, parachurch (interdenominational) organizations, and political advocacy coalitions—would embrace the evangelical label, creating an enormous evangelical institutional footprint. True to the culture-positive vision of the original evangelical leaders in the 1940s, the leaders of these institutions were culturally savvy and college-educated, with many holding advanced degrees. And when the media sought out people to speak for evangelicalism, they interviewed this upper echelon of elite evangelicals—journalists, college presidents, CEOs, authors, pastors, and denominational leaders. To the degree that the theologically, geographically, and regionally diverse evangelical movement had any coherence, it was offered by these establishment leaders.

So when we come to an event like the Capitol Riot, some analysts were quick to note the many signs and signals of evangelical piety and Christian nationalism in the crowds. But some evangelical leaders and their allies pushed back, arguing that while some of the rioters and their crowd of supporters may have been using evangelical symbols or invoking evangelical shibboleths, they were *not* representing "evangelicalism."

For instance, the NAE put out a statement dutifully condemning the January 6 riot, saying, "The National Association of Evangelicals (NAE) denounces the violence at the U.S. Capitol as well as the nation's longstanding vices that led to this chaos." But when it came to identifying some of the rioters as evangelicals, the NAE was more equivocal: "The mob at the Capitol was provoked by leaders, including President Trump, who have employed lies and conspiracy theories for political gain. *Evangelicals are people who are committed to truth and should reject untruths.*"[3] So if the riot was premised on a lie, and evangelicals are "committed to truth," then evangelicals who joined the riot must, at the very least, not have been good evangelicals, right?

The most forthright of these arguments came from veteran Christian religion reporter and commentator Terry Mattingly, who, a week after January 6, would write in an editorial that he could see no discernible pattern of connections between the rioters and establishment evangelical institutions: "Anyone who studies 'evangelicalism'—white or otherwise—knows that we are talking about a movement based on the work of powerful denominations (this includes megachurches), parachurch groups, publishers (and authors) and major colleges, universities and seminaries." Mattingly went on to hazard that those Christians who did join the riot were "people from small, possibly independent, congregations with zero connections to institutions of evangelical power" and that "almost certainly means that these people are part of a smaller niche and are not, again, linked to or even influenced by power centers inside evangelicalism."[4]

Mattingly here is very much reflecting the journalistic and academic conventional wisdom about American evangelicalism: that evangelical Christianity exerts its cultural, political, and religious influence through weighty institutions and large voter blocs. It follows that if we want to understand the trendlines and zeitgeist of evangelicalism, we must continue to look to those institutions and their representative spokespeople. Hence, if establishment evangelicalism was not, in any way, directly tied to or even supportive of the riot, some who participated may have been evangelicals in some sense, but they were not representing "true evangelicalism."

This establishment approach to understanding American evangelicalism has almost entirely misapprehended the mystical ties that bind so many evangelicals to Donald Trump. Evangelical elites—the institutional leaders and muckety mucks who align around the NAE and whom Mattingly suggests guide and manage the "power centers" of evangelicalism—were actually outposts of resistance to Trump early on.

During the 2016 campaign, even as Trump was winning over huge swaths of evangelical voters on the ground, the evangelical elites generally wanted nothing to do with him. Trump's evangelical support, particularly early on in that campaign, came not through the power centers but the grassroots.

This divide between elite evangelicalism and populist evangelicalism was evident at *Christianity Today*, the most respected news outlet speaking for and to the evangelical community. I've talked to multiple reporters and editors who worked at *Christianity Today* during the 2016 election, and they've described the staff as shocked when Donald Trump won the election, especially by the fact that he received such stalwart evangelical support. Mark Galli, the *Christianity Today* editor at the time, would later describe the post-election sentiment in his elite evangelical circles as "Who are these people? I know hardly anyone, let alone any evangelical Christian, who voted for Trump."[5]

Pause for a moment and consider that statement: the editor and reporters at the most historic and august evangelical publication in America were befuddled by and relationally distant from the groundswell surge that led to 81 percent of white evangelicals voting for Trump.

Donald Trump exposed a stark divide between elite establishment evangelicals (the genteel and media-savvy leaders) and grassroots evangelicals. Many of the elite evangelicals, over time, followed suit and came around to tentatively supporting Trump—eventually—but the evangelical alignment around Trump has not not emanated from elite evangelicalism. No, it came burbling up from the evangelical hoi polloi. If anything, the 2016 campaign left the elites of the evangelical establishment in the position of the fabled leader in the French Revolution who said, "There go my people. I must find out where they are going so I can lead them."

While this institution-tracking conventional wisdom—which the NAE and *Christianity Today* embody and which Mattingly gamely follows—may have been well suited to understanding evangelicalism in the twentieth century, it is seriously outdated and creates dangerous knowledge gaps in the twenty-first. This analytical default misconstrues the tectonic shifts that have upended evangelical power and evangelical politics in the past twenty years. It fails to recognize the insurgent forces that are rapidly redistributing power within American evangelicalism, and it pushes toward a conclusion that an episode like January 6 was marginal or fringy instead of a searing warning about the state of American evangelicalism.

I have tracked dozens of prominent evangelical Christian leaders—some of them, like Ché Ahn and Cindy Jacobs, national and international celebrities with incredible reach and influence—who were in the crowds around the Capitol that day. These leaders do not hail from the institutions of the elite or recognized evangelical establishment. They have not been covered systematically or comprehensively in any media reporting about January 6. Yet all these characters are firmly ensconced in that particular segment of evangelicalism that we call the Independent Charismatic or fourth-quadrant world.

And no figure has been more important to theologizing Christian Trumpism for the charismatic and evangelical masses than Lance Wallnau.

A Pastor in Search of a Program

Like many Independent Charismatic leaders, Lance Whitaker Wallnau has a biography that is both murky and perpetually refashioned. He says that he worked for a Fortune 500 company before transitioning to a career in ministry, though I can find nowhere that he names that company. An online bio of Wallnau, evidently of his own creation, says that he worked "20 years as an entrepreneur in the Oil Industry," though that math is pretty iffy given that, by the time he was thirty-seven, he was working as a full-time pastor in Rhode Island.[6] Lance's father, Carl Wallnau, was a World War II veteran who served under General Patton, then earned a law degree and worked as a vice president at Meenan Oil before becoming CEO of Swan Oil Company in Pennsylvania, perhaps undergirding Lance's claims to have pursued a career in that same industry.[7]

Similarly, Lance's undergraduate degree-granting institution is unspecified. He claims to hold a master's in theological studies from "South West Christian University," a school name that does not exist but appears to be a reference to South*western* Christian University, a Pentecostal school in Oklahoma. In 2012, he also received a doctorate from Phoenix University of Theology. That school, which primarily serves midcareer independent and Pentecostal pastors and ministry leaders, offers academic credit for "experiential learning," a practice that leads some scholars to label the school a "diploma mill."[8] My point is not that Wallnau doesn't possess any of his claimed credentials; it's simply that a conventionally orderly and respectable résumé is not the criterion for leadership in Independent Charismatic circles. No, the coin of the realm is one's ability to communicate compellingly, exercise the gifts of the Spirit in interesting ways, and hold an audience's attention—and those qualities Lance Wallnau has in spades.

Somewhere in his itinerant early adult life, Wallnau met Esther Mallett, a major West Coast leader from the Latter Rain movement and founder of Community Chapel World Outreach, a Latter Rain network of charismatic churches. Wallnau would call Mallett his spiritual mother, and she trained him in the Latter Rain teachings about apostles, prophets, and the end-times movement of God.[9] Mallett set Lance up as pastor of one of her churches in Cranston, Rhode Island.

So in the mid-1990s, Wallnau was serving as the pastor of Word of Life Covenant Church in Cranston. In his speaking today, he frequently references this phase of his life in disparaging ways, joking about how he was hoping for it to become a megachurch, hoping for revival, hoping to significantly impact the local community, but nothing materialized. There are remarkable parallels between Wallnau and Ché Ahn and Lou Engle: all three men were washed-out charismatic pastors in the 1990s who longed to have greater influence and to lead an exciting revival but who felt constrained by the limitations of traditional church structures.

In 1996, evidently seeking a creative outlet, Lance and his wife, Annabelle, created Lance Wallnau Ministries, a nonprofit headquartered at their church.[10] You can see the Latter Rain influence peeking through in the charter documents for Wallnau's ministry. For instance, he described the purpose of Lance Wallnau Ministries in 1998: "To establish an apostolic mission . . . providing for church planting . . . establishing spiritual covering for and authority over members of the five fold ministry and groups seeking association in the fellowship."[11]

This could easily be the charter for Ché Ahn's HIM apostolic network, likewise founded in 1996. But Wallnau wasn't in Wagner's NAR mentoring circles at that time. He was trying to forge his own model of what "apostolic" ministry could look like.

It was in this disillusioned and discontented phase that Wallnau encountered a concept that would radically alter his life and bring him into the upper echelons of charismatic celebritydom. In 2000, at the age of forty-four, Wallnau met a man named Loren Cunningham, a revered figure and elder statesman of Independent Charismaticism. Cunningham was the founder of Youth With A Mission (YWAM), a charismatic youth organization famous for sending short-term Christian missionaries to troubled areas around the world. Cunningham told Wallnau a story of something that happened to him twenty-five years earlier, in 1975. This story has been told and retold so many times—by Cunningham, Wallnau, and others—that it's taken on a mythical quality, leaving its factual origins hard to discern. But here are the contours.

In August 1975, Loren Cunningham and his wife, Darlene, were vacationing in Colorado, and while there, they had scheduled dinner with Bill Bright and his wife, Vonette. Bright was the founder of Campus Crusade for Christ, now simply called Cru, which was a more mainstream evangelical college ministry. According to Wallnau's rendition of the story, it was a major donor to both Campus Crusade and YWAM who insisted the two leaders meet for dinner.[12] The night before their meal together, when Cunningham was praying, he felt that God was giving him a revelation for how to "disciple the nation."[13] In this revelation, which Cunningham has described as a sort of auditory download, God told him about seven spheres of influence—basically areas of society—into which Christians should go to spread Christianity's impact in the world. The seven spheres of influence Cunningham received were: the home; the church; the schools; government and politics; the media; arts, entertainment, and sports; and commerce, science, and technology.[14]

The next evening, as they were getting ready to meet the Brights for dinner, Loren Cunningham wrote these seven spheres on a sheet of paper so that he could share them with Bill Bright. But in Cunningham's telling, before he could do that, Bill had pulled out his own list of seven areas of cultural influence, which God had revealed directly to *him* the previous day. As the two compared lists, they saw slightly different phrasings but more or less the same set of ideas.

Cunningham viewed this as a miraculous work of God, who simultaneously revealed the same game plan to two key evangelical leaders the same day. Cunningham would also narrate how, a few days later, he would compare the seven spheres he and Bright had agreed on with another list he heard articulated by Francis Schaeffer, an evangelical philosopher and theologian who served as a major intellectual of the religious right. Schaeffer's list was evidently in agreement with theirs.

Cunningham would sometimes refer to the seven spheres as the "seven mind molders of culture," and he began using them in YWAM trainings. The basic idea emerging from Cunningham and Bright was that Christians should not only be involved in the church sphere or the home-family sphere, but they should try to have a positive influence in all spheres of society. For Cunningham, you "disciple nations" by getting Christians to branch out and make positive influence in all the seven spheres of society.

To be fair, the idea of dividing society up into different spheres of authority and imagining Christian influence in each goes back a long way in Protestant theology, at least to the thought of Abraham Kuyper, an early twentieth-century Calvinist theologian and Dutch prime minister. You could trace some elements of this idea back to John Calvin himself, in the sixteenth century. By the 1970s, when Bright and Cunningham were conferring, these ideas were enjoying a resurgence through the spread of Christian Reconstructionism, the Calvinist movement that was pushing dominion theology and would provide many of the theological underpinnings for the religious right in America. But what Cunningham added to the Kuyperian/Reconstructionist concept was a charismatic and prophetic gloss: God has now revealed these important political concepts mystically in the late twentieth century.

What's interesting is that the seven-spheres concept has been around since at least 1975, but it didn't really gain much of a following until Lance Wallnau heard about it. When Wallnau learned this story directly from

Cunningham in 2000, he found the seven spheres magnetic. This was the signature concept or teaching for which Wallnau had been searching. But he wouldn't merely transmit the seven-spheres concept to his own audiences; no, Wallnau would put his own spin on it.

Prophetic Memes and Meme Makers

When Wallnau heard Cunningham's account of the seven spheres or "seven mind molders of culture," he linked it with another story he had just heard. In this other story, which a friend of Wallnau's had recounted to him, a Christian man in Georgia had a heart attack and near-death experience in which he had a vision of seven islands emerging out of the ocean. The seven islands became seven mountains, and the voice of God spoke to him, saying, "Those are seven world kingdoms that shape the world." God told the between-death-and-life man that one particular mountain was "the government mountain, and you are called to go into it." After all this, the man's spirit returned to his body, and he went on to be elected to the Georgia state legislature.[15]

So Wallnau took the seven-spheres Cunningham-and-Bright list from 1975, combined it with the "seven mountains" near-death-experience vision, and the Seven Mountain Mandate was born. He would also later acknowledge, like Cindy Jacobs, that these ideas of discipling or transforming nations resonated for him because of the Latter Rain theology in which he was already steeped. Almost as soon as he assembled these ideas, Wallnau began teaching and lecturing about this concept, using his Lance Wallnau Ministries platform to start spreading this framework.

Like many Independent Charismatic leaders, Wallnau was not so much creating something new but rather repackaging older ideas. Yet there is a significant if subtle shift in rhetoric between the spheres imagery that Cunningham and Bright used and the mountains image that Wallnau brought. To be sure, Cunningham taught Christians to strategically move into the "spheres of influence" by pursuing careers in media, the arts, government, and the other spheres. He encouraged Christians to try to bring Christian leadership to those different sectors of society. Yet it remained, implicitly, a grassroots approach to cultural change, with influence growing as more and more Christians bore witness to their faith in each sphere.

Wallnau's mountain imagery, on the other hand, brought with it a whole new provocation to conquest and strategy for battle. Who will conquer and hold the *top* of each mountain of culture? Who will govern from the high places? As Wallnau once put it, "There are a remnant of people at the top of each sphere who control power over 90 percent of the influence that happens in their sphere. These people are called 'kings.' Jesus says the gospel goes to kings. For some reason, the church focuses on taking the gospel only to the poor and completely forgets about taking it to rulers and world authorities. . . . The key here, if you can capture the high places, you can shape a culture."[16] If Cunningham imagined transformation from below, growing up through the grassroots, Wallnau proclaimed the need for Christians to assert control of society in a top-down, vanguard maneuver.

To understand how Lance Wallnau took up this idea of the Seven Mountains and made a new career out of it, we have to think about how ideas and theology move around in the Independent Charismatic world. As we saw in chapter 1, this decentralized fourth-quadrant landscape is distinct and has its own media, culture, and ethos. In most traditional forms of Christianity, theology is passed on or developed either through systematic scholarly reflection (*systematic* theology) or through denominational and confessional creeds and statements of faith (*creedal* theology). But the Independent Charismatic world is dispersed. What unites people across congregations and ministries are not shared statements of faith but shared experiences (the spiritual gifts) and shared desire for revival.

One of the unifying ideas that also binds this subculture together is the belief that God still speaks through prophecy. So you have all of these different leaders—some, like Cindy Jacobs, who outright call themselves prophets; some who just say they're "prophetic"; and some who have little prophetic insights or interludes—and they're all pushing their ideas into the charismatic media marketplace. Most of the prophecies from this cacophony never take hold, and some are so vague ("It's going to be a year of prosperity" or "God has a special work for you to do") that they can be neither proven nor refuted. But a select few prophecies or prophetic images become iconic and supremely influential. These classics get picked up by different prophets and other charismatic media figures, who then riff on them, elaborate them, and repackage them.

I call these celebrated, durable prophecies *prophetic memes.* These prophecies are like internet memes in that they keep getting repurposed and utilized in different ways, but they're also theological and ostensibly revelatory, given by God to the prophets. They aren't quite what we would call theological doctrines, in a "statement of faith" sense, but they come close in terms of importance.

For instance, one of the Kansas City Prophets named Bob Jones (not to be confused with Bob Jones University) created a major prophetic meme in the 1980s called the "billion-soul harvest." It promises that in some fast-approaching future, a revival will break out that will lead one billion people to convert to charismatic Christianity. This "billion-soul harvest" language resurfaces anytime there's a new revival, and it's frequently paired with another popular prophecy about a global Third Great Awakening. Huge swaths of people across the charismatic world believe in various prophetic memes so that the memes become part of the assumed vocabulary and culture even though they might have very little grounding in the Bible or traditional Christian theology.

The Seven Mountain Mandate is one of the most important prophetic memes in all of global Independent Charismatic Christianity today. It has become the organizing structure for how millions of Christians think about politics and the relationship between the church and the world. If you attend Christian nationalist gatherings or listen to Christian political podcasts, you'll hear perpetual talk of the Seven Mountains: strategies for taking the government mountain, how to conquer the education mountain, and on and on.

If you are hearing about the Seven Mountains for the first time as you read this, you may be especially shocked by the facts to come. Sociologist of religion Paul Djupe conducted a survey in March 2023 to see how many Americans believe in modern-day prophecy. In the survey, he included a question about the Seven Mountains. Respondents were asked if they agree or disagree with the statement "God wants Christians to stand atop the '7 mountains of society,' including the government, education, media, and others." Note the very specific phrasing, which includes Wallnau's mountain metaphor, rather than vague language about Christians influencing society.

In Djupe's survey, 20.4 percent of all respondents—from a sample of all Americans, not just Christians—either "strongly agree" or "agree" with this statement.[17] Even more revealing is the fact that among the survey respondents who said they believe in modern-day prophecy ("Modern-day prophets continue to reveal God's plans to humanity"), fully two-thirds agree with the Seven Mountain Mandate.[18]

Pause for a moment to let this sink in. In 2000, Lance Wallnau heard Cunningham's story, blended it with a dubious near-death experience report, and created a charismatic prophetic meme. Today, *more than one-fifth of all Americans* recognize and endorse that concept. And among prophecy believers, which undoubtedly includes most Independent Charismatics, along with other charismatic-leaning Christians, two-thirds share Wallnau's vision of Christians conquering the high places in society.

So how did an idea—albeit a sticky and prophetically amplified one—move from something being taught by an obscure Rhode Island pastor to become a core political theology for millions of modern Christians? Perhaps unsurprisingly, C. Peter Wagner reenters the story here.

A Meeting of the Minds

It was in 2001, just about a year after Wallnau began teaching about the Seven Mountains, that C. Peter Wagner heard Wallnau speak at a prophecy conference. As a practiced navigator of the Independent Charismatic world by then, Wagner had a good ear for solid, catchy prophetic memes, and he recognized that Wallnau was in possession of one. Wagner would eventually call Wallnau "one of the most creative thinkers in the church today."[19] And Wallnau would later say that Peter Wagner "is probably the first father I had in the Spirit," paying tribute to the man who celebrated and championed Wallnau's own originality.[20]

Most of the members of Wagner's inner circle—people like Cindy Jacobs, Ché Ahn, Chuck Pierce, Becca Greenwood, and Dutch Sheets—had long-running ties to Wagner, often going back to the 1980s or 1990s. Wallnau was the exception. He had previously been appreciative of Peter Wagner and his teachings on prayer and spiritual warfare, but they only met in 2001.

The encounter between Wagner and Wallnau was a true meeting of the minds, and Wagner would later openly talk with others about his strategy for "drawing Lance more closely into our circles."[21] He invited Wallnau to bring his Seven Mountains teaching to the ICA, where it was enthusiastically received by the group. Wallnau would officially join the ICA in 2004. Wagner would also cultivate a mentoring relationship with Wallnau, eventually inviting him into EVAT, the molten core of the NAR, around 2007. But, relatively speaking, Wallnau was a late arrival to the NAR.

As they had for Ché Ahn, Wagner's NAR programs and networks would prove to be the launching pad that Wallnau needed to become one of the top charismatic personalities in the world today. Cindy Jacobs rose to prominence through her preternatural prophecies. Ché Ahn ascended through building his HIM network. Lance's rise had everything to do with the Seven Mountains idea. "There are people who, once they have an idea, for better or for worse, everybody's gonna get it," Wallnau eulogized Wagner after his death. "So what Peter did was he endorsed an idea, that, I'm convinced, gave that whole Seven Mountains thing legs that went global, because then Dutch Sheets would say it and then Cindy Jacobs would say it, Chuck [Pierce] would endorse it. . . . Everybody that was in alignment with [Peter] would go with it, pretty much. So everywhere I went, I heard about it."[22]

The NAR networks, touching tens of thousands of churches and ministries at that point, took Wallnau's prophetic meme and spread it all over the Independent Charismatic world. And I do mean "world" quite literally. Today you'll find the Seven Mountains concept talked about and cherished in charismatic communities all around the globe.

Peter Wagner was extremely fond of the concept of paradigm shifts, and, in his memoir, he describes at least fifteen discrete paradigm shifts he personally underwent, including key pivot points we've observed in his biography like his embrace of church growth theory, his rejection of cessationism through his partnership with John Wimber, his move into strategic-level spiritual warfare, and his migration toward apostolic and prophetic governance for the church. So we should not take it lightly when Wagner describes the changes in his own thinking after meeting Wallnau in 2001 as "what I now consider to be the most radical and potentially world-changing paradigm shift of all."[23]

Wagner's meeting with and patronage of Wallnau developed around the same time that Wagner was beginning to embrace the Reconstructionist-originated ideas of *dominion theology*. Dominion theology is an assertive vision of Christianity, forecasting Christians taking over whole societies from the control of the devil and structuring society around Christian values and theology. As I noted in chapter 2, these dominion theology, or Kingdom Now, ideas had been circulating around Independent Charismatic networks and cross-pollinating with the Latter Rain prophecies for at least a couple of decades before the NAR got off the ground, and some of Wagner's disciples, particularly Dutch Sheets, Bill Hamon, and Cindy Jacobs, seem to have adopted them before meeting Wagner. But Wagner, as a newcomer to the Independent Charismatic scene, was slow to embrace these dominion ideas. He would even write in his notes from a 2003 meeting with some of his NAR mentees and EVAT members, "I need help on 'dominion theology.' Concepts. Criticisms. Sources."[24] Wagner clearly wanted to get his theological bearings before wholeheartedly embracing these ideas.

Part of Wagner's hang-up about dominion theology was that he was a perennial pragmatist, and he seems to have struggled to know what the practical application of a charismatic dominion theology would even look like. Lance Wallnau's Seven Mountains framework solved this problem for Wagner, offering a fairly detailed program for how the church should go about systematically conquering and "discipling" different sectors of society.

Observe the many synchronicities between Wallnau's Seven Mountains concept and this dominion style of interpretation: in both cases, Christians are divinely mandated to take back control, or dominion, over all creation and all society from Satan. In both cases, there is spiritual warfare as well as very concrete, real-life competition between the forces of darkness and the forces of light to enact God's kingdom on the earth. In both cases, there is an assumed top-down dimension of governance. For Wagner, the Seven Mountain Mandate became the accessible, detailed program for how to implement dominion theology. As Wagner once put it:

> So, once we have a mindset for taking dominion and discipling whole nations and reforming our society. . . . We're ready for action. . . .

> Fortunately God, here in the Second Apostolic Age, has brought Lance Wallnau. And Lance Wallnau was the one who began

to teach us and popularize a way to simplify this, and Lance Wallnau says that society is controlled by Seven Mountains. And that helps us all, because as soon as we look at these Seven Mountains, we can see where we fit. And then, when we know where we fit, we can begin to transform society.[25]

What you see happening around the mid-2000s in the NAR leadership circles is an elaborate programmatic and theological entwining of charismatic dominion theology and Wallnau's more digestible and memorable Seven Mountains concept, all toward the ends of strategizing for global Christian supremacy.

The Seven Mountains Everywhere

In late 2007 and early 2008 came a very intentional public rollout of these Seven Mountains and dominion theology ideas, which had already been incubating inside NAR circles for years. In his December 2007 address to the ICA, Wagner spoke rapturously about the dominion-Seven Mountains "paradigm shift," saying, "Our apostolic movement is entering a new season that many of our older apostles could not have imagined. Rather than 'building our own kingdom' as critics might say, today's apostles are intent on building the kingdom of God, and many are willing to take whatever steps, radical as they may be, to help make that happen."[26]

In the same address, Wagner touted the publication of nine new NAR-authored books about these ideas all published within the space of about a year, including Cindy Jacobs's *The Reformation Manifesto* and Becca Greenwood's *Destined to Rule*. Likewise, Wagner highlights that Johnny Enlow, a prophet-pastor who was close to Wallnau and Ché Ahn, was on the cusp of publishing the first book explicitly about the Seven Mountains concept, titled *The Seven Mountain Prophecy*. A month later in January 2008, Wagner released *Dominion! How Kingdom Action Can Change the World*, in which he cheerfully espoused an undisguised form of dominion theology, linked it with his apostolic-and-prophetic and strategic-level spiritual warfare frameworks, and bound it all together with Wallnau's Seven Mountain Mandate.

Wagner and Wallnau were so mutually influential that, at times, it can be difficult to discern what is original to Wallnau and what came in through Wagner. Consider this rousing memo that Lance Wallnau wrote to his fellow apostles in 2008 shortly after the "apostolic alignment" ceremony with Todd Bentley at the Lakeland Outpouring and before the major scandals about Bentley broke in the news:

> We now come into this era of the Apostolic. The apostolic is all about a final governing presence in the body of Christ. . . . In other words, the Apostolic is a colonizing force that reproduces the culture of a conquering kingdom.

> So Jesus is the Apostle who comes from heaven to colonize earth with heaven . . .

> There are 7 spheres that shape nations, 7 realms that control the minds of the multitudes. . . . The Apostolic assignment is to take those spheres, and bring them under the dominion of the Embassy of Heaven, the Kingdom of God.

> My encouragement to you is grab everything. Park yourself in the anointing, go in the flow with God, get filled with the Spirit of God, but let God take this glory to where it's never been. Take it to the top of the mountains, because that's an apostolic assignment that will bring Jesus' inheritance into the earth.[27]

This is a neat encapsulation of how entwined the NAR, Seven Mountains, and dominion theology had become: with the advent of modern-day apostles, Christianity is primed to truly colonize the earth with heavenly culture by conquering the tops of the Seven Mountains in every society. As these ideas percolated through the NAR networks and beyond, you can see an accompanying politicization of those networks.

Even in Wagner's already quite radicalized circles—where strategic-level spiritual warfare and the spiritual oligarchy of apostles and prophets were de rigueur—these Seven Mountains ideas proved contentious. Some leaders in the ICA and the other NAR institutions started pushing back when it came to dominion theology. One apostle and longtime ally of Wagner withdrew from the ICA and WLI, writing in a long letter to Wagner, "I became disquieted at the time when you platformed and affirmed as your own belief in the dominion based eschatology."[28]

A lot of leaders were on board with the idea of church networks being led by apostles and prophets, but a program aimed at world domination gave them pause. The inner core of Wagner's followers, however, especially his EVAT group, embraced this new, colonizing, dominion modality.

Not by happenstance, this campaign to spread the Seven Mountains framework coincided with an unprecedented political opportunity for the NAR. In August 2008, John McCain, the Republican nominee for president, plucked a folksy and charismatic, in both senses of the word, Alaskan governor named Sarah Palin out of obscurity to be his vice-presidential running mate. Palin, who was baptized as a child at the Wasilla Assembly of God, a Pentecostal megachurch, had spent more than two decades stewing in Independent Charismatic and NAR teachings. The Toronto Blessing had swept through one of her churches, and Palin belonged to a "spiritual warfare network" created by Mary Glazier, a member of Cindy Jacobs's ACPE. Glazier claimed that she had helped inspire Palin's entry into local politics.[29] From Peter Wagner and other NAR leaders' perspectives, someone who evidently shared their aggressive theology and looked to the apostles and prophets for leadership was on the cusp of being elevated to one of the highest offices in the land.

Of course, McCain and Palin lost that election to Barack Obama and Joe Biden, but the 2008 election still gave the NAR leaders a taste of partisan politics and ensconced many of them in right-wing Christian activist circles. Wagner would again address the ICA a month after the election, where he said, "I have never experienced a personal emotional moment attached to politics that matched listening to Palin's nomination and her acceptance speech. I felt that it was a nudge from the Holy Spirit."[30] He urged his fellow apostles not to be discouraged but to remain hopeful: "We will see our cities and our nation transformed if we accelerate our commitment to be Holy Spirit driven revolutionaries!"[31]

Wallnau, for his part, rode the wave of NAR enthusiasm for his ideas all the way to charismatic stardom. He took his Seven Mountains schtick to every megachurch, apostolic gathering, and charismatic conference that would have him. Wallnau's presentations have a real motivational speaker vibe, with Wallnau almost always using a whiteboard or large sheet of paper to draw the Seven Mountains and illustrate his ideas. While he was still technically pastoring the little church in Rhode Island, his nonprofit, Lance Wallnau Ministries, jumped from an income of $131,000 in 2004 to $955,000 in 2008, driven largely by Wallnau's speaking fees, conference honoraria, and CD sales.[32] Shortly thereafter, he officially left his Rhode Island church, moved to Texas, began casting himself as a business consultant, and took to speaking and teaching full time.

In the span from 2008 to 2015, Wallnau became a household name in Independent Charismatic circles. In 2013, he coauthored and coedited a short volume with Bill Johnson—Ché Ahn's close friend, Revival Alliance partner, and the apostle over Bethel Church in Redding, California—titled *Invading Babylon: The 7 Mountain Mandate*. Peter Wagner and Ché Ahn were also contributors to the book.

The Seven Mountain Mandate was the goldmine prophetic meme that put Lance Wallnau on the map. But it wouldn't be his last.

Donald Trump and the Cyrus Anointing

It is easy to forget, in retrospect, how controversial Donald Trump was among evangelical Christians in the 2016 campaign. There were seventeen candidates at the height of the Republican primary, and a number of them— Ben Carson, Ted Cruz, Marco Rubio, Rick Perry, and Mike Huckabee— had personal evangelical bona fides and were popular with and respected by evangelical elites.

Donald Trump was different. After he announced his presidential bid in June 2015, he cursed and cussed, he stumbled over his Bible references, he said he didn't ask God for forgiveness, and he couldn't name his favorite Bible verse. All of these signals were read by elite evangelicals and by educated analysts of evangelicalism as being antithetical to avowed evangelical piety and values. So the elite evangelicals, particularly those from the noncharismatic first and second quadrants, excoriated Trump, ignored him, or publicly supported the other Republican candidates.

Yet polls kept showing that a plurality of evangelical voters were gravitating toward Trump. For sure, when you have such a divided field, some of those pluralities were very low, such as a poll in July 2015, a month after he entered the race, that showed Trump leading the field among white evangelical voters but still only getting support from 20 percent of them.[33] It was this dynamic—Trump's burgeoning popularity with grassroots evangelicals and his vileness to evangelical elites—that drove the ongoing befuddlement of the mainstream evangelical media (like *Christianity Today*) and the secular media. These dynamics also governed which evangelical leaders met with or endorsed Trump early on.

Anthea Butler, a scholar and sharp observer of evangelical politics, summed it up well: "Trump went to what I laughingly referred to . . . as the D-list. He went to prosperity gospel people. He went to lower-named Pentecostal preachers. He went to charismatics who were outside of any denominational construct. And he brought all of those people together."[34] Among those "D-list" charismatics living "outside of any denominational construct" was one Lance Wallnau.

In September 2015, Lance received an invitation to meet with Trump at Trump Tower, at one of the meetings convened by Paula White, along with a group of televangelists, prophets, apostles, and a messianic rabbi. The story goes that Wallnau attended as an observer, mostly out of curiosity. He did not plan to support Trump, thinking he'd probably endorse one of the more evangelical candidates. But Lance says that God spoke to him during the meeting to say, "Donald Trump is a wrecking ball to the spirit of political correctness." After the gathering, when Wallnau returned home, he also heard God say, "Trump is a Cyrus."[35]

This image of Cyrus—or the "Cyrus Anointing," as Wallnau sometimes phrases it—would become a central pillar of Christian Trumpism. When the Jewish people were conquered by the Babylonian Empire in the sixth century BCE and taken away to exile in Babylon, their deliverance came through a messiah (the term *messiah/mashiach* is Hebrew for "anointed one") in the person of the Persian emperor, Cyrus. Cyrus conquered the Babylonians, and he was the one who sent the Jewish leaders back to rebuild

Jerusalem. Wallnau anchored his new Trumpian prophetic meme in Isaiah 45. Here's Wallnau's interpretation of the passage:

> The Lord took me to Isaiah 45 and he said, "The next president will be the 45th president, I want an Isaiah 45 Cyrus" . . . Cyrus was prophesied in Isaiah 45 one hundred years before he was born. The prophet Isaiah called by name the political leader who would go into Babylon, who would literally, overnight, take occupation of Babylon, and who would decree freedom for the Jewish people, with this audacious statement, "I've anointed him; I'm going to break open the gates; and he doesn't know me." This is Isaiah 45. So I said, "Wait a second. God anoints political leaders, for his purposes, that do not know him?"[36]

To play out Wallnau's analogy, the ancient Jewish people were in exile in Babylon, and conservative Christians in 2016 were in cultural exile in the United States. God anointed Cyrus, the Persian emperor, to conquer the Babylonians and send the Jews back from exile. For Wallnau, Donald Trump is the Cyrus, the heathen warrior king, who will come in and beat up conservative Christians' enemies and send evangelicals back from exile. In their second meeting at Trump Tower that fall—once again with a group of D-list evangelical leaders—Wallnau shared this prophecy directly with Trump. "Here's what the Lord told me about you. Isaiah 45 talks about 'Cyrus, my anointed,'" Wallnau says he told Trump. "Now Mr. Trump, I know and you know that you're not really an 'evangelical,' but the Bible says that 'though [Cyrus] know me not,' God's got his hand on him."[37]

What sense did Donald Trump make of these wild prophetic associations and scripture references that were almost certainly beyond his level of biblical literacy? We can only guess. This was only one of the first of many instances of a Pentecostal or charismatic prophet speaking words of prophecy over Trump. He has always seemed game to hear and absorb another positive revelatory image of himself.

Whether you attribute Wallnau's insights to his shrewd instincts or to prophecy is likely a matter of theology. But in any case, what Wallnau intuited and touted in the fall of 2015, even as most evangelical elites were irked and outraged by Trump, was that the masses of American evangelicals was not looking for a pious evangelical statesman. They wanted a bare-knuckled brawler. Wallnau had a theological worldview and a skill at packaging messages that were ready-made to underwrite a figure like Trump.

Wagner, Wallnau, and Trump

Wallnau became one of the first evangelical leaders to openly endorse Donald Trump, and he did it using this new wrecking-ball "Trump as Cyrus" prophetic meme. For several months, through early 2016, Wallnau was one of the few Christian leaders making a positive, "biblical" case for supporting Trump over and against the other dyed-in-the-wool evangelical candidates. At a time when most evangelical elites were exceedingly wary of the insurgent Trump campaign, Wallnau came forward with a Bible reference and a prophecy that resonated deeply with the pro-Trump evangelical grassroots.

Marvin Olasky, a noncharismatic evangelical leader and editor of *World* magazine, a smaller parallel publication to *Christianity Today*, would later tell the story of how, when he made a principled, evangelical, biblical case that Trump was "unfit to be president" in October 2016, he received an unprecedented number of letters from readers—some two thousand letters. According to Olasky, 80 percent of the letters were angry and argumentative, and one rationale he heard across the board was this analogy between Trump and Cyrus.[38]

The "Trump as Cyrus" meme synchronizes handily with Wallnau's Seven Mountains teaching. In Wallnau and Wagner's understanding, the government was a different mountain than the religion mountain, so they needed an anointed *government* leader, not a pastor—to conquer that mountain. To borrow a Freudian analogy, while most evangelical elites were following their superego, eschewing the uncouth Trump for his moral deficiencies, Wallnau used prophecy and the Bible to indulge the evangelical id. He was saying, in essence, "Trump may be a bastard, but he can be *our* bastard." He cloaked his realpolitik reasoning in the Seven Mountains and this Cyrus Anointing idea.

Throughout the 2016 Republican primary, Wallnau took a lot of heat, particularly from evangelicals, because nonevangelicals would probably not have heard of Wallnau—for being one of the foremost Trumpian Christian voices. And even though Peter Wagner was dying at the time, as we've seen, he actually decided to leap into the fray to defend his mentee. I noted in chapter 2 how, in February 2016, Wagner posted on Facebook his own endorsement of Donald Trump. Now, with the background of these prophetic memes, let me share the core reasoning of that post. Here's what Wagner also wrote:

> God is not limited to using Christians to accomplish His purposes. We need only to recall Cyrus, the idolatrous king of Persia, whom God used to help get His people back to Jerusalem. . . .
>
> Let me point out that influence is related to spirituality in the Religion Mountain, but this is not true in any of the other six mountains that are the molders of culture. The chief producer [of] influence in the six non-Religion mountains is not spirituality but success. The most successful people are the most influential. Success? In the Business Mountain and the Media Mountain Trump has accumulated 8–10 billion dollars. He knows how to influence. I want to vote for a commander-in-chief, not a bishop-in-chief.[39]

Wagner's endorsement was almost entirely premised on Wallnau's theology. After Wagner's Facebook post, the other EVAT leaders, like Cindy Jacobs and Ché Ahn, jumped on board the Trump bandwagon. Becca Greenwood told me that the EVAT members were pretty divided at the time over which 2016 Republican candidate to support but that Wagner's endorsement helped to galvanize the EVAT circle around Trump because they believed that "Peter had the ability to see things apostolically ahead of time."[40] From that moment forward, the leaders of the NAR have been the tip of the spear of Christian Trumpism.

Sometimes journalists or other analysts of the NAR say that the Seven Mountains framework is "theocratic" or that it's about creating a "theocracy." That's not precisely true. In the common understanding of theocracy, priests or other clergy or clerics rule over a society or community in the name of God. Part of the Seven Mountains concept, as Wallnau and Wagner articulate it, is that each mountain (each segment of society) has its own culture and rules, so you have to play by the rules of that mountain if you want to conquer it. A religious leader, a priest, or even a Christian apostle or prophet might not have the skill set to take over the government mountain or the business mountain. Similarly, voters or political consultants shouldn't try to import "religion mountain" rules—such as ethics and expectations for moral righteousness—into the conquest of the government mountain.

In the Seven Mountains frame, a leader in one of the nonreligion mountains doesn't have to be pious or even necessarily religious to govern according to the kingdom of God. They just have to exert their power in conformity with Christians' (here, conservative charismatic Christians') interests. Of course, this means that the Seven Mountains prophetic meme was a political theology ready-made for someone like Donald Trump. Trump is big on dominion and being domineering, on winning. Trump is clearly not a devout Christian, by any conventional definition—Wallnau says he told Trump, "You're not really an 'evangelical,'" and he would openly question whether Trump was a Christian at all. But Trump was willing to govern according to the desires of conservative Christians. Calling Trump a Cyrus implicitly acknowledges that his approach to power and governing mentality are not *Christian* in any ethical or moral sense. But from Wagner and Wallnau's perspective, Trump had already succeeded in dominating—"conquered," so to speak—two of the other Seven Mountains: business and media. So why not make him the champion of the government mountain too?

Wallnau and Wagner promoted and leveraged these two prophetic memes—the Cyrus Anointing and the Seven Mountain Mandate—to consolidate charismatic support, and eventual broader evangelical support, around Donald Trump in 2016. If you go into charismatic circles and listen to how people talk about Trump, these two memes will come up over and over and over again. Many different factions from a lot of different segments of American Christianity have glommed on to Christian Trumpism, but charismatic support for Donald Trump is premised on these two pillars: the Cyrus Anointing and the Seven Mountains. They both can be traced back to Lance Wallnau, with a notable assist from Peter Wagner.

The Prophet Pundits of *FlashPoint*

From the point of his endorsement of Donald Trump all the way up to the present, Lance Wallnau has been one of the leading Christian proponents—and propagandists—of Trumpism. At the end of September 2016, Wallnau self-published a book, *God's Chaos Candidate: Donald J. Trump and the American Unraveling*, where he lays out his pro-Trump Seven Mountains and Cyrus Anointing memes at length.

About a week after *God's Chaos Candidate* was published, the *Access Hollywood* October surprise hit the news, with Donald Trump claiming blithely on video that he could "grab [women] by the pussy" with no consequences. This was a crisis for Lance Wallnau, who had made himself the prophetic face of Christian Trump support.

Wallnau, ever the cagey operator, grabbed his cell phone and recorded an impromptu Facebook video, where he passionately argued that God had not left Trump: "This isn't God exposing something. This is the devil strategically exposing information in order to destroy a candidate," Wallnau told his followers. "God can do more with Samson than he can do with Jezebel. God could do more with a carnal prophet. God could anoint the jawbone of an ass and slay his enemies, better than he could anoint Jezebel to advance his prophetic agenda."[41]

Once again, riffing on the Samson and Jezebel stories, Wallnau was constructing a commentary that existed in the space between a prophecy and a biblical principle to uphold his ongoing Trump support. This is the real brilliance of Wallnau's propaganda: for charismatic evangelicals, who prize prophecy and prophetic illuminations of scripture, Wallnau's claims to oracular authority and insight into the spirit realm create a sense that God has a special hand on Trump. Yet the Bible references and biblical imagery also speak to more mainstream evangelicals, who might not buy in to all the prophecy business but are looking for "biblical" reasons to support Trump. This crossover appeal—to those both inside and outside of the more narrow charismatic niche—has helped skyrocket Wallnau to even greater fame and prominence.

Throughout the Trump era, Wallnau perfected the art of hot-take Facebook Live rants, where he comments on the day's news and mixes in his own prophetic insights. A lot of these insights are still based on the Seven

Mountains and the Cyrus Anointing memes. But Wallnau is very creative, and he has operated as an ad hoc generator of new prophetic memes regarding Donald Trump. Within the charismatic media sphere, Wallnau, who was already popular before Trump, has become the go-to Trump defender and commentator. Many people scoff at Lance Wallnau, labeling him a crazy right-wing preacher or prophet-pundit. But we write him off as a fringe voice at our own peril.

Like Cindy Jacobs, Wallnau was also heavily involved in the POTUS Shield spiritual warfare gatherings in Washington, DC, in January 2017. That same month, at a conference of NAR leaders at Chuck Pierce's church, Wallnau offered a new prophecy referencing their recently deceased mentor Wagner. He verbally imagined a future in which his and Peter's vision of the Seven Mountains would take over huge slices of American Christianity and where prophets could develop whole YouTube channels to provide an alternative to secular news media, which he alludes to being dominated by a demonic spirit called Leviathan:

> So here's what I think Peter would say today, and to those
> of you who love his legacy, I'd encourage you to think about
> this. I think he'd say the 7M model is more important than
> ever before, because the nature of the power of media and
> Hollywood upstream to shape popular culture. Jon Stewart
> did more to disciple millennials and then Bernie Sanders came
> along and cleaned it up. It's popular culture on television and in
> comedy and in news especially that Christians are going to have
> to go into.

> And I can virtually prophesy—and, Chuck, I encourage you
> to help me pray into this—I think we could have YouTube
> channels that do our own version of commentary on what's
> happening, and because we are such a large body, it will go viral
> through the internet channels, even though it won't be honored
> by MSNBC or CNN, and there'll be millions of views on witty,
> anointed, prophetic commentary, exposing the soft underbelly
> of Leviathan.[42]

Through his own Facebook Live rants and punditry, Wallnau spent the four years of the Trump presidency living into that prophecy, actively propagandizing his fellow Christians through viral videos and prophetic memes.

As the 2020 election ramped up, Wallnau energetically campaigned for Trump. He traveled through the swing states with his close friend Ché Ahn to urge every pastor and Christian to openly advocate for Trump. He told audiences that for the brief window of the Trump administration, Christians had controlled the tops of some of the Seven Mountains. God only knew what would happen if Biden became president.

Then, in the fall of 2020, just weeks before the election, Wallnau's prophecy about a prophetic commentary YouTube channel from January 2017 would come to fulfillment. Kenneth Copeland, one of the old lions of the Word of Faith-prosperity gospel movement, had a Christian television channel called Victory Channel, and that fall he launched a new political commentary show called *FlashPoint*. Broadcast on Copeland's Victory Channel and also posted on YouTube, *FlashPoint* adopted the slogan "Where Politics and Prophecy Align."[43] Most of the people who were invited on as commentators also cast themselves as prophets. *FlashPoint* was an unwavering, pro-Trump, Big Lie, conspiracy-spreading religious broadcast through the period between the 2020 election and January 6. And the forerunner—the leading voice on *FlashPoint*—was, of course, Lance Wallnau.

What little numerical data is available about *FlashPoint* in this era shows a staggeringly rapid adoption of this charismatic prophecy show. While they don't break out the numbers show by show, Victory Channel had virtually no YouTube presence before *FlashPoint* launched in late September 2020. That month, Victory Channel videos received 56,000 views on YouTube. In October, it was 152,000 views. In November, 1.4 million views. In December 2020, 6.1 million views. And by January 2021, the month of the insurrection, they received 32.4 million views on YouTube.[44] These numbers are mirrored in what you see on social media in the same time period: *FlashPoint* flooded the charismatic media space in the lead-up to January 6.

And it's still going strong. If you suspect that my characterizations of *FlashPoint* or of Wallnau and his peers' commentary are hyperbole or caricature, I would encourage you to watch any episode of *FlashPoint*. There you will discover the epicenter of prophetic Christian Trumpism and charismatic

Christian nationalism today. If you do hazard entry, be prepared to experience a topsy-turvy world where down is up, where Christians are simultaneously imperiously persecuted and gloriously triumphant, where prophetic memes replace actual news reporting, where right-wing politicians mingle with charismatic prophets. *FlashPoint* is Lance Wallnau's worldview and ambition made manifest.

What Lance Did on January 6

Throughout that season, between the November 2020 election and January 6, 2021, Wallnau delivered nearly daily rants on Facebook, his podcast, *FlashPoint*, or any other venue that would have him. Like Cindy Jacobs, Lance Wallnau was one of the speakers at the December 12, 2020, Jericho March event on the National Mall. Unlike Jacobs, Wallnau actually attended in person. "You are the privileged generation that is called to endure the contradiction along with Donald Trump and see America restored," he told the crowd. "This is not a weak movement. This is the beginning of a Christian populist uprising! There is a backlash coming. We are going to continue to build this as a groundswell from now till 2022. You will be on the news; they will not be able to ignore you. . . . There is a Great Awakening coming! This is the spark that is starting it right now!"[45]

I have sorted through hundreds of social media profiles of Christians who were present for the riots and protests at the US Capitol on January 6. Strikingly, a common denominator you can find across many of those accounts are clips of Wallnau's Facebook Live rants and links to episodes of *FlashPoint*. If we are looking for the key mobilizers that got Christians enraged and activated enough to drive or fly, sometimes cross-country, to the US Capitol on January 6, we have to look at Lance Wallnau and his *FlashPoint* platform, two of the most important and influential conduits of that mobilization.

With the popular fixation on Donald Trump's speech at the rally on the Ellipse on January 6, it's easy to forget that it was only one of three rallies that Stop the Steal organizers had planned. The first major rally was the one on January 5—the Rally to Revival—at which Ché Ahn spoke. Trump's Ellipse "fight like hell" rally was the second. The third rally event was planned for 1:00 p.m. on January 6 at the Capitol itself. Evidently, the organizers of the Stop the Steal election denial campaign anticipated that the real action would be at the Capitol that day, and they had strategized to put maximum pressure on the lawmakers then meeting inside the Capitol Building by staging another rally just outside.

This third event, at the Capitol, had to be canceled because of the rioting that broke out. Yet the list of planned speakers at the event is revealing. It's a veritable who's who of up-and-coming Christian nationalist politicians and activists, including political schemer Roger Stone, Pennsylvania state senator and then-future gubernatorial candidate Doug Mastriano, Representative Lauren Boebert, Representative Marjorie Taylor Greene, and, naturally, Lance Wallnau.

On the morning of January 6, 2021, inside his Trump International Hotel room, Lance bundled up against the cold and headed out to the Ellipse to see Donald Trump's speech. He posted a picture of himself on social media giving a thumbs up near the stage.

When that rally was over, Lance made his way across the National Mall with the throngs of angry rioters. He was ready to rile up the crowd even further at the afternoon rally, eager to keep the crowd at a low boil of rage. But it turned out Lance's further services weren't needed; the pot had already boiled over, and Trump supporters were rioting at the Capitol. So Lance watched the protests and furor for a bit and then headed back to his hotel room.

That evening, he would broadcast live as a panelist on a special one-and-a-half-hour edition of *FlashPoint*. Predictably, he spoke about the Seven Mountains and the need for Christians to rise to "the top of the sphere of influence that they're in and not being ashamed of the gospel." But amid debriefing the violence and chaos everyone had witnessed, Wallnau went further. "We have to know that the national news cycle is a spirit, is the false prophets of Baal. They're trying to make today's incidents in the Capitol something which is attached to us," he said on *FlashPoint*. "The devil will have his media. We may not be able to turn around corrupt media, but we can create another narrative by our presence and our power that plants the gospel in cities and in communities and in territories, where it contradicts the deception that is in the land."[46]

Lance Wallnau, chief Christian propagandist of the MAGA movement, has been steadfast in advancing that narrative ever since: Christians are the embattled and beleaguered cultural exiles *and* a populist force to be reckoned with. Christians are the real Americans and the destined leaders at the tops of all the mountains of influence.

If we want to know what implementing this Seven Mountains blueprint in a pluralistic democracy looks like, look at what its proponents did in the crucible of the 2020 election and its aftermath. That was a moment of supreme crisis and opportunity, from their perspective.

Ché Ahn has been an outspoken enthusiast of the Seven Mountains framework since it first entered the NAR bloodstream in the mid-2000s. He contributed a chapter to Lance Wallnau and Bill Johnson's Seven Mountains book. In late November 2020, as all this battling over the election results was going on, Ché posted on Instagram, "There's no separation of church and state. God's kingdom involves all the 7 Mountains of Influence."[47]

Johnny Enlow, a close prophet associate of Wallnau's and a longtime leader in Ché Ahn's HIM apostolic network, was the first to write a book on the Seven Mountains. In the aftermath of the election, Enlow would argue that anyone opposing Trump's attempt to hijack the election was guilty of "treason" and that such traitors were legally "executable" by Trump.[48] Other key Seven Mountains proponents, like Cindy Jacobs and Becca Greenwood, were there at the Capitol, leading spiritual warfare to keep Trump in office.

And, of course, there's Lance Wallnau, Mr. Seven Mountains himself. Wallnau took Loren Cunningham and Bill Bright's dreams, branded them with the imagery of mountains, brought these ideas into Peter Wagner's inner circle, and became the paramount exponent of the 7M prophetic meme for twenty years and counting. No Christian leader has done more to personally and theologically bolster the cause of Donald Trump than Lance Wallnau. After the 2020 election, no Christian leader has been a more prominent spokesperson for the Stop the Steal, Big Lie, epistemic discombobulation among evangelical Christians than Lance Wallnau. And of course, he was there, on the site of the Capitol Riot, watching the havoc ensue.

As much as Wallnau and his NAR fellows might proclaim that their battle is with demons, the front lines of opposition they meet is not from cosmic principalities and powers. It is actual people and democratic systems that take the brunt of their aggression. So if we want to know what applying the Seven Mountains concept looks like in a pluralistic democracy—a diverse nation governed by the rule of law, where separation of church and state is enshrined in the constitution—we need look no further than January 6.

The Most Important Evangelical Political Theologian of Our Time

Since the Capitol Riot, Wallnau's star has, if anything, continued to rise. He is now helping run a Colorado Springs–based organization he cofounded in 2017 called the Truth and Liberty Coalition. Truth and Liberty's mission is, forthrightly, "to educate, unify and mobilize believers in Jesus Christ to affect the reformation of nations through the seven mountains of cultural influence."[49] Their list of influencers and partner organizations are the banner carriers of the new charismatic-power-inflected religious right—a religious right reborn in the Trump era with an Independent Charismatic leadership core. The organization trains Christians on how to run for office and how to strategically engineer takeovers of local city councils and local school boards, which represent the government and education mountains.

Wallnau was invited to campaign on stage with the NAR-aligned Christian nationalist candidate Doug Mastriano in his ill-fated bid for Pennsylvania governor in 2022. He has spoken at the ReAwaken America events led by Michael Flynn. Right-wing politicians like Kari Lake, Marjorie Taylor Greene, Lauren Boebert, and even Donald Trump book appearances on *FlashPoint* to reach the charismatic, prophecy-believing audiences that Wallnau has spent decades galvanizing. And, incredibly, one-fifth of all Americans have embraced his Seven Mountains schema.

Wallnau's career as a pastor, a prophet, a pundit, and a political theologian has been lived in defiance of the buttoned-up evangelical institutions that putatively guide and speak for "evangelicalism." I would even argue—and I know how controversial this statement will be—that Lance Wallnau is the most important evangelical political theologian of the twenty-first century so far. He will not be gracing the stage at the annual meeting of the academic Evangelical Theological Society anytime soon. As of this writing,

Christianity Today has mentioned his name only once, and that was slightly mockingly in connection to the failed 2020 Trump prophecies.[50]

But can anyone find a Christian leader more in sync with the id of American evangelicalism than Lance Wallnau? His ideas and his prophetically glossed theology have become the battle anthem of the religious right and MAGA evangelicalism. So if you want to answer the question "Where is American evangelicalism going next?" you can, like many commentators, go on watching the evangelical institutions of power, forged during the twentieth century. You can go on listening to the elites who purport to speak for evangelicalism. I'll be watching Lance Wallnau.

6

WORSHIP IS A WEAPON

IN JULY 2020, a couple of hundred Christians gathered on the Golden Gate Bridge to sing worship songs, to pray against the spread of COVID-19, and to demonstrate their freedom to worship. This was just weeks after George Floyd's murder by a white police officer, and Black Lives Matter protests were roiling. It was also four months into the pandemic lockdowns. It was a tempestuous, confusing time in America, and many Christians found great hope in this brazen, impromptu Golden Gate concert.

This musical gathering was inspired and led by a young, long-haired, charismatic worship leader named Sean Feucht. It would serve as a catalyst for a far-reaching harmonizing of right-wing politics and charismatic Christian worship music. This dynamic would crescendo six months later on January 6 and continue very much to the present. Feucht titled the July 2020 Golden Gate gathering—and the ensuing tour, during which he took similar in-person worship concerts to dozens of US cities—Let Us Worship. Begun as a defiant protest against local and statewide COVID-19 restrictions, Let Us Worship has resulted in three chart-topping albums and hundreds of events, many with thousands in attendance. It has also slingshotted Feucht (pronounced *foyt*) to iconic status in the religious right, making him a national celebrity and first-order right-wing provocateur.

Sean Feucht is hardly anyone's stereotype of a reactionary Christian leader. He's not a straight-laced, activist pastor like Jerry Falwell, or a televangelist like Pat Robertson, or a psychologist and family expert like James Dobson, or a political operative like Ralph Reed. No, Feucht is a sunshiny, flaxen-haired, hippie-looking millennial worship leader who loves posing for pictures with his guitar. Yet Feucht, who is just a shade past forty years old, could reasonably be included in the company of these top-tier captains of conservative religious indignation.

Anyone who has spent time around modern American evangelicalism knows that worship music is big business. Contemporary worship songs, designed to be sung in churches or for personal devotion, now make up a significant fraction of the billions of dollars American Christians spend annually on specifically Christian retail products. Major worship-music brands, from Bethel to Hillsong to Passion, rake in millions of dollars in sales each year, and headliner worship leaders can draw crowds that rival major rock concerts.

But a shift has occurred over the past decade, accelerating greatly since 2020: worship is now political. Today many right-wing and Republican rallies have taken on the ethos and aesthetic of a charismatic worship service, with worship leaders deploying styles of music and participation that were developed to spark Christian faith formation to now enliven Christian nationalism. Sean Feucht is at the forefront of this shift.

Where did Sean Feucht come from? How did he rise from being a standard-issue charismatic worship leader to one of the preeminent religious celebrities in the United States in just a few short years? What is the connection between charismatic worship and Christian extremism? And what does the fusion of Christian worship music and right-wing politics augur for the future?

Even if you have encountered news about Sean Feucht before picking up this book, you might still be surprised to learn just how deep his affinities and associations with the NAR are. While he does not explicitly call himself an apostle or a prophet, Feucht has grown up under the mentorship of people like Ché Ahn, Lou Engle, Cindy Jacobs, and Lance Wallnau. But Feucht has also been deeply imprinted by leaders of another major Independent Charismatic brand that is adjacent to but distinct from Peter Wagner's NAR networks, namely, the Bethel Church empire headquartered in Redding, California.

In this chapter we will look at the ways that Feucht, by regurgitating and repackaging many of the NAR frameworks we've explored in previous chapters—along with a few he picked up at Bethel—embodies the broader charismaticization of right-wing politics. If the old adage is true that everyone is the hero of their own life story, we can learn by examining, to the degree possible, Feucht's life story as he narrates it himself.

Beyond the bounds of his own psyche, Sean Feucht is also a hero to many contemporary American Christians—most of whom would, no doubt, both balk at being characterized as extremists and love to talk about what Feucht means to them. But we must get inside his own hero's narrative—the one *he* constructs—to truly understand his power and reach. Then we will look at how Christian worship, particularly charismatic worship music and experiences, has in recent years become a fast-track vehicle for Christian radicalization, with people like Feucht leading the charge. So let's rehearse—and then problematize—Sean Feucht's hero's journey narrative on the way to apprehending the centrality of charismatic worship to today's right-wing politics.

A Prophetic Journey

Sean Feucht was born in 1983, on the older end of the millennial generation, and his birth has an important backstory. One year earlier, his older brother, Christopher, was born. But then, after only ten weeks of life, little Christopher mysteriously suffocated and died in his sleep. This tragedy devastated the Feucht family, and they leaned into their Assemblies of God (Pentecostal) church community for support. At Christopher's memorial service, one of the pastors began to prophesy over the family, telling them of a vision of a new baby who would bring joy in the midst of their sorrow. Exactly one year, to the day, of Christopher's death, Sean was born. So from his earliest moments of cognizance, it was impressed on Sean that he had an exceptionally purposeful role in the world. To borrow one of Sean's phrases, he was on a *prophetic journey*.

As a teenager, Sean dedicated his life to a radical Christian lifestyle. He was passionate about worship music and learned to play guitar. He began leading the worship sessions in his church youth group. Expressive, emotional worship is central to most forms of evangelical aesthetic and sense of belonging, and Pentecostals and charismatics have been the up-to-the-minute pioneers in worship music since at least the 1970s. Due in part to Feucht's leadership and passion, the youth group's weekly attendance surged from one hundred to more than four hundred some weeks.[1]

In high school, Sean was a blond-haired, handsome football quarterback at a Christian school. He contemplated, from a young age, becoming a missionary. He started dating his first serious girlfriend (and eventual wife),

Kate, who also happened to be a cheerleader. A pastor's daughter, Kate was also passionate about global missions.

During high school, Sean was given a burned CD—it was the nineties after all. But this was not a bootlegged music album; it was a prophecy recording, made by Lou Engle and some of the planning team and speakers for The Call DC. Sean was transfixed: the CD "contained some of the wildest prayers, prophecies, and decrees I had ever heard," Feucht would later write. "The prayers for revival coming out of The Call were exactly what our hearts longed for."[2] So seventeen-year-old Sean and his girlfriend, Kate, helped organize charter buses from their church to attend the September 2000 event in DC.

Across legions of interviews and in written reflections, Sean returns again and again to The Call DC as an utterly transformative experience: "There was an energy and expectation that was palpable! You could almost feel the electricity of the crowd! . . . It was the most intense twelve hours of nonstop worship, prayer, and fasting for revival in America I had ever been part of."[3]

Prostrated there on the National Mall, swallowed in the massive crowd, Feucht had a vision of the whole earth in the palm of God's hand, with small fires of worship burning around the globe. In the vision, God inhaled the smoke of the worship fires, and then "He began to blow the wind of revival upon the earth."[4] Feucht dedicated his life to seeing this vision fulfilled.

It was also at The Call DC that Sean cemented a deep antiabortion commitment. He was especially moved that day by the rhetoric of Lou Engle, who called the Supreme Court's 1973 *Roe v. Wade* decision a "death decree" over America that was keeping the nation chained to murder and immorality. So taken was Sean with Lou Engle and Ché Ahn's leadership that day that he began to volunteer for future events of The Call, thus beginning a friendship with and mentorship by both men that has spanned three decades now. Feucht has even called Lou Engle a "spiritual father."[5]

Sean attended Oral Roberts University in Tulsa, the school founded by the famed faith-healing evangelist. It was a Christian school with a robust worship culture, yet Sean describes a season of disillusionment when he tried out for multiple bands and worship leading opportunities and was roundly rejected. His faith came back to life when he found his "own personal Cave of Adullam": a biblical reference to a cavern where David, who had been anointed as king but not yet crowned, hid out from his aggressive rival King Saul.[6] David is believed to have written a couple of the biblical psalms from that cave. For Feucht, his psalmic refuge was a stairwell in his dorm, where he could unabashedly play his guitar and where the "most raw, honest, and passionate sounds, melodies, and lyrics poured from my heart."[7]

Sean began hosting worship sessions in his dorm room for his fellow charismatic students. Colloquially, the group began calling the gatherings The Burn, hearkening back to both Sean's near obsession with The Call and also his vision of a world on fire with revival. Sometimes sessions of The Burn would last more than twenty-four hours. This impulse toward raw, prolonged worship and prayer sessions at Oral Roberts University dovetailed with other charismatic centers that were then experimenting with 24/7 prayer and worship, petitioning God for revival. Sean sensed that somehow The Burn was part of his prophetic journey.

Itinerant Firestarter

After college, in 2005, Sean married Kate and started a real-estate business in Tulsa with some friends, but he couldn't shake his own sense of calling. So Sean and Kate, in an act of faith, decided to take The Burn, his college-based worship sessions, on the road. They traveled the country, leading worship and prayer at churches and relying on the hospitality of their hosts. Eventually, Sean and Kate created a nonprofit called Burn 24-7 that would keep perpetuating these Spirit-filled prayer and worship sessions in the United States and abroad. The Burn 24-7 website says that the movement "carries the Amos 9:11 and Acts 15:16 Davidic calling to 'rebuild again the Tabernacle of David' so that the 'rest of humanity may seek the Lord.'"[8] Translated, this means that Burn 24-7 utilizes particular styles of worship to create an environment akin to the Tabernacle in ancient Israel.

From roughly 2007 to 2019, Burn 24-7 was Sean Feucht's worship and missions platform, and he took it everywhere, traveling to more than sixty nations and countless US cities and churches by the time he was thirty-seven. Along the way, Sean and Kate had four children, and they frequently took their young kids along on their trips abroad. The Feuchts were

Christian social media influencers before that was even a category, displaying their charming, sold-out-for-Jesus, fervidly worshipping family at every opportunity.

In 2009, Feucht encountered another NAR apostle named Charles Stock. Stock was a longtime Peter Wagner associate who taught classes alongside Peter at WLI. By 2009, Stock was serving, together with Lou Engle and James Goll, on the leadership team of Ché Ahn's HIM network, which already comprised eight thousand ministries spread around the globe. Stock was also the pastor of a large Independent Charismatic church in Harrisburg, Pennsylvania, called Life Center. Sean was so impressed with Charles Stock that shortly after their meeting, when Sean felt he heard God say, "Surround yourself with joyful fathers in this season!" he knew his young family needed to move to Harrisburg—despite the fact that they had few other connections there.[9] Stock would become another in a series of spiritual fathers to Feucht.

Several times in his life, Sean has received prophetic words about Isaiah 22:22 ("The key of the house of David I will lay on his shoulder; So he shall open, and no one shall shut; And he shall shut, and no one shall open"). So he found the idea of moving to Pennsylvania, known as the *Key*stone State, to be a rich prophetic development.[10] Though he didn't, as far as I can tell, officially align Burn 24-7 with Ché Ahn's apostolic network, being in the HIM orbit in Harrisburg launched Sean into a new web of relationships and opportunities. For a time, Burn 24-7 even had an Apostolic Council, separate from its board of directors, and this council included Mike and Cindy Jacobs, Charles Stock, and several other NAR or NAR-adjacent leaders.[11]

If you were to draw a Venn diagram of all the NAR networks intersecting in Pennsylvania, Stock's church, Life Center, would be at the overlapping heart of all the circles. The apostles and prophets Peter Wagner mentored sometimes cycled through there. In fact, it was while visiting Life Center one week that a Canadian NAR prophet (an ACPE member) named Stacey Campbell prophesied, shouting over Feucht, "You, Sean, are a man of war! I see blood all over your hands. You were made for the day of battle and you will be misunderstood by many."[12] At first, Sean found this prophecy confusing and off-putting. But over time he would embrace his calling as a "man of war."

Throughout this intermediary stage in Feucht's growth and evolution, he was becoming increasingly well known in Independent Charismatic circles. As we've seen, climbing into leadership in that world is both a matter of personal charismatic branding (prophetic memes, catchy songs, distinctive speaking styles) and of relational capital (who you know). If you track Sean's social media postings throughout these years, you can see him hanging out and leading worship and prophecy conferences with James Goll, Cindy Jacobs, Dutch Sheets, Ché Ahn, Lance Wallnau, Lou Engle, and many other core NAR leaders. Through Burn 24-7 and his close ties to these leading NAR figures, Feucht became a known quantity in a vast web of loosely affiliated churches around the country. He has matured and become popular in the shade cast by the NAR, with multiple central NAR leaders serving as his dearest mentors and spiritual parents.

On Earth as It Is at Bethel

Those who have tracked Feucht's more recent ubiquity, especially throughout the 2020 election, may be surprised to learn that he was not very politically involved during the 2016 campaign. He did support Trump and reposted a video on Facebook of an NAR prophet in Las Vegas prophesying over the candidate a few days before the election.[13] But against the backdrop of what NAR figures like Lance Wallnau or Cindy Jacobs did to amplify Trump's cause, Sean's support seems relatively tame. Throughout the summer and fall of 2016, the Feuchts were in the middle of a pivotal life transition, joining up with the Bethel empire in Redding, California.

Bethel Church—and its many subsidiaries—is easily the most prominent apostolic-and-prophetic charismatic hub in the United States. Some scholars and analysts have characterized Bethel as part of the NAR, but I think it's more helpful to think of Bethel as another fivefold ministry brand, one that grew up alongside and cross-pollinated with Wagner's NAR networks.

The Bethel apostle Bill Johnson grew up as a pastor's kid at Bethel Church in the 1960s and 1970s, when it was a medium-sized Assemblies of God church in the small city of Redding, near the California–Oregon border. Like his father, Bill discerned a call to ministry and took over pastoring a different small Assemblies of God church in the nearby tiny mountain town of Weaverville. He was there through the 1980s. Like Ché Ahn, Lou Engle, and Lance Wallnau, he was a mildly successful charismatic pastor.

Then Bill Johnson and his wife, Beni, heard about the Toronto Blessing, and they traveled to Toronto in 1995 to experience the holy-laughter revival. As it had been for Ahn and Engle and countless other pastors, Toronto proved to be the spiritual kick in the pants that Bill Johnson needed. On his way to Toronto, he prayed, "'God if you will touch me again, I'll never change the subject.' . . . I would make his outpouring the only thing I would give myself to."[14] Shortly thereafter, Bill was invited back to Redding to take over his father's former church.

Bill and Beni Johnson returned to Redding in 1996 and began building the post-Toronto Bethel amalgamation that is, today, one of the most influential and emblematic brands in all of global Independent Charismaticism. They would eventually take Bethel Church out of the Assemblies of God denomination in order to pursue the fivefold apostolic-and-prophetic model.[15] In 1998, they founded Bethel School of Supernatural Ministry (BSSM), a training school that very much mirrored WLI, founded the same year, with its emphasis on apostolic-prophetic themes. But BSSM always explicitly aimed to expand the supernatural repertoire and skills of young charismatics. Indeed, as it says on its website, "The mission of BSSM is to equip and deploy revivalists who passionately pursue world-wide transformation in their God-given spheres of influence."[16]

If that "spheres of influence" language sounds familiar, it's because there is a deep Seven Mountains slant at Bethel. In fact, the Seven Mountain Mandate is one of the major concepts Bethel has borrowed from its NAR friends. Bill Johnson coedited the book *Invading Babylon: The Seven Mountain Mandate* with his friend Lance Wallnau in 2013. Since the mid-2000s, when the Seven Mountains framework swept into Bethel, it has been Bethel's underlying political theology and mode of cultural influence.

Thousands of students have cycled through BSSM's programs, with 2,600 students enrolled (pre-COVID-19) and 40 percent of its student body international students. That means that every year, hundreds of students from all over the world descend on remote Redding, California, to receive hands-on training from Bill Johnson and his network of apostles, prophets, evangelists, and revivalists.[17] A core part of the curriculum at BSSM is worship, and students participate in extensive prayer and worship sessions that are so engrossing they sometimes border on trance-like. Bethelites sometimes claim that they collectively see "glory clouds" in the midst of worship: inexplicable gold dust or angel feathers suddenly materializing and floating around in the sanctuary.[18]

Again, according to the BSSM website, students are "immersed in a revelatory culture where the Holy Spirit becomes the chief instructor and tour guide," and they are instructed "how to read, understand, and 'do' the Bible—how to practice [God's] presence, to witness, heal the sick, prophesy, preach, pray, cast out demons and much more."[19] The students are encouraged to take those new techniques and go out into the streets of Redding to pray for healings and to spread the gospel through supernatural manifestations. Bethel is cultivating what we could call "a culture of the everyday miraculous," training up the next generation of supernaturally empowered revivalists who expect miracles for breakfast, lunch, and dinner.

Building on the success of Bethel Church and BSSM, Johnson and the Bethel leadership have also created and crafted Bethel Music into one of the most important worship-music collectives in the world. They entrusted leadership of Bethel Music to Bill Johnson's son Brian Johnson and his wife, Jenn. Taking music written by worship leaders at Bethel, Bethel Music began releasing albums and flooding the worship-music market with captivating and expressive songs. In a recent study of the thirty-eight most popular Christian worship songs used by churches from 2010 to 2020, music brands associated with four megachurches utterly dominated the list: Bethel, Elevation, Hillsong, and Passion. Hillsong and Passion each had nine, and Bethel was in the lead by far, with thirteen of the top songs.[20]

So despite its geographical isolation and its mid-tier megachurch size, approximately five thousand to six thousand members, Bethel punches way above its weight. Most churches in the United States rely on donations from congregational members to make up more than 90 percent of their budgets, but at Bethel, that dynamic is reversed. As of 2013, only 19 percent of Bethel's thirty-seven-million-dollar annual budget came from member donations. The other thirty million dollars each year comes from students' BSSM tuition, music and DVD sales from Bethel Music, Bethel conferences, and other subsidiary interests.[21] Every week, thousands of churches in the United States and around the world sing Bethel's catchy and compelling worship anthems in their services, adding more money into Bethel's coffers through licensing fees churches must pay. Bill Johnson's lonely outpost in Northern California has, in the words of one observer, "defined the soundtrack of contemporary Christian worship."[22]

When Sean Feucht's father abruptly died of brain cancer in 2010, Beni and Bill Johnson reached out and invited Sean and Kate to spend some time at Bethel as they grieved. While there, Sean and Bill connected on a deep level as Bill's father had passed away with a similar affliction. By 2016, they were inviting the Feuchts to make Bethel their home base.

By all accounts, the Feuchts fit right in in Redding. Sean would later reflect that Bethel "is a community that can tolerate and even celebrate taking your children to a war zone on spring break. . . . We felt covered, championed, and looked after."[23] Sean began releasing worship albums with Bethel Music, and he became very close to both Bill and Beni Johnson and their son and daughter-in-law, Brian and Jenn Johnson, frequently spending time together socially beyond their many ministry collaborations.

As the Trump presidency was playing out in the nation, Feucht was becoming one of the recognizable faces of Bethel, and he was on a glide path to becoming a very respectable celebrity worship leader. Then he started receiving prophecies that he was supposed to run for Congress.

Sean for Congress

Since young adulthood, Sean Feucht has held conservative political views—especially, in connection with his transformative experience at The Call DC, on abortion. But in 2019, at a Bethel Music conference, a charismatic Republican operative approached Sean to say, "I really believe you are going to run for US Congress. It's all over you, man. We need a long-haired, Jesus-loving worship leader in there. . . . You *are* the change."[24] Bolstered by this and other prophetic words, and supported by a cadre of veteran staffers who had worked on the Pat Robertson and Ben Carson campaigns, Sean decided to, once again, seek out his prophetic destiny. It didn't go well.

From the start, Feucht knew that taking on the political establishment in California's 3rd District, both the Democrat then holding the seat and other Republican challengers, would be a "David versus Goliath" endeavor.[25] With no background in politics or policy, Sean would later admit, "I did not physically have time nor space to research all the topics that came up on the campaign trail."[26] He had prominent supporters and endorsers, including Mike Huckabee, but Feucht was unprepared for the onslaught of campaign demands and fundraising. His campaign was unique, choosing what Sean would describe as a "'Jesus People Movement' bohemian vibe" that staffers thought would appeal to millennials in Northern California.[27] He also endorsed dismantling or reducing school vaccine mandates, a topic that, even pre-COVID-19, was popular in the region.[28] In Feucht's own telling, he also wasn't prepared for the degree of backlash from his fellow Christians, whom he imagined would leap to support him. But while many charismatic friends around the country celebrated his prophesied entry into politics, many other Christians saw Sean as unnecessarily politicizing the faith.

The most iconic moment of Feucht's campaign came when he joined a group of sixty charismatic worship leaders for a White House visit in December 2019. Ostensibly, the meeting was about religious liberty, but the group wound up leading a high-powered worship session, with Mike Pence and other Trump administration staffers in the room.[29] This gathering was smack dab in the middle of Trump's first impeachment proceedings and was, not unreasonably, read as a pointed statement of ongoing charismatic support for Trump even amid his trials. Bethel Music's Brian and Jenn Johnson were there, as was Hillsong's Brian Houston, and Paula White joined the group. In a photograph from that day, sixty hip young worship leaders stand arrayed around Trump in the Oval Office, with Trump seated at the Resolute desk. Among the group, Sean smiles and leans toward the center, his hand conspicuously outstretched to touch Trump's sleeve.

Feucht lost badly in the primary, getting only 13.5 percent of the vote. He was heartbroken. "Out of all the ministries, seasons, initiatives, and adventures I had chased after in my life, running for political office was the one endeavor that included the clearest directive and word from God," he writes in his memoir.[30] It was a decimating season, although one that Sean had very little time or space to process. Immediately after his defeat, the pandemic hit.

The California primary was held on Super Tuesday, March 3, 2020. The next day Governor Gavin Newsom declared a state of emergency due to an alarming rise in COVID-19 cases. Two weeks later, most of the country was on lockdown.

Sean would later conclude that God *was* at work in getting him to run but not because he was intended to win the election. No, God had orchestrated this episode to awaken Sean to reality: "I saw behind the veil of the political realm," he would later tell Ché Ahn in an interview. "I knew the agendas."[31] Prior to his campaign, Sean was political but not politically active. After his campaign, and as COVID-19 restrictions engulfed the world, Sean began blending political activism and worship in a way that would help to transform modern right-wing American politics.

Let Us Worship

So by early 2020, Sean Feucht was a failed congressional candidate, a relatively popular charismatic worship leader and recording artist, and an ideological hybrid of Bethel and the NAR. Feucht's resistance to COVID-19 restrictions was inspired, in part, by what he saw Ché Ahn and Harvest Rock Church doing in Southern California, and he decided to do something similar in Northern California.[32]

But Sean didn't defy the California statewide COVID-19 restrictions by embedding himself in a congregation and continuing to defiantly run services the way Ché Ahn did at Harvest Rock. The Bethel approach is more provocative and flamboyant, which mirrors Feucht's own instincts and aesthetic. Sean chose to defy Governor Gavin Newsom's COVID-19 restrictions on the most quintessential piece of Americana in Northern California: the Golden Gate Bridge.

Feucht put out a call on social media and led a group of two or three hundred worshippers to walk out onto the middle of the bridge to sing, pray, and prophesy. Evidently, many in the group were Bethelites. Sean branded the event with the hashtag "Let Us Worship," but he also talked about it as a "NEW Jesus people movement," hearkening back to the hippie revivals of the 1960s and early 1970s and also to Feucht's recently terminated campaign. Soon a slickly edited video of the group singing was posted on YouTube and Facebook.[33] The very next day, Sean staged a similar Let Us Worship event at Huntington Beach in Southern

California. This time, a thousand people showed up to stand on the beach and worship.

These Let Us Worship events struck a chord with evangelicals across the nation. After four months of COVID-19 restrictions and lockdowns, people were tired of feeling cooped up. Churchgoers—especially charismatic churchgoers, for whom ecstatic and absorbing communal worship sessions are a core pillar of their spiritual routine—longed to go back to their churches. California had some of the most stringent COVID-19 restriction policies in the country. Particularly galling to avid worshippers in California was a July 3, 2020, mandate from Governor Gavin Newsom restricting singing at all gatherings—due to growing understanding of the airborne spread of the disease—because this seemed targeted at churches.[34]

Sean took Let Us Worship on the road, staging low-budget, high-energy events in city after city. By the end of July, they had hit seven California cities, including Redding. Then they really revved things up, moving out to different states and cities across the country. Early on, a young pastor named Jay Koopman joined the embryonic Let Us Worship movement, taking on most of the preaching at the events and acting as a hype man for Feucht. He also led altar calls and baptisms that invited participants to commitment and conversion. Koopman was, at the time, an associate pastor at Ché Ahn's Harvest Rock Church and had to get Ché's permission to join the Sean Feucht roadshow, a further sign of the deep congruence among the NAR, HIM, and Feucht's efforts.[35]

Sean's years of itinerant ministry among far-flung charismatic churches, his connections through Ché Ahn's networks, and his popular Bethel platform meant that hundreds of churches around the country were eager to host or help stage a Let Us Worship event. Let Us Worship was becoming a movement.

Feucht's worship protest movement was originally framed as a demonstration for religious freedom, arguing that the US Constitution and natural, God-given rights should guarantee worshippers' ability to gather, even in the face of a global pandemic. Feucht would frequently make references back to his years of leading worship sessions abroad, highlighting places where Christians were persecuted and claiming that "the greatest opposition we have ever experienced" occurred not in any other country but here in the

United States during COVID-19.[36] He often insinuated or outright declared that nefarious demonic forces or anti-Christian politicians' ulterior motives were actually driving the policies. He knew this, he suggested, because while running for office, he had seen "behind the veil" of how politics really works.

Local authorities, especially Democratic authorities who were urging caution, often didn't know how to respond to Feucht's traveling worship spectacles. He proudly, and half tongue in cheek, states that he "became the number one COVID violator in twenty-eight states. . . . I wear that as a badge of honor."[37] Sean and his staff often did not apply for permits, and while Feucht didn't explicitly encourage or discourage mask-wearing, Let Us Worship participants generally didn't wear masks.

More than ten thousand people congregated at some of the events, which were frequently in violation of local COVID-19 restrictions. Sometimes police would show up to attempt to prevent the events, but the participants would claim this was a violation of their First Amendment rights.[38] Public health officials would warn that these concerts were superspreader events, with high risks of local COVID-19 outbreaks following in their wake. Sometimes authorities would even launch investigations, threatening legal penalties. Various municipalities levied thousands of dollars of fines against Feucht, but from Sean's perspective, these were just tactics to scare Christians and keep them at home.

Through all this opposition, Sean felt more and more like he understood Stacey Campbell's prophecy over him: "You, Sean, are a man of war! . . . You will be misunderstood by many."[39] While many American Christian leaders and pastors fought back against COVID-19 restrictions, with some like Ché Ahn even taking their cases to the Supreme Court, Sean Feucht and Let Us Worship became the primary public face of Christian COVID-19 resistance, taking the fight to the streets.

Riots to Revival

If Let Us Worship began as a series of religious freedom protests, the political causes multiplied from there. When Feucht took the show outside of California, some of the states and municipalities he went to did not have such strict COVID-19-related gathering regulations, and local Republican officials often allowed or even welcomed the events. All of this raises the question: If these concerts were not straightforwardly about taking a stance against local high-strung COVID-19 policies, what was the point?

The Let Us Worship events were occurring throughout the summer and fall of 2020, as the ongoing uprising against police violence and racism wracked US cities following the murder of George Floyd. Feucht was invited by friends in Portland, Oregon—a center of protests and clashes with the police—to bring Let Us Worship there in August. Sean agreed, reasoning, "I felt that, in the same way God had sent us into war zones across the world, we now needed to take His light into this area of darkness in our own nation."[40] They added new branding into this event, calling it Riots to Revival.[41]

Upward of five thousand people showed up at the first Portland Riots to Revival / Let Us Worship event, and Feucht would later exuberantly recall, "The sight of it was staggering—it was an *army!*"[42] Sean became a regular guest on Fox News, speaking not only to the vision behind Let Us Worship but also dramatically recounting any opposition they faced. Local and national news outlets began covering each of Feucht's events, further publicizing the phenomena.

The Portland event shifted the focus of Let Us Worship away from merely protesting COVID-19 regulations to also "bring healing to cities upended by racial unrest."[43] Feucht's rhetoric frequently castigates cities, especially cities led by Democratic politicians, as depraved and deprived places that need revival. After the shooting of Jacob Blake, a Black man, by police in Kenosha, Wisconsin, Feucht brought his Let Us Worship tour to Kenosha. Likewise, when protesters occupied a few blocks in downtown Seattle, keeping out police and calling it the Capitol Hill Occupied Protest (CHOP), Feucht decided to host a Let Us Worship event inside CHOP. From Sean's perspective, "We and three thousand of our friends entered the epicenter of chaos and lawlessness. We were coming to declare that Jesus was Lord over their 'occupied territory.'"[44] This event led to actual violence, with CHOP protesters attacking the Let Us Worship equipment, breaking their drums and guitar pedals. Feucht supporters physically pushed back. Sean posted on Instagram, "THE CHURCH REFUSED TO BE INTIMIDATED AND GOD KEPT POURING OUT! . . . we made it out of the lion's den of CHOP alive . . . [thank you to the burly bodyguards]."[45]

At many places Feucht and Koopman took their tour, they encountered great resistance, but they also found legions of supporters. At every
stop, hundreds—or more often thousands—of Christians would show
up to sing passionately. After a *Rolling Stone* article irritably dubbed Sean
Feucht "Jesus Christ, Superspreader," Sean started selling T-shirts emblazoned with that title. When other Christians claimed what Sean was doing
was unbiblical and quoted a famous passage from Romans 13, in which
the Apostle Paul calls the church to submit to governing authorities,
Sean responded that such a citation "was taken out of context and felt
manipulative."[46]

The 2020 Let Us Worship tour, which hit dozens of cities, reached
its zenith at an event on the National Mall on October 25, 2020. Sean saw
that date as prophetic. Not only was it just eight days before the national
election; 10/25, for him, corresponded with Hebrews 10:25, which instructs
Christians to "not forsake[e] the assembling of ourselves together."[47]

Just in case the parallels between this event and Sean's seminal spiritual awakening at The Call DC in 2000 weren't obvious—Christian protest
events, on the National Mall, at the height of presidential elections—Sean
invited Lou Engle to help lead the DC Let Us Worship crowd from the stage.
Engle had the huge crowd gather in small groups: "The blood [of Jesus] is
our weapon. Just begin to pray the blood of Jesus over your state, over your
city. Go, brothers and sisters, we're before the throne of God. . . . Pray for a
pro-life government."[48] After the concert, Feucht and Engle led a group in
prayer and worship in front of the Supreme Court, a sort of proto-Jericho
March, to intercede against abortion.

The gathering in DC also happened to occur at the exact time that
the confirmation debate over Supreme Court nominee Amy Coney Barrett
was occurring in the US Senate. Missouri Senator Josh Hawley took a break
from the proceedings inside the Capitol to come out and address the crowd.
Feucht introduced him by saying, "I feel like [Hawley] is a sign and a wonder of a new generation. He is the youngest member of the Senate. He's on
fire for Jesus. He's a revivalist filled with the Spirit of God, and he's taking a
stand for the things we all need to be taking a stand for."[49] Just a few months
later, Hawley was one of the handful of senators to object to the certification
of the presidential election, and he was memorably photographed walking

past the gathering crowds outside the Capitol with his fist defiantly raised in the air.

By the end of 2020, Let Us Worship was still somewhat about religious freedom, but it was also about healing racial strife, declaring the lordship of Jesus over American cities, changing the Supreme Court, and overturning *Roe v. Wade*. What holds all these disparate purposes together? Well, given Sean's deep background in NAR and Bethel circles, it should surprise no one that the most fundamental layer of his political theology is the Seven Mountain Mandate.

Feucht grew up in an environment shaped by the Seven Mountains teaching, so while he frequently references the 7M framework, he rarely pauses to explain it. He just assumes his audiences are acquainted with the popular meme. He'll talk about "expanding spiritual territory," a Peter Wagner–inspired phrase if I ever heard one, and say things like "Why shouldn't we [conservative, Spirit-filled Christians] be the ones leading the way in all spheres of society?"[50] Sometimes he'll invoke Wallnau and Johnson's *invasion* image, telling audiences, "We need to believe that God's called us to invade this mountain of government, and bring his kingdom and bring his presence, and bring heaven's solutions. There are solutions that can only be fixed in this state from heaven."[51]

More than anything, the message of Let Us Worship was that American Christians needed to make public demonstrations of the power of Christianity, to squarely defy any opposition, so as to instigate the next revival. As Sean would report to a group of NAR leaders, including Cindy Jacobs and Chuck Pierce, who had gathered on New Year's Eve—seven days before the Capitol Riot—Let Us Worship is "the greatest revival movement in my lifetime. . . . We have really found the value and the passion to fight for future and for the prophetic destiny of America, not just for us but for our children's children."[52]

Kingdom to the Capitol

Sean Feucht joined at least one of the Global Prayer for Election Integrity conference calls, in which apostles, prophets, and Trump advisers strategized and prayed together (described in chapter 3).[53] On January 5, 2021, Sean was on the road in Texas and posted on social media his support for Josh Hawley amid the outcry over his planned objection to the vote count the next day. Sean was vaguely supportive of the efforts of the protesters, and he expressed outrage at how Trump was censored by social media companies after January 6. But unlike the other characters of this book, Sean Feucht had little direct involvement in the events of January 6.

Without a doubt, Sean's 2020 Let Us Worship tour leapfrogged him up many tiers in charismatic celebrity circles. In 2019, when he was already a fairly recognizable worship leader with a Bethel platform, Feucht struggled mightily to raise even $300,000 to sustain his congressional campaign. His umbrella organization, Sean Feucht Ministries, raised around $284,000 that year, which was average compared with what he had done in previous years. But by 2020, Sean Feucht had become a media and social media sensation, and Sean Feucht Ministries raised $5.3 million that year alone.[54] To date, Sean has released ten different albums based on his Let Us Worship tour, three of which have reached number one on iTunes top albums charts for daily music sales in the United States.[55] Feucht's many years traversing Independent Charismatic communities had made him a known quantity within those fourth-quadrant networks. But 2020 launched him into the stratosphere, making him famous in broader evangelicalism.

After the Biden inauguration, Sean has, if anything, become more recognizable on the religious right. He has carried on with Let Us Worship, in various iterations, long after the pandemic was no longer a concern. His cheerful smile and his shrewd quarrelsomeness have made him an in-demand spokesperson for any conservative resistance cause.

Sean has also become a Republican tastemaker, speaking to and for the combative Christian far right. On New Year's Eve at the end of 2021, Sean held a concert in Miami, and he brought Florida Governor Ron DeSantis and his wife, Casey, out on stage. Casey was battling cancer at the time, and Sean and Jay Koopman offered prophetic healing prayers over her and gave Ron DeSantis a "Defender of Freedom" award for his antagonism toward COVID-19 restrictions.[56] Not to be outdone, Donald Trump also hosted Sean Feucht at his Florida estate, Mar-a-Lago, and even signed a guitar for him there.[57] Other name-brand right-wing politicians like Jim Jordan, Lauren Boebert, and Marjorie Taylor Greene have made it a priority to be photographed with Feucht, to appear as guests on his podcast, and to attend his worship events.

Feucht has also appeared on stage and led worship at the ReAwaken America tour, where Lance Wallnau has also been a featured speaker. In fact, the figurehead of the ReAwaken tour, Michael Flynn, Trump's former National Security Advisor, has become friends with Feucht. He told Sean in a recent interview, "You're a warrior. When I first met you and got to know you, I was like: Wow! We've got these different warriors that have different talents."[58] I'm not sure if Sean would call this statement from Flynn a prophecy, but I'm confident he would see it as a fulfillment of one.

In 2022, a documentary film crew that had been following Feucht's Let Us Worship tour released a film about Sean with the sardonic title *Superspreader*. It opened in 235 theaters nationwide. The film, which also features interviews with Ché Ahn, Jay Koopman, and Bill Johnson, was produced by a religious nonprofit. It casts the Christian COVID-19 resisters as heroic, conscientious leaders confronting tyranny, with the director explaining its purpose as "giving believers the courage to stand up for truth."[59]

Also in 2022, Sean created a nerve center for the activist and lobbyist side of his work by buying a Washington, DC, row house on Capitol Hill, just steps from Congress and the Supreme Court. He named this new project Camp Elah, Elah being the name of the stream from which David chose the stones to slay Goliath. Camp Elah was designed be a staging ground for charismatics to spiritually impact lawmaking through worship, prayer, and lobbying.

Within weeks of the launch of Camp Elah, something Feucht had spent decades praying for, fasting for, campaigning for, and lobbying for became reality. The US Supreme Court reversed its 1973 *Roe v. Wade* decision with its *Dobbs v. Jackson Women's Health Organization* decision. Sean, who was in Washington, DC, the day of the decision, was ecstatic, posting on social media:

VICTORY IN JESUS!!!
50 YEARS OF PRAYER ANSWERED!!!!!!
THE DEATH DECREE REVERSED!!
History belongs to the intercessors!!![60]

By early 2023, Sean had taken Let Us Worship to 175 cities around the United States. Then he announced the latest evolution of Let Us Worship, this time called Kingdom to the Capitol. The plan was to bring Let Us Worship-style events to every one of the fifty state capitols before the 2024 election. As with previous events, these new Kingdom to the Capitol stops have been met with resistance and protest, but Feucht remains undeterred. As he recently put it,

> We have to wake up: We're living in a spiritual war. . . . As
> I've gone city to city in America, and even now, we've faced
> threats from Satanists, Antifa, drag queens, from tyrannical
> governmental leaders. It seems like they're all in bed together,
> they're all pushing this agenda. And here's the reality: These
> globalist companies, they do have a religion. Their religion is
> the rainbow religion. It's the LGBTQ, wokeness, Satanism,
> whatever you want to call it. . . .
>
> The Bible says, when you encounter wicked deeds of darkness,
> expose them. Don't tolerate them. It's like David: David didn't
> go try to tolerate the giant. He came into a nation full of apathy
> and said, "That giant needs to fall down." So, as we go capitol
> to capitol, that's our same message. We want to see the giants
> of human trafficking, the giants of abortion, the giants of
> perversion, the giants that indoctrinate our kids with Satanic
> ideology. We want to see those come down, and we are seeing
> them come down.[61]

If Let Us Worship originated in a declaration of Christian freedom, by now it has a long list of enemies. And Sean Feucht crusades on.

A Modern David?

I have endeavored to capture Sean Feucht's own narration of his journey, with some NAR miscellany and points of interest thrown in. This narrative has endeared him to so many, and it inspires thousands of people to show up in city after city to join his movement. Knowing his story, you may find it easier to see how American Christians who feel that the culture has turned against them find Feucht's version of bold, aggressive, public Christianity invigorating and inspiring.

You might have also noticed that while Sean compares himself and his movement with many biblical figures (including Nehemiah, Esther, Gideon), he has a particular personal attachment to the character of David. This is not terribly surprising: David is the shepherd boy anointed young and set on a unique prophetic journey. David is the courageous teenager who stands up to Goliath and delivers his people. David is the psalmist presented as the author of many biblical hymns. The warrior-poet, frequently beset by his enemies, David triumphs over them all.

Naturally, Sean Feucht—with his own story of prophetic destiny, his identity as a musician, and his sense of embattlement and persecution—resonates with the David story. Sean's college dorm stairwell where he can retreat to vigorously play his guitar becomes his own "personal Cave of Adullam." His Burn 24-7 movement is spiritually rebuilding the tabernacle of David. His congressional campaign is David (Sean) versus Goliath (the political establishment). David was a biblical "man of war" with blood on his hands, and evidently, according to Stacey Campbell's prophecy, Sean is too. Sean's life verse is Isaiah 22:22, about the Key of David. And, most tellingly, his Washington, DC, forward-operating base is Camp Elah: the metaphorical source of stones to kill giants.

In his self-portrayal, Sean's righteousness and willingness to boldly follow his prophetic destiny have also made him a running list of enemies: Christians who didn't vote for him, local officials trying to enforce legal COVID-19 restrictions, Christians who kowtowed to these regulations, any supporter of abortion rights, Satanists, Antifa, drag queens, atheists, Black Lives Matter protesters, the LGBTQ community, Christians who disagree with his politics. That's the thing about having a prophetic destiny: chosen-ness engenders enemies.

Hundreds of thousands, probably millions, of American Christians have accepted Sean Feucht's prophecy-driven hero narrative, for he performs it very compellingly. Amid the chaos of COVID-19, the heart-wrenching 2020 election, and our ongoing turbulent politics, Sean, the happy-go-lucky troubadour of unregulated Christian worship, has given many Christians an image of hope. I have read Feucht's books, interviewed people who know him, and spent innumerable hours listening to him speak. And I maintain that the more people who see Sean Feucht as a hero, the more dangerous he becomes.

I want to be very precise about what I find objectionable, even malignant, about Sean Feucht. I'm absolutely fine with Sean holding his political views on abortion. That is entirely his right. I have no objection to Feucht running for office—an opportunity afforded to every citizen in a democracy. You don't have to vote for them, but far-right Christians like Sean Feucht should have full freedom to mount campaigns like he did.

Likewise, Feucht and other Christians have every right to object to government policies and regulations and to give voice to those objections publicly. The Let Us Worship protest events, purportedly, began as a cry for equality and religious freedom, in opposition to what the protesters believed to be an overreach by Gavin Newsom's COVID-19 regulations. People can reasonably disagree about the legitimacy of this cause. Personally, I think that Newsom's and California's COVID-19 restrictions were overwrought, in hindsight, but understandable in the context of what was known at the time. And we can reasonably disagree about Sean's tactics. I think he recklessly put a lot of people's health in danger. But those debates—about the legitimacy or tactics of his work—are fair game under the freedoms of the First Amendment. Religious freedom and free speech are not what's at issue here.

What deserves our prolonged attention and concern is a subtle change that occurred during the course of Let Us Worship in 2020 because it is a beguiling and commonplace move being made by Christian nationalists and Christian supremacists. If Let Us Worship began as a religious freedom campaign, within about a month, Feucht was already revamping the tour with his Riots to Revival tag and targeting cities marked by racial unrest. He intentionally took the roadshow to Portland, and to Seattle, and then on to other restive cities wracked with protests around police violence, where confrontations with Black Lives Matter protesters would be almost inevitable. Recall that Feucht envisaged his Portland crowd of supporters as "an *army*" and that he explicitly targeted the protester-occupied section of Seattle "to declare that Jesus was Lord over their 'occupied territory.'" Those hardly sound like peaceful, upbeat religious freedom events.

Indeed, all this talk—of spiritual warfare, of armies of worshippers, of invading the government mountain, and of killing giants—makes Let Us Worship, and its new Kingdom to the Capitol variant, sounds less like a joyful worship concert tour and more like a guerrilla warfare campaign. Sean will sometimes unabashedly state that "worship is our weapon." It's apparent from the track record of Let Us Worship that he's not out to deploy the worship weapon defensively but rather to "expand spiritual territory."[62]

This is a prime example of the rhetorical crossover from religious freedom to Christian supremacy. It's a move from "Christians deserve the same rights as everyone else," which is a perfectly constitutional and democratic claim, to "we are fulfilling America's prophetic destiny by conquering the Seven Mountains," which represents a deeply antidemocratic agenda. At some point along the way, despite his many invocations of the biblical character of David, the harassed and beleaguered shepherd boy, Sean Feucht started looking a lot more like Goliath, the taunting, bullying giant just itching for a fight.

In the summer of 2021, Sean decided to bring Let Us Worship back to Portland, Oregon, to commemorate the first anniversary of the start of the Riots to Revival subcampaign. This was six months after January 6, and tensions were still running high between right-wing and left-wing political groups in Portland. This time, Feucht put out a call for local Christians to come and provide security for the event. Sean and Jay Koopman posed for a picture with a group of men, many of them clad in tactical gear, whom Sean said were "all ex-military, ex-police, private security & most importantly LOVERS OF JESUS & freedom."

Careful observers noted that many of the men in the group photo were actually Proud Boys—including at least one who was then undergoing prosecution for his involvement in January 6—or members of other local right-wing militia-style groups. Sean joked on social media, "If you mess with them or our 1st amendment right to worship God—you'll meet Jesus one way or another."[63]

Sean Feucht is only one man, but he is also something of a pied piper, having drawn hundreds of thousands of supporters and followers with him down the path of grievance politics that leads to Christian supremacy. So we must ask: Why has Sean Feucht's quite obviously extreme and chauvinistic version of Christianity found such fertile ground among his fellow evangelicals?

Feucht's schtick works as well as it does because it plays on two weaknesses in American evangelicalism. We could think of them as evangelicals' twin political Achilles's heels: the power of charismatic experiences and the evangelical persecution neurosis. Let's look briefly at both.

The Power of Charismatic Experiences

If you were to ask a wide range of evangelicals the question "At the most basic level, how do you know what you know?" you would no doubt get an eclectic range of answers. But I'd wager that most of those answers would circle around the Bible. The Bible is, for evangelical Christians, *the* definitive source; as the children's song says, "Jesus loves me, this I know, for the Bible tells me so."

But there is another dimension to evangelical epistemology—how they know what they know—that gets talked about less: *experience*. While virtually all evangelicals profess reliance on the Bible as the guide to their beliefs, most evangelicals also build their spirituality around interior or communal experiences of the divine. On the less charismatic side of evangelicalism, this can include things like listening for the inner promptings of God, meditating on the Bible, and actively participating in communal worship. On the more charismatic side, it might look like speaking in tongues, praying for miracles, listening to words of prophecy, and engaging in ecstatic worship. For most evangelicals, spiritual experiences are a vital, nourishing side dish that complements their main epistemic dish of the Bible.

Part of what makes Pentecostals and charismatics distinctive among evangelicals is that they put a special emphasis on experiences—particularly experiences of the supernatural—as central to their knowing of God and of the world. A famous charismatic evangelist named Leonard Ravenhill once wrote, "A man with an experience of God is never at the mercy of a man with an argument, for an experience of God that costs something is worth something and does something."[64] In other words, experiences of God bypass our rational and argumentative knowing and anchor us in something deeply reassuring, a primal truth.

One major reason that Pentecostal-charismatic churches are growing so rapidly around the globe is that these churches deliver powerful, immersive worship experiences—of catharsis, of ecstasy, of healing, of inner peace, and other such goods. This is deeply attractive to many, especially in an era of disillusionment with organized religion. Even those of us who have left behind charismatic belief and worship often find significant charismatic experiences from our past to be evocative memories, ones that are attached to deep emotions.

With its culture of the everyday miraculous, Bethel, Sean Feucht's current home base, has been at the forefront of promoting this experience-first style of charismatic evangelicalism for the past two decades. What Bethel offers its congregants, its legion of students, and its distant supporters and worship imitators are captivating, soul-uplifting, rapturous experiences. The lowering of epistemic barriers in pursuit of the miraculous is a near obsession at Bethel.

I'm not interested in quibbling over whether these experiences are objectively real or scientifically verifiable. It is enough that they are real to and behavior-shaping for the people who believe in them. And as long as these charismatic experiences, whether individual or corporate, remain in the realm of religion and personal devotion, or even in the domain of individual civic decision-making, I have no deep concerns. Everyone has all sorts of rationales for choosing the politics they choose; if some charismatics want to vote for Donald Trump because they feel led to do so by God, that is their freedom as citizens. Democracy is not about parsing voters' motives but about establishing stable systems for adjudicating disagreements and guaranteeing space for all citizens to participate in the political process.

As I see it, the problem occurs when these energetic charismatic experiences are publicly leveraged and antidemocratically politicized. Mesmerizing charismatic experiences have a way of bypassing our analytical filters. Such experiences can smuggle ideas and practices across the semi-rational blood-brain barrier to convince people that some things are real or true, even if we have no evidence for them otherwise. When leveraged for political muster, this is profoundly destabilizing to a democracy.

When groups of people using the evidence and assuredness from charismatic experiences enter the public square, as protesters and contenders in political arguments, those experiences can become a monkey wrench to democratic debate. Democratic politics requires a certain down-to-earth humanism—a willingness to keep the intergroup conversation in the realm of the mundane. But if, as Ravenhill notes, spiritual experiences are invulnerable to argument, then how do we publicly debate or adjudicate them?

For the brief moment that Feucht's Let Us Worship events were about a policy debate—over whether California should have stringent COVID-19-related regulations on congregational gatherings—that was a cognizable democratic dispute. But when Feucht and Let Us Worship folded in conceptions of hyper-politicized revival, declaring Jesus's lordship over cities, and Jericho March–style prophetic demonstrations against abortion or LGBTQ rights, Let Us Worship left the realm of policy debates and moved toward intangible aims like "expanding spiritual territory." How are local political authorities or voters supposed to respond to such claims? Such Let Us Worship protests might still be permissible as free speech, but they are neither using democratic means nor pursuing democratic ends.

Similarly, the NAR and other Independent Charismatic prophets claimed that God had revealed to them that Donald Trump was destined to win the 2020 election. How do you dispute that apart from ad hominem attacks on the prophets? How would you publicly and democratically arbitrate such claims? The Trump prophecies rely on the authority of charismatic experience—which, for many of the prophets' followers who showed up on January 6, sidestepped all evidence or rational inquiry.

I don't know how else to put this than to say that we are in the midst of an epistemic crisis. Many Trump supporters, particularly right-wing Christians, have become unmoored from reality. From early 2021 to the present, approximately three in ten Americans persistently and falsely believe that Donald Trump won the 2020 election, despite a host of legal rulings, congressional hearings, and investigations that show the opposite. Among all white Americans, this number is slightly higher than among the general population—36 percent. But among white evangelicals, it's double the general population. That is, 60 percent of white evangelicals "believe that the election was stolen from Trump."[65] I would argue that charismatic experiences are playing a starring role in creating this discombobulation about what constitutes truth and how we know it.

Two recent groundbreaking surveys bear this out. The first, conducted by sociologist Paul Djupe after January 6, set out to assess what share of American Christians believe in modern-day prophecy and what impact such beliefs have on political behavior. Djupe correlated belief in prophecy ("God reveals his plans to humans through prophecy") with willingness to support violent behavior on behalf of one's group. Statements like "I would participate in a public protest against oppression of my group even if I thought the protest might turn violent" or "I would support any org[anization] that fights for my group's rights even if they sometimes resort to violence" are highly relevant in the case of Let Us Worship, where protests have sometimes turned violent.

Djupe discovered that even among the large group of Americans who might identify with some "Christian nationalist" sentiments, those who believed in modern prophecy were much more likely to express support for such extreme actions. Similarly, Djupe found that among self-identified Republicans—a group that is primed to believe Trump's election lies—prophecy believers were far more likely to believe the 2020 election was stolen: 82 percent of Republican prophecy believers thought the election had been stolen, while only 40 percent of Republican non-prophecy believers agreed.[66] If we want to understand why Independent Charismatic Christians were so overrepresented in the crowds on January 6, I would suggest that we start here.

A second study, conducted for the Public Religion Research Institute by a group of scholars with expertise in Pentecostal-charismatic Christianity, focused on people's exposure to charismatic practices or experiences. They discovered that 56 percent of American evangelicals had personally witnessed or experienced at least three out of four identified charismatic practices: "speaking in tongues, receiving direct revelation from God, divine healing, or receiving a definite answer to prayer."[67] What they found correlated with those experiences is, again, striking. Among Christians who are not charismatic and not evangelical, only 3 percent support laws that would discriminate against LGBTQ individuals in terms of housing, public accommodations, and jobs. For noncharismatic evangelicals, it was 17 percent, and for charismatic evangelicals, it was 24 percent. Likewise, 10 percent of noncharismatic, nonevangelical Christians supported the most extreme position on abortion (it should never be permitted by law). Among noncharismatic evangelicals, it was 12 percent, but among charismatic evangelicals, twice as many (24 percent) supported this most extreme position.[68]

One takeaway from these two studies is that charismatic experiences and theology—the things that separate charismatic evangelicals from other evangelicals—are accelerants for more extreme political views and behavior. Put differently, the epistemic confidence of charismatic experiences adds a premium of radicalization for folks who might otherwise incline toward extreme views. We simply cannot make sense of the ongoing radicalization of right-wing groups and individuals without also attending to the increasing integration of charismatic Christians and charismatic practices in right-wing political mobilization. If you are truly and experientially convinced, beyond all argumentation, that God anointed Donald Trump to be president for two terms, why wouldn't you fight tooth and nail to see the will of God enacted? If you believe through direct revelation that the legality of abortion is a spiritual "death decree" holding America in bondage, why wouldn't you do whatever you deem necessary to see that reversed?

Charismatic experiences can be wonderful, life-affirming, cathartic, transformative parts of an individual's spiritual life; they can also be a political Achilles's heel for evangelicalism. When charismatic experiences are projected onto the scrum of American politics, and when they are leveraged to become motivators of extreme political behavior, they can destabilize a society. Sean Feucht's provocative and inciting behavior is emboldened by a compelling set of prophecies that have told him he is special, a modern-day David destined by God to win his battles.

The Evangelical Persecution Neurosis

Sean Feucht's Let Us Worship tour also plays heavily on a persecution neurosis among American evangelicals. While the proportion of the US population identifying as Christians is rapidly declining, Christians still make up a strong majority—more than 63 percent of all Americans in 2022.[69] Roughly 24 percent of all Americans identify as evangelical or born-again Protestants, making evangelicals one of the most potent segments of the Christian majority.[70] Christians are hardly a persecuted minority in the United States.

One only needs to look at places like North Korea, India, or Afghanistan to see what actual persecution of Christians looks like.

David French, an evangelical lawyer and commentator who spent years advocating for religious freedom, has recently argued that in the United States, "religious liberty has never been more protected under federal and constitutional law." French points to a long series of Supreme Court decisions and other legal rulings that have thoroughly enshrined religious freedom as a paramount concern in US law.[71] Even more salient is the fact that evangelical Christians wield immense influence over the Republican Party, one of the two dominant American political parties, and over its agenda. Considered from a wide angle, Christians are not persecuted in the United States. There are occasional incidents of anti-Christian bias, but any claims about widespread persecution or discrimination against American evangelicals must be held up to the bigger picture.

I am not the first to argue that while evangelicals are not persecuted in the United States, they do have a persecution complex. Indeed, evangelical Christians in the United States frequently articulate a sense that they are being targeted for their faith. In 2016, a survey of American evangelical leaders found that 36 percent claimed that they had experienced persecution for their faith, while 76 percent anticipated that they would be persecuted in the coming years.[72] Similarly, a recent survey found that 59 percent of white evangelical Christians say that there is "a lot of discrimination against Christians" in the United States. This was significantly higher than the portions of white evangelicals who said there was a lot of discrimination against Muslims (49 percent), Jews (48 percent), and lesbian and gay people (42 percent).[73] In many evangelicals' minds, they are the most vulnerable minority in America. The sense of being embattled, harassed, and discriminated against, whether real or imagined, is actually quite useful communally: it keeps evangelicals motivated to evangelize more, to lean into their churches and ministries, and to stand firm against a menacing, secularizing society.

Against this backdrop, it becomes clear that Feucht activates these evangelical fears especially by comparing "persecution" in the United States with many places he's been where Christians are minorities and do face regular persecution. Feucht's oratory erases the real-world privileges US Christians enjoy, positioning American evangelicals as the perpetually harassed who need champions and defenders.

The in-your-face, confrontational strategy of Let Us Worship brings down on Feucht the disapprobation that many evangelicals continually expect. Sean casts himself as a martyr, a Jesus freak (to borrow a phrase made famous by the Jesus People movement), a principled Christian who courageously stands up for his faith. But I have never seen another Christian martyr so eager to throw himself to the lions, then turn around and criticize the lions on social media for attacking him, then hang out with his right-wing celebrity friends who congratulate him for exposing the lions' lion-ness, and, finally, rake in a small fortune from credulous supporters of his lion-jousting antics.

I would not characterize Sean Feucht as a huckster, a term frequently levied by his critics and critics of the NAR. No, I think Sean is something more pernicious and hazardous than a huckster. Hucksters don't have a sense of prophetic destiny; their motive is profit and acclaim. Sean strikes me more as the sincere, true-believer type. And he also reveals the mercurial nature of the evangelical persecution complex. Underneath and behind Christian anxiety about being persecuted is a simmering indignation. Feucht presents as a cheerful golden retriever for the Lord, but he's also fuming at a long—and growing—list of enemies. He's the sort of person who can joke: mess with me and my crew, which happens to include some Proud Boys, and we'll make sure you meet Jesus one way or the other.

So much of what gets spun as Christian persecution or Christian pleas for religious freedom today is nothing but assertions of Christian privilege and Christian dominance. In truth, the COVID-19-related restrictions on congregational gatherings were not deployed uniquely against Christians. Jewish, Muslim, Buddhist, and even nonreligious in-person gatherings were all similarly sanctioned for public health reasons. And no matter how you evaluate his policies in retrospect, it's politically absurd to think that Governor Newsom was enacting his COVID-19 policies to hurt Christians, who still make up 63 percent of the population of California.[74] Feucht used Christian rage about losing access to in-person worship as a funnel to capture Christian indignation and redirect it straight into culture war issues: abortion, LGBTQ rights, Black Lives Matter protests, and public education curricula.

In his vision at The Call DC in 2000, Sean saw "little fires breaking out all over the world," an image that very much describes what has transpired since 2020.[75] The sparks thrown off from Sean Feucht's flinty behavior have fallen on the dry kindling of deep-seated evangelical narratives of persecution and discrimination. Today American evangelicalism—especially, but not exclusively, white evangelicalism—is aflame with anger and resentment. There were many entrepreneurial evangelical arsonists long before Feucht came on the scene, but no one has been more effective at making American evangelicals burn (24/7) in recent years than this guitar-strumming, long-haired, self-proclaimed Jesus freak.

A New Archetype

Nurtured and incubated in the bosom of the NAR and Bethel, Sean Feucht braided together charismatic worship, the Seven Mountains political theology, and militant Christian mobilization during COVID-19 to create a new defiant archetype for religious right leadership. So meteoric has been his rise that, despite being virtually unknown outside of Independent Charismatic networks in 2018, today he numbers among the most recognizable faces of American evangelicalism.

Again, Sean Feucht did not have a direct hand in the Capitol Riot, but we should not underestimate the impact that his city-by-city crusade had in fostering the psyche and ethos of January 6. Strange as it may seem, many charismatics expected that there would be a literal Riots to Revival transformation that day—we'll see more of that in the next chapter. Multiple groups of people in the crowds surrounding the besieged Capitol sang charismatic worship songs, including Bethel songs and others written by some of the same worship leaders who joined Feucht at the White House in 2019.[76] January 6, 2021, was less than six months after Feucht launched Let Us Worship on the Golden Gate Bridge. By then, he had become the standard-bearer for this integration of Christian worship and far-right politics.

Today you can hear charismatic Christian songs sung not only in church sanctuaries or local concerts, but they also have become the anthems belted out at right-wing political rallies. As a *New York Times* piece put it, "Worship is increasingly becoming a central feature of right-wing events not aimed at exclusively Christian audiences."[77] In the 2022 midterm elections,

Sean Feucht led worship at campaign rallies for two Christian-nationalism-fashioned gubernatorial candidates: Doug Mastriano in Pennsylvania, who is close to many people Sean knows from his time in Harrisburg, and Kari Lake in Arizona. Likewise, the ReAwaken America tour, headlined by Sean's friend Michael Flynn, blends charismatic Christian worship, baptisms, intense Christian nationalist rhetoric, QAnon, and COVID denialism. Sean Feucht has led worship for at least ten ReAwaken events.

Many leaders—pastors, worship leaders, politicians—have been party to today's merger between charismatic worship and right-wing politics. After all, sixty other worship leaders and worship industry icons joined Sean Feucht for that White House visit in December 2019. It would be simplistic to act as though one man or one movement was solely responsible for these shifts, but Feucht is the undeniable heavyweight champion of politicizing worship.

Feucht spins, and seemingly believes a narrative that puts him in the position of the beleaguered and persecuted one. He is David harassed by Saul or facing off with Goliath. He is the warrior-poet squaring off with the powers and principalities. But somehow, in all of these instances, Sean also identifies deeply with the prophecy about being the "man of war [with] blood all over your hands." He's the bully, forcing himself into public spaces, permits be damned. He's the superspreader, who won't encourage his worshippers to wear masks to protect the immunocompromised and elderly. He's the long-haired innocent, standing with Proud Boys and threatening his enemies with their violence.

Sean Feucht is a Goliath with a David complex. It turns out that's been Donald Trump's secret sauce too.

7

A GOVERNMENTAL WAR

THERE'S STEEP COMPETITION for what qualifies as the most outlandish meeting to occur in the White House during the Trump administration. But one of the strangest had to be a meeting that took place on December 29, 2020, eight days before January 6. At this meeting, which reportedly lasted more than two hours, fifteen apostles and prophets of the NAR met with top leaders from the Trump administration. The group included two of the most recognizable faces in the prophecy and spiritual warfare world: Becca Greenwood and Dutch Sheets, both members of Peter Wagner's EVAT.

Much of what transpired that afternoon remains shrouded in mystery.[1] The participants in the meeting clearly agreed that they were not supposed to discuss it publicly. The more loose-lipped among them, however, have let slip some details. They describe traveling to DC on very short notice because of a prophetic dream given to one of the members of the group. They claim that they were prophesying and making apostolic decrees inside the White House while also receiving "strategy" from "people in the know."[2] They believed that Washington, DC, in the season surrounding January 6 and the presidential inauguration, was the epicenter of a massive, invisible spiritual battle, and they were at the White House as the *ekklesia* (a Greek word usually translated as "church") to bring "warring angels" down to aid in the battle.[3]

What motivated this group of NAR leaders to schedule a last-minute trip to Washington, DC, on what turned out to be the threshold of the Capitol Riot? How did they get that level of access to the White House, and who were they meeting with? And what does it signal when religious leaders, invoking prophecies and spiritual warfare, are directly coordinating with elected officials or staffers tasked with running the nation's government?

I have saved this most harrowing tale of the NAR and January 6 for last because the context of the previous chapters helps us apprehend how seriously we should take it. At the very least, the existence of this meeting proves that people in Trump's White House staff were actively coordinating with Christian nationalist leaders and intentionally stirring the pot among prophecy believers in the lead-up to January 6. But this episode also represents just how perilous the charismaticization of right-wing politics is and how close we could be to another Christian-prophet-led effort to supplant American democracy.

At the center of this story is Dutch Sheets. We've encountered Sheets a few times in the previous chapters: He was a friend of the Texas prophet Cindy Jacobs in the 1980s and met Peter Wagner through her. He spoke at The Call DC in 2000, alongside his friends Ché Ahn and Lou Engle. He was part of the planning team for Paula White's One Voice Prayer Movement, the intercessory adjunct to the 2020 Trump campaign. But now we will dig more deeply into Sheets's background, his theology, and his role in January 6. I maintain that no single Christian leader did more to mobilize Christians for the insurrection than Dutch Sheets—although, as we will see, he wasn't even really focused on January 6.

Sheets lives at the nexus of all the dynamics we've looked at: modern prophecy, strategic-level spiritual warfare, apostolic governance of the church, the Seven Mountain Mandate, and the utilization of charismatic worship experiences for right-wing political ends. But Sheets is also a prophet-apostle who believes that he has the unique spiritual authority to fashion the outcomes of American elections through prayer and spiritual warfare. So buckle up for what might be the most madcap Christian story of January 6.

Christ for the Nations

William "Dutch" Sheets grew up in Ohio, the son of an itinerant Nazarene evangelist and pastor; the Church of the Nazarene is a predominantly noncharismatic evangelical denomination. Dutch and his younger brother, Tim, both played football in high school, with Dutch at quarterback. "I went through a rebellious phase, and everything I believed in was shaken," he remembers. But this phase didn't last long, and, after a couple of years, he "got slammed by the Holy Spirit" through the Jesus People movement:

"Suddenly it became real to me. [God] was alive to me. I could talk to him, and I knew he was listening, and I heard his voice."[4]

Dutch went to Bible college at Christ for the Nations Institute (CFNI). Founded in Dallas in 1970 by the Healing Revival proponent Gordon Lindsay, CFNI has been an anchoring institution for the Independent Charismatic sector for half a century. After Gordon Lindsay died in 1973, his widow, Freda Lindsay, took over and became the paradigmatic leader there for two decades.

Dutch's younger brother, Tim, similarly attended CFNI, and it was also there that Dutch would meet his wife, Ceci. They married while they were still students. Ceci has been a lifelong ministry partner, co-pastoring churches with Dutch and helping to run his various ministries.

Throughout the 1980s, Dutch felt that his calling was to teach and to pastor. He worked for and taught at CFNI while also serving as prayer and missions director at a nearby charismatic church called Church of the King. Church of the King was then pastored by a man named Jim Hodges, who had been one of Dutch and Ceci's Bible professors at CFNI. Inspired by the Latter Rain ideas, Hodges was already teaching about fivefold ministry and the anticipated return of modern apostles and prophets at CFNI in the late 1970s.[5]

The 1980s was the era in which the Reformed Reconstructionists' extreme ideas about dominion theology were cross-pollinating with Independent Charismatic networks' Latter Rain revivalism, producing what was then called Kingdom Now theology. I interviewed a CFNI staffer from that time who described to me how Hodges's Church of the King was the local hub of this insurgent Kingdom Now teaching, with professors like Jim Hodges and Dutch Sheets spreading these controversial and imperious theologies into the CFNI student body—much to the chagrin of Freda Lindsay and many other faculty.[6]

Sheets and Hodges would both later join EVAT. For some of the people who came into Peter Wagner's orbit in the 1980s and 1990s, this shift into apostolic-prophetic mode and then embracing dominion visions of global conquest represented a radicalizing altered trajectory. For Dutch Sheets and Jim Hodges, Peter Wagner simply amplified what was already ingrained in their ministry, life, and theology.

Colorado Pastor, Prayer Warrior

In 1992, Dutch Sheets received an unusual invitation. A pastor named Bob Stennett, who was connected to these same Kingdom Now circles, had founded a church called Springs Harvest Fellowship in Colorado Springs in 1986. Then Stennett felt that God spoke to him, saying that Dutch Sheets was supposed to take over as senior pastor and that he should become Dutch's associate pastor.[7] Needless to say, this is a very unconventional process for selecting one's successor and boss. Dutch chose to accept this word, and he and Ceci moved their family to Colorado Springs to commence with this new assignment from God. He would be the pastor of Springs Harvest Fellowship until 2010.

This interesting tidbit from Sheets's biography highlights the important role prophecy plays in the warp and woof of Independent Charismatic life. There are all kinds of charismatic prophecies. Some are just basic encouragements and affirmations ("God wants you to know he sees you"), but some prophecies have life-altering potential. If you are open to ongoing and even personalized revelations from God, then you have to be ready for those revelations to upend your life. It was the next year, 1993, that Cindy and Mike Jacobs would also move to Colorado Springs, in part to join Dutch's Springs Harvest Fellowship.

Colorado Springs carries special prestige in American evangelicalism. By the mid-1990s, approximately eighty national and international evangelical Christian ministries had their headquarters in Colorado Springs, making this relatively small city a concentrated hub of evangelical power. According to Cindy Jacobs, many of these national evangelical leaders, particularly the charismatic ones who were open to modern prophecy, attended Dutch's "rapidly growing congregation," positioning an ambitious young pastor like Sheets to have innumerable networking opportunities there.[8]

As Wagner got to know Sheets, he pushed the younger pastor to begin writing books. Wagner knew from experience that writing books—particularly books speaking to evangelical spirituality and mixed with practical guidance—could multiply your influence. Despite the fact that Dutch had never gotten better than a C on any paper he'd written, Wagner's encouragement harmonized with several prophetic words he'd been given that he should write.[9] Dutch's first book, *Intercessory Prayer,* was published in 1996, and Peter Wagner wrote the foreword.

It's worth spending a minute on Sheets's view of prayer because it will factor centrally into his involvement in January 6. In the book, Dutch argues that "God Needs Our Prayers."[10] In other words, in Sheets's theology, God relies on human prayers to decide when and how to act. "Though God is sovereign and all-powerful, Scripture clearly tells us that He limited Himself, concerning the affairs of Earth, to working *through* human beings," Sheets writes.[11] This is not what all Christians or even all evangelicals believe. Evangelicals, like all monotheists, debate about how much of world affairs and individual lives is foreordained by God and how much is left to human agency and free will. Sheets's conception of prayer very much emphasizes human agency, even to the point where God almost absents Godself from the affairs of the world apart from Christians' prayer interventions.

Intercessory Prayer was a breakout hit and has sold more than a million copies worldwide. Sheets's personable and unpretentious but rousing tone of empowerment, along with his inspiring stories of prayers being answered, struck a chord with evangelicals, even evangelicals who weren't necessarily in the Independent Charismatic camp. *Intercessory Prayer* also proved to Dutch that writing was part of his calling; to date, he has authored at least sixteen more books and coauthored or contributed to many more.

In 1996, at the urging of Cindy Jacobs and others, Peter and Doris Wagner chose to move to Colorado Springs. The Wagners eventually became members of Dutch Sheets's Springs Harvest Fellowship church, which meant that Peter was serving as Dutch's mentor and Dutch as Peter's pastor.[12] Chuck Pierce also relocated to Colorado Springs from 1998 to 2000 to work alongside the Wagners.[13]

Hundreds of charismatic leaders and thousands of charismatic churches were eventually involved in the early NAR. But from 1998 to 2000, it was this quadrumvirate of leaders—Peter Wagner, Cindy Jacobs, Chuck Pierce, and Dutch Sheets—who laid the foundation for the NAR through their collaboration in Colorado Springs.

The 2000 Election

To understand the behavior of Dutch Sheets and the other NAR leaders in the aftermath of the contested 2020 presidential election, we can look at what they did in the aftermath of the contested 2000 election. Throughout the 1990s, Peter Wagner and Cindy Jacobs had built a tremendous global prayer network. By the year 2000, there was an international Strategic Prayer Network, overseen by Wagner, and a subsidiary USSPN, with fifty state coordinators, managed by Cindy Jacobs and Chuck Pierce.

These statewide strategic prayer coordinators were often local apostles or prophets or high-profile pastors, and they, in turn, oversaw dozens of regional coordinators in each state with hundreds or even thousands of intercessors following along. These prayer coordinators were not mere facilitators; they were frontline charismatic activists who were often cultivating relationships with local politicians and even governors. Through emails, phone calls, and faxes, Wagner and his fellow leaders could very quickly mobilize thousands of Americans to be praying and advocating for the same cause. Up until 2000, the USSPN prayer coordination was mostly focused on global missions, especially the 10/40 Window, and on local revivals or crises.

After Cindy Jacobs and Peter Wagner created the ACPE in 1998, this company of recognized prophets—including Chuck Pierce, Lou Engle, Dutch Sheets, and Bill Hamon—became convinced during the 2000 election that "God desired that George W. Bush be elected president of the United States."[14] This was part of what inspired Lou Engle and Ché Ahn to gather the massive crowd of fasting prayer warriors on the National Mall at The Call DC in September 2000.[15] There were also prophecies in the group about Florida, particularly Tallahassee, being "the high place of our nation."[16] So, well before the election, the NAR networks began focusing on Florida and Tallahassee, galvanizing existing prayer networks and hosting conferences there.

In the midst of this, Dutch Sheets describes a transformative experience of intercession in October 2000, where he wept for three and a half hours, prophetically sharing in God's heart for the future of America. He felt God was calling him to "issue a national call to prayer for the upcoming presidential election," and he created a document urging churches to pray and fast for twenty-one days leading up to the election. Though Sheets doesn't name Bush in the prayer alert, the subtext is pretty clear: "There must be a turning in this nation toward righteousness, and this will only happen if God's man is elected into office."[17]

Using the communications infrastructure of the USSPN and all the proto-NAR networks, Wagner, Pierce, Jacobs, and Sheets distributed this alert so that "within 24 hours, no fewer then [sic] one million individuals had this document in their hands." The prayer alert also earned Sheets a lot of publicity, and he was invited on Pat Robertson's *700 Club*, a flagship tel-evangelism show, three times before the election to "trumpet these alerts."[18]

But Wagner, Sheets, and other NAR leaders also believed in something called the "openness of God," or open theism, which holds that while God is all-powerful, God does not always get what God wants. This is very much related to the view of prayer that Sheets holds: God relies on intercession. As Wagner put it, "God's purpose may be thwarted or it may be accom-plished depending, to one degree or another, on the obedience of His people and their willingness to use the weapons of spiritual warfare that He has provided."[19] Stated simply, Wagner and Sheets believed that God relies on prayer warriors and apostolic generals to accomplish God's will on the earth.

Relatedly—and this is widely misunderstood—among these folks, the concept of prophecy does not mean "God foretelling future events through prophets"; rather, prophecy entails God revealing God's will and desire for the future. God's will might be thwarted if the enemies are too strong or if God's people don't muster enough spiritual warriors.

So the ACPE collectively believed that God wanted George W. Bush to be president, but when the election results were hanging in the balance with a recount in Florida—coordinated out of the state capitol in Tallahassee—God's will and America's destiny seemed to be suspended on a knife's edge. The ACPE prophets, believing that their prayers and their prophetic declarations had real power in the spiritual realm, gathered in late November 2000, and they declared "together in agreement that George W. Bush, Dick Cheney, and Colin Powell would be positioned for the future of our nation."[20] They believed that this helped turn the tide.

Along similar lines, Dutch Sheets had been given many prophecies—including from Lou Engle and Chuck Pierce—about Isaiah 22:22, the same verse about holding keys that can open doors that Sean Feucht perpetually references, or other prophecies about the number 222.[21] So Sheets became convinced that, on December 2, 2000 (12/2/2000), he needed to go to the White House to "decree that the door to the White House was open to

George W. Bush, and that he would enter it as the president of the United States."[22] So Dutch made the trek to DC with two other intercessors, and, standing on the White House grounds, they spent thirty minutes praying intensely: "A few days later, the Supreme Court made its decisive ruling and Vice President Al Gore conceded."[23]

Now, I do not believe that NAR leaders—through spiritual warfare, intercession, and standing next to the White House praying about keys—threw the 2000 election to George W. Bush. But *they do believe it.* The ACPE members and Wagner collectively wrote an entire book titled *Destiny of a Nation,* laying out their prophetic evidence and why they think they were the crucial factor in swinging the election. At the end of the day, whether you or I believe in political prophecies matters far less than the fact the prophets and their followers believe in them—and act accordingly.

And one more historical footnote from this era: Katherine Harris was the Republican Florida secretary of state who made the exceedingly controversial decision to end the Florida recount and declare Bush the winner, which was then struck down by the Florida Supreme Court but later upheld by the US Supreme Court. In 2006, Harris gave an interview to *Charisma Magazine* in which she name-checked Dutch Sheets, Cindy Jacobs, and Kimberly Daniels (a Florida NAR apostle) as "godly friends and mentors."[24] She even called Sheets "her 'Mordecai' [who] because of his ongoing counsel and encouragement, recently gave her a large metal key as a symbol of Florida's role in turning the nation around." Mordecai is the biblical character who urges his niece Esther to intervene in Persian politics to save the people of Israel. Now, Dutch Sheets and Cindy Jacobs may well have met Harris *after* the 2000 election, so this is not definitive proof that they influenced her decision. But you never know when a prophecy believer might be in a crucial place at just the right time.

The 50-State Tour

Part of what made the NAR such a significant force in Independent Charismatic circles in the 2000s was its distributed, mesh network of leaders in every one of the fifty states. In late 2002, Dutch Sheets and Chuck Pierce mutually discerned that God was giving them a new assignment—they were to travel to each of the fifty US states and do the following:

- *Gather and network intercessors and leaders in each state.*
- *Seek specific insight and messages for every state. . . .*
- *Receive and deliver prophetic discernment relating to prayer, events, actions, and strategies for breakthrough in each state.*[25]

So during 2003 and 2004, Sheets and Pierce visited each of the fifty states, delivering prophecies. Twenty years before Sean Feucht crisscrossed the country with Let Us Worship and Kingdom to the Capitol, Dutch and Chuck were laying the foundation. The two prophets averaged a different state every two weeks, and they agreed not to develop prepared or repeated remarks but to listen to what the Holy Spirit was saying in each location.

Through the tour, they mobilized other prophets and apostles in each state because, as Pierce summarizes, "when strategic intercessors are aligned with apostolic leaders, breakthrough begins. Intercessors carry the burden of God, prophetic people make key declarations, and apostles set the decrees in motion. In other words, intercessors keep the heavens open; prophets begin to express God's heart, making key declarations into the atmosphere; and apostolic leaders pull upon that revelation or blueprint of Heaven and bring it into an established form in the earth realm."[26] You may want to read that quote again because, from the NAR leaders' perspectives, that is how a spiritual warfare campaign works. That is the underlying framework for much of what we witnessed on January 6.

This 50-State Tour invigorated and buoyed the state-by-state prayer networks. Sheets and Pierce's state-focused prophecies were written down and distributed. Prophetic artists took the two prophets' words for each state and made artworks depicting them. In charismatic circles, people still talk about this as The 50-State Tour, almost as if it were a favorite album tour by a rock band. Some of the USSPN state coordinators who helped organize this tour would also be in Sheets's group that prophesied at the White House days before January 6.

One of the prophecies that Chuck Pierce delivered about Florida in 2003 said, "There is a shaking at Lakeland. A new anointing is about to come. . . . In the midst of Lakeland, My waters will spread across this state."[27] This prophecy would seem especially prescient a few years later in 2008, when revival broke out in Lakeland. However, the Lakeland Outpouring would also prove quite disruptive within the NAR leadership networks, and it would even drive a wedge into the relationship between Peter Wagner and Dutch Sheets.

As the Lakeland saga unfolded in 2008 and Wagner and the NAR leadership debated whether to get involved, Dutch Sheets became the leader of those voicing concerns, writing in an email to Wagner that Todd Bentley's heedlessness could harm their whole movement: "I'm very reticent to do anything" about Lakeland, Sheets wrote to Wagner, and he was hearing from other leaders who "believe that this is not only going to have a very adverse effect on the prophetic movement, but what is perhaps more alarming is their strong opinion that it could bring great damage to the apostolic movement as well."[28]

Dutch was personally on the fence about whether Lakeland was really a Holy Spirit–led revival, so he declined to be involved in commissioning Bentley. In August, as scandal after scandal broke, Sheets wrote a very public and very pointed letter saying that "some of my dearest friends and co-laborers" have made "huge mistakes." He tried to honor Peter Wagner—"I would defend the character of Peter and Doris Wagner as vigorously as anyone I know. . . . It remains my great honor to be associated with them and call them a spiritual father and mother"—while also saying they made "wrong decisions."[29] If the unwritten rule of the NAR spiritual oligarchy was that apostles and prophets did not publicly disagree, Sheets was frustrated enough to violate that rule.

This Lakeland fallout created a fracture between Wagner and Sheets. Sheets had long disagreed with some of Wagner's church growth ideas, feeling that obedience, not growth, was the biblical criterion of church success. But Lakeland widened the rift. Sheets would write to Wagner in 2010, "I believe the disagreements we had over Lakeland and . . . over the church growth movement have inflicted wounds on you and Doris that make it difficult to move forward in this relationship . . . [I] feel it is the appropriate time for me to step out of EVAT."[30]

Wagner responded, acknowledging that this was not a huge surprise and that "our primary apostolic alignment had begun lacking true substance" for some time.[31] It was very unusual for a member of EVAT to resign. After all, these were Wagner's spiritual sons and daughters. Wagner and Sheets remained friends until Wagner's death in 2016, but Sheets had a distinct, national profile by that point, and his independent and hardline streak had finally won out.

Ironically, because Wagner maintained a strict cap of twenty-five members in EVAT, Sheets's withdrawal from the group cleared the way for a much younger acolyte of Wagner and Cindy Jacobs's to join the inner circle: Becca Greenwood. Twelve years later, Greenwood and Sheets would be together at the White House strategizing and prophesying for Trump's reinstatement, another sign that while Sheets may have left EVAT, he did not leave the NAR guild.

Ekklesia Theology

We must stop at two more waypoints before we get to Dutch Sheets and Donald Trump, and both are examples of what I've called prophetic memes. Both were constructed by Sheets in the season after he split off from EVAT. The first is a Greek word, and the second is a flag from American history.

The word *ekklesia* in Greek is often translated as "church," but the word had a range of meanings in the ancient world. Literally, *ekklesia* translates as "assembly" or "congregated group," and it functioned in the first-century Jewish usage of Greek as a synonym for *synagoga*, from which we get the modern word *synagogue*. The Jews have their synagogues, and the Christians have their churches. This is why theology about the church in Christianity is usually called *ecclesiology*.

But earlier Greek uses of the word signify more an "assembly," in a political sense, as in "the assembled representatives"—similar to how some American states still designate their legislative body a "state assembly."

Dutch Sheets focuses his own interpretation of *ekklesia* on one particular passage in Matthew 16—the same passage Ché Ahn used in his January 5 speech. There, Jesus famously tells Apostle Peter, and the other apostles gathered around, "You are Peter, and on this rock I will build My church [*ekklesia*], and the gates of Hades shall not prevail against it. And I will give you the keys of the kingdom of heaven, and whatever you bind on earth will be bound in heaven, and whatever you loose on earth will be loosed in heaven"

(Matt 16:18–19). It's worth noting that in this passage, Jesus is alluding to Isaiah 22:22, Dutch Sheets's life verse, and offering a similar promise to the Apostle Peter about keys that can lock and unlock heavenly realities.

I have found some handwritten notes from various meetings that Peter Wagner had with Dutch Sheets and some of Sheets's associates around 2010. In those notes, you can see a potent new theological idea forming for Sheets: he reinterprets the term *ekklesia* by hearkening back to the older Greek usage. Sheets told Wagner that *ekklesia* should be translated as "a governing body" and that Jesus employed the term to mean "my governing body in the earth." He said it was time for the church to move from a "congregational mindset to a congressional mindset."[32] In other words, the apostles and prophets were supposed to "legislate in the spirit, [then] implement in the natural."[33] This is a radically different vision of the church from what most Christians hold.

Over the next few years, Sheets would begin teaching and talking about this idea, refining it, and bundling his whole theology around it.[34] In Sheets's *ekklesia* theology, the church, as led by apostles and prophets, is God's appointed spiritual government on the earth. He argues that Jesus intended in Matthew 16 to invoke the imagery of Roman colonization. When the Roman Empire would conquer new territory, according to Sheets, they would send some of their Roman citizens to be the local *ekklesia,* as in governing assembly, and thereby impose the culture of Rome on the new territory. He argues that Jesus meant for Christians to become his colonizing *ekklesia,* bringing the culture of heaven to earth.

This *ekklesia* theology functions as a sort of charismatic dominion theology 2.0. In fact, Sheets traces many of the same themes of older dominion theology, now aligned around this new term, so that the *ekklesia* "by its very definition is an invading force," and the "ekklesia concept is the restoration of the dominion mandate of Genesis 1."[35] Just as dominion theology and the Seven Mountain Mandate say Christians are supposed to conquer all parts of society, Sheets's *ekklesia* concept puts Christians in charge of the earth in the spiritual realm, an authority they can use to "legislate"—that is, change reality—in the natural realm.

I have searched in vain for any respected biblical scholarship to back up this interpretation of *ekklesia.* As far as I can tell, this exegesis is original to Sheets. For readers unfamiliar with Christian theology, let me just observe how far in the opposite direction this points from most Christian under-standings of Jesus. Sheets is arguing, largely based on his retranslation of a single word in a single verse, that Jesus—the first-century Jewish peasant living under Roman colonial rule, the sacrificial leader who was executed by the Roman Empire and who said "My kingdom is not of this world" (John 18:36)—looked at the pitiless, colonizing model of the Roman Empire and said, "*That's* the image I want my followers to imitate."

Sheets started teaching this *ekklesia* idea around 2011, and other NAR leaders and networks have amplified it. While not as ubiquitous as the Seven Mountains, it has likewise been carried through charismatic media to become a major prophetic meme. Today you can hear this theology on the lips of many charismatic leaders, including Sean Feucht, who recently, off the cuff, quoted Matthew 16 as "on this rock I will build my *ekklesia*: the ruling body government. The gates of hell shall not prevail."[36]

After he split off from EVAT, Sheets went through an aimless and lim-inal season. Wagner didn't invite Sheets to take over any of his networks on Wagner's retirement. Sheets also handed off pastoral leadership of his church in Colorado Springs in 2010. He continued writing books and maintained an extensive speaking schedule, but he would later describe this period in his life, saying, "I [was] in transition for a couple of years. I knew I was between assignments and didn't know exactly what the Lord was planning next."[37]

In early 2012, he moved back to Dallas to lead his alma mater, CFNI, as executive director. This arrangement didn't last long, however. Reading between the lines, one might surmise that Sheets was restless at CFNI, frus-trated that the demands of the job didn't fit his personality and were inter-fering with his writing and speaking. Within two years, in 2014, he was announcing the end of his tenure there.

Yet during this short time back at CFNI, something happened to Sheets that would alter the iconography of the religious right in America: he was given a flag.

An Appeal to Heaven

For the 2013 CFNI graduation, Sheets had invited one of his spiritual sons, US Army captain and lawyer Bill Ostan, who had just returned from serving in Afghanistan, to be the speaker. During the ceremony, the captain paused to share a gift with "Papa Dutch." The flag had a white background, a plain evergreen tree at the center, and the phrase "An Appeal to Heaven" written across the top.

Ostan explained that this phrase had been a rallying slogan in the American Revolutionary War and that it was a quote from the philosopher John Locke. When a person or community has had every appeal to unjust human authorities rebuffed, Locke suggested in a 1689 treatise, they must make "an appeal to heaven": that is, go to war and let God judge.[38] This flag was commissioned by George Washington to fly over the Massachusetts Navy during the war. Ostan made the case that because this flag was commissioned before the official start of the Revolutionary War, and because it predated the Stars and Stripes, "in many ways, it is the banner under which America was born."[39]

Sheets, who is prone to gauzy theological readings of American history, was immediately taken with this flag and this story. "I felt the presence of the Lord come on me very strongly," he later wrote. "Though I was seeing this flag for the first time, it confirmed and amplified a revelation God began giving me over a decade ago. I sensed it's [*sic*] weighty significance. Little did I know, however, this flag would also represent God's next great assignment for my life."[40] Indeed, for the next decade of his life and right up to the present, the Appeal to Heaven flag would become the driving symbol of Dutch Sheets's life and political activism.

When, in May 2014, Dutch Sheets announced his resignation from CFNI, he said, "The No. 1 passion of my life is seeing America experience a third great awakening. This has been my primary calling from God for over 20 years. . . . I believe there is a two- to three-year window for us as a nation to see certain things change. I feel a great responsibility and stirring in my spirit to be a part of leading in this." Even there in the spring of 2014, Sheets was already focusing on "a new assignment for America leading up to national elections in two years."[41]

Sheets abhorred the Obama administration, viewing the Obama presidency itself as a judgment from God on America. He wrote in a 2009 memo that "the current administration and Congress have the most radical anti-Christian, anti-Bible agenda in the history of our nation."[42] At least once, he parroted the right-wing falsehood that Obama was a Muslim.[43]

So as he departed CFNI, he began rolling out this new Appeal to Heaven flag meme and prayer campaign and driving toward a Republican victory in the 2016 election. As they had with the Seven Mountains campaign, the NAR networks jumped into promoting this new prophetic meme, with Lou Engle, Cindy Jacobs, and many others spreading the flag image all over the country.

Sheets turned the Appeal to Heaven flag into a Christian nationalist totem, of sorts—"a movement designed to wake up the body of Christ and let them know: When it comes to America, it ain't over."[44] He published a book in 2015 titled *An Appeal to Heaven*, and he began, once again, traveling around the country through his many networks and sharing this new meme.

From 2015 to the present, you can increasingly see these Appeal to Heaven flags popping up all over the place at right-wing and Christian nationalist rallies.

Some Christian lawmakers display them in their offices and on social media accounts, and they have even flown over the Illinois State Capitol, as well as inside the Arizona and Arkansas State Capitols.[45] In 2015, Sarah Palin wrote an opinion piece in *Breitbart* urging lawmakers and judges to fly the flag over courthouses and legislative buildings, and she thanked her "special friends, Pastor Dutch and Ceci Sheets, [who] presented me with an Appeal to Heaven flag of my own. It has stirred my heart and will stir millions more once the significance of this flag is understood."[46]

There's a double entendre in the use of the Appeal to Heaven flag that is important because it creates plausible deniability for public figures who embrace it. When lawmakers have been accused of promoting Christian nationalism by flying the flag, they'll often demur that it's simply a piece of American or Revolutionary War history. But to people on the inside, the flag signals a prayer-and-spiritual-warfare driven form of American Christian nationalism.

At the same time that he began rolling out the Appeal to Heaven flag meme, Sheets also created a smartphone app called Give Him 15. The premise was a daily devotional on the app and the associated website that would include a set of prayers and prophetic declarations, which millions of believers could decree and pray in a coordinated fashion every day.

Well before Donald Trump ever declared his candidacy for the American presidency, Dutch Sheets was gearing up for a knockdown, drag-out spiritual battle for the 2016 election, with his new *ekklesia* theology, the Appeal to Heaven flag, and the Give Him 15 devotionals as his primary strategic spiritual weapons for that battle.

The 2016 Campaign and Trump Presidency

By 2016, the NAR leaders had developed a whole playbook for coordinated prayer and spiritual warfare during an election year. In February 2016, as mentioned in chapter 2, Cindy Jacobs, Lou Engle, Dutch Sheets, and others launched a unified As One national call to prayer, with daily digital prayer guides, forty-day fasts leading up to the election, and concerted events. Tellingly, the subtitle of the As One campaign was "A National Appeal to Heaven," and the evergreen tree was at the center of the logo.[47]

Unlike some of the other NAR leaders who were quick to embrace Lance Wallnau's Seven Mountains and Trump-as-Cyrus prophecies as rationale for supporting Trump in the Republican primary, Sheets was more of a holdout. He supported other candidates in the primary, who were eliminated one by one. Over the course of the 2016 campaign, Sheets would travel "to seventy-seven cities holding rallies, not for Trump but for righteousness to prevail."[48] Along the way, the Appeal to Heaven flag increasingly became part of the iconography of political prayer in America.

But by the time it came down to Hillary Clinton versus Donald Trump, Sheets was 100 percent in the Trump camp. At an Appeal to Heaven conference on October 21, 2016, the same day Peter Wagner died, Sheets excoriated Christians who, disgusted by Trump's behavior, said they might sit out this election. "Enough of this religious 'I'm not gonna vote at all cause I don't like anybody,'" he chided. "In the days of the *ekklesia* in biblical times, you were not allowed, as a member of the *ekklesia* to not show up and vote. . . . You're not voting for a personality. You're voting for the Supreme Court."[49]

When the election was called for Trump a few weeks later, Sheets was effusive, posting an image with himself holding an Appeal to Heaven flag: "Never have I seen so much prayer for an election . . . this was a miracle, pure and simple. . . . Angelic visitations, dreams, prophetic words, strategies, and

Holy Spirit-inspired prayers gave me much confidence that God was willing to give us mercy, not judgment."[50]

But we get an interesting insight into how Sheets was thinking about Trump's actual presidency in remarks he gave a couple of months later, at a conference of NAR leaders on New Year's Eve, three weeks before Trump's inauguration. Sheets, looking toward the next four years, predicted:

> We're going to enter into a new level of warfare . . . we're going to face new levels of demonic desperation. It's going to manifest in people. . . .
>
> We had better not put our faith in man or in a political party or system. They will fail us, and if we don't pray for them they'll be overcome by the same principalities and powers that overcame those in the past. . . . We gotta birth for them what they don't know how to birth. We gotta pray into being things they don't understand.
>
> [Trump] is, at best, a baby Christian, with very little understanding of scripture, stumbling his way along . . . trying to find God's will. We're going to have to birth it in him! We're going to have to pray it into him! We're going to have to pray the spirit of wisdom and revelation into him! . . . We're going to have to go to a new level of kingly declarations and decrees.[51]

Undeniably, Sheets was a major Trump supporter. But his support was built around engineering as much social and spiritual transformation in the United States as he and the other NAR leaders could accomplish in the four-year window opened by Trump's success.

While some prophets and apostles took on advisory roles to the Trump administration, Dutch Sheets and Cindy Jacobs were at the heart of the prayer and spiritual warfare mobilization surrounding the Trump presidency. Sheets helped start POTUS Shield, the prophet-driven spiritual warfare initiative. When Trump's Supreme Court nomination of Brett Kavanaugh appeared to be in danger, Sheets and a group of intercessors showed up at the hearing to do spiritual warfare on Kavanaugh's behalf. Sheets posted pictures of himself in the Senate gallery with the hashtag #AppealToHeaven.[52] And in November 2019, Sheets was in the handpicked group of intercessors invited to the White House to strategize for Paula White's One Voice Prayer Movement.

If all these prayer and spiritual warfare efforts were to enlist an army of intercessors, Dutch Sheets was serving as the intercessory commander-in-chief, directing the attention and efforts of the massive charismatic spiritual warfare networks that he built alongside Peter Wagner and Cindy Jacobs. By the time the 2020 election rolled around, more than half a million people had downloaded Sheets's Give Him 15 app, signaling at least some intention on their part to follow along and join in declaring his daily decrees as the *ekklesia*.

On October 18, 2020, Donald Trump was on the campaign trail in Las Vegas, Nevada, and he attended the Sunday morning service at a large Independent Charismatic church led by an NAR apostle-and-prophet couple. This was one of the churches Sheets and Pierce had visited and activated on their 2003–2004 tour. One of the pastors, Denise Goulet, prophesied publicly and directly to Trump that morning: "The Lord said to me, 'I am going to give your president a second win . . .' The Holy Spirit makes you able to finish. Take this to the end, Mr. President."

Later in the same service, her husband, Paul Goulet, was preaching, and he brought out an Appeal to Heaven flag. He pointed at Trump and said, "I saw this flag hanging out on the fence of the White House. It's time to appeal to heaven . . . I am appealing to heaven right now to bless this president."[53] Someone snapped a photo of Paul Goulet holding the Appeal to Heaven flag with Donald Trump's head silhouetted in the foreground, and the image went viral on charismatic social media. Dutch Sheets triumphantly reposted it.[54]

A few days later, Trump issued a statement that he was no longer a Presbyterian, the denominational church he was raised and professedly confirmed in. He was now a nondenominational Christian.[55]

Give Him 15

When the 2020 election was called for Joe Biden, and Donald Trump refused to concede, Dutch Sheets clearly saw a strong parallel to the 2000 election. He believed that his and the other NAR leaders' prayer and spiritual warfare efforts had turned the tide in Bush's favor. Sheets now threw everything into Appeal to Heaven high gear.

Recall that for Dutch Sheets and the NAR—and these views extend to many prophecy believers in the Independent Charismatic world—prophecies are not simply self-activating; Christians must intercede and do spiritual warfare so as to enact God's will. This is what the Jericho Marches and shofar-blowing and prayer gatherings in the interval between the 2020 election and January 6 were all about: bringing the prophecies into fulfillment through, as Sheets would put it, the authoritative mobilization and declarations of the *ekklesia*.

In 2000, Sheets had relied on the USSPN distribution network and Pat Robertson's *The 700 Club* televangelism interviews to spread his message, but now he had built a direct-to-prayer-warrior dissemination network through his Give Him 15 app. Yet until the 2020 election, Give Him 15 was fairly siloed. You'd have to download the app or visit the web page to see the daily updates. So the day that Biden was declared the winner, Sheets began recording himself reading his Give Him 15 daily reflections and posting these videos on YouTube, where they could be easily shared on social media. This revolutionized Sheets's relationship with his networked audience, making his sober-but-reassuring daily admonitions must-watch viewing for charismatic prayer warriors around the country.

In the daily videos, Sheets would layer together prophetic words and dreams he was hearing about from his vast networks of intercessors, updates on the legal wranglings from Trump's team of lawyers, and decrees for the *ekklesia*. These seven-day-a-week videos consistently got 100,000 views each and sometimes more than 300,000 in the weeks leading up to Biden's inauguration.

Sheets's Give Him 15 videos are laced with his signature theological memes: the Appeal to Heaven and the *ekklesia*. There is almost always at least one Appeal to Heaven flag behind him in the shot, and he regularly invokes *ekklesia* language. Here is one passage from his December 20, 2020 video (the day after Trump first tweeted summoning his followers to DC on January 6):

> Please understand that our current battle is regarding the U.S. government—our battle in these elections and much of the prayer that is taking place right now . . .

The war over Planet Earth is a governmental war—who will
rule the earth? The battle for humankind is governmental—
who will be their lord and master? The battle for the heavens
is governmental—who will be the Most High? God is not
into politics. The political spirit is a perversion of government,
but he *is* into government, big time. To believe otherwise is
to forfeit his righteous influence on earth. And, of course, the
very word he used to describe us in scripture, *ekklesia*, means
government.[56]

I have been through hundreds of social media accounts from Christians who were there, in the crowds, on January 6, and their webs of supporters, and there are certain golden threads you can find stitched through most of them. One common denominator that you see across so many of them is Lance Wallnau: Lance's Facebook live streamed rants and clips of the news-style *FlashPoint* show of prophet-punditry that Wallnau helped create. Starting in December 2020, Dutch Sheets became a regular panelist, alongside his friend Lance, on *FlashPoint*, so he also appears in many of those clips.

The other golden thread you can find spooling out through Christian January 6 participants and into their networks of friends and supporters are these Give Him 15 videos. They were shared and reshared across Facebook and Twitter and Parler.

Frequently, in the Give Him 15 videos, Dutch would collate different prophecies or prophetic dreams that friends had sent him. Give Him 15 became a sort of prophecy clearinghouse, where Sheets would instruct and update his viewers using the latest Trump prophecies. Day by day, as you get closer to January 6, these prophecies and dreams become more and more about Washington, DC, and the Capitol Building.

On January 1, 2021, five days before the insurrection, Sheets recited a dream on Give Him 15 from a close associate and prophet named Gina Gholston. Gholston's dream involves Dutch and other apostles and charismatic prayer warriors riding like generals, on the backs of horses, into battle in front of the US Capitol. They see the hand of God come down and open the dome of the Capitol Building, and a dark, smoke-like demonic entity rises out of the roofless Capitol. They hear a cavalry bugle sounding to charge, and so they advance on the Capitol. Written on the ground in front of them are the words "Don't stop."

Sheets goes on to interpret Gholston's dream: "We have become a strong army, capable of responding quickly. . . . The darkness is an alliance with evil spirits—probably a principality . . . God is coming to cleanse our government. Many in our Congress need to go. And, finally, Holy Spirit said to us, 'Don't stop.' . . . Using the authority of Christ's name, [we must] command the darkness to leave our Congress and our government."[57] This was the imagery flooding hundreds of thousands of social media accounts in the lead-up to January 6. This was the prophetic propaganda reaching people as they made plans to travel to Washington, DC.

The Contested-State Tour

Happening in tandem with Sheets's Give Him 15 propaganda blitz was another track of his prayer warfare mobilization. Sheets described, in an early December 2020 interview, how, a couple of weeks prior, he got a call from "some people in Washington, DC," who "work in the current administration there, [but] don't want to be identified or talk about who they are." These mysterious Trump administration officials or staffers invited him to come to DC to pray with them that week. Once in DC, these same people urged him, Sheets recounts, "Maybe the Lord is asking you to go to all of these contested states and take a prayer team."[58]

In a separate letter to his financial supporters, Sheets summarized the conversation this way: "They made an appeal for me to join the natural to the spirit since what we do in the spirit directly affects what happens in the natural, basically marrying civil and spiritual government. They suggested I go to each of the seven election-contested states, and call the *ekklesia* of the Lord to come together, joining us to pray for America from each state."[59] In addition to Sheets's much more prominent profile and platform, this was another difference from what played out in the 2000 election. In 2000, the nascent NAR's spiritual warfare to swing the contested election in Bush's favor was autonomous and marginal; in 2020, government officials were trying to bolster, harness, and steer their spiritual warfare at particular targets.

While Sheets protects the identities of these government officials, it is evident that their words really spurred him on. Immediately he reached out to a team of about twenty intercessory prayer leaders, primarily apostles and prophets, from all over the country to join him on a whirlwind tour of the contested states where the Trump legal team and local MAGA activists were fighting over vote counts and slates of electors. This team of twenty prayer generals was a potpourri of apostles and prophets from the networks that Peter Wagner built, with three EVAT members (Sheets, Greenwood, and Jim Hodges); Dutch's brother, Tim Sheets; state coordinators from Wagner's USSPN; and others from Dutch's own apostolic network.[60]

If Sheets and Pierce's 50-State Tour in 2003–2004 was logistically impressive, this contested-state expedition was truly remarkable. Sheets was in Washington, DC, on November 20, with Trump officials whispering this idea in his ear, and by the next night, the team had been recruited and assembled from all over the country in Atlanta. It was a frenetic tour: November 21—Georgia, November 22—Michigan, November 23—Arizona, November 24—Wisconsin, November 29—Nevada, November 30—New Mexico, December 1—Pennsylvania, December 13—Georgia again. At every stop, the group of prophetic intercessors would stage a massive prayer meeting at a local church—often the same churches that Sheets and Pierce had visited during the 50-State Tour and places where Sheets could call in a quick favor. This was at the height of the COVID-19 pandemic, and these prayer meetings were packed with hundreds of unmasked people. These meetings were also broadcast live on Facebook and YouTube, with more than 100,000 people around the nation live streaming sessions on YouTube and sometimes an equal number of viewers on Facebook.

These "prayer meetings" are not what many people imagine when they hear that term. They averaged around three hours, and after an hour of intense worship music, Dutch would get up to give some brief remarks. Then he'd invite up the intercessory team, and these apostles and prophets would take turns prophesying about God's view of the 2020 election. These prophecies, as is common practice in Independent Charismatic churches, are often spoken over swelling, tonal, mesmerizing keyboard chords, giving them an aura of otherworldliness. Here are a couple of samples.

Jacquie Tyre in Pennsylvania:

I'm calling up the minutemen, the kingdom militia . . . to
move across this nation. And even out of this Keystone State,
even out of Pennsylvania, there is rising up a militia, that is
connecting to the battlefield states, that will uncover, even
beginning this night, the fraud, the corruption, the infiltration
of evil from Pennsylvania to Georgia, from Georgia to Nevada,
from Nevada to Arizona, from Arizona to New Mexico, from
New Mexico to Wisconsin, to Michigan. God, we declare, that
the militia men, the minutemen of the kingdom of God, are
rising up in this hour! And, Father, we declare and decree in this
place that there is no demon in hell and there is no voice out of
government that can topple the kingdom of our God![61]

Don Lynch in Arizona:

And to the rulers and principalities, the *ekklesia* now reveals the
multifaceted wisdom of God. And God said, "Do you have the
stomach to finish the job? Put your foot on his chin, and expose
the neck. Pick up that weapon and find you are strong enough
to wield it. Finish this! Finish this!" I say, "Finish this!". . . .

For the God tonight gives you a new weapon, in a new season,
for a new era, and a rebirthing of the *ekklesia*. . . . For God said,
"The strongman of the Supreme Court must be made stronger
by those who decree from heaven's court. Expose the neck,
swing the sword, finish the job." For God says, "No chicken-
legged Philistine is going to become the most powerful political
leader in the world!"[62]

This raging prophesying, full of images of militia and swords and bat-
tlefields and decapitations, went on night after night, state after state, live
streamed to hundreds of thousands of Christians. It's hard to overstate how
violent this rhetoric became, how frenzied the crowds in the videos get. The
camera would occasionally pan to the audience during the prophesying, and

they are screaming and shouting and speaking in tongues in fervent agreement with the unrestrained prophecies. If you doubt it, go look them up; as of this writing, the videos are still on Dutch Sheets's YouTube and Facebook pages.

It may be difficult to comprehend that this scale of Christian radicalization was going on inside twenty-first-century America. Watching those videos, I can't help but think of the energy in the crowds on January 6. And it's not just the violent language or the religious furor that calls January 6 to mind; it's the ecstasy and hope, the boundless optimism that this violence, spiritual or otherwise, will bring about the long-awaited revival.

Part of what is so striking about these contested-state prayer meetings was how unabashed and out in the open they were. Dutch Sheets and his team of militant prophets crisscrossed the country, night after night, issuing invective-filled prophecies that electrified hundreds of thousands of Christians. If you listen to the entirety of that Arizona Don Lynch prophecy I quoted—an extended prophetic allegory of the David and Goliath story, with Lynch physically acting out the chopping off of the giant's head—it comes pretty darn close to being a prophetic death threat on Joe Biden, "the chicken-legged Philistine" who is on the cusp of "becom[ing] the most powerful political leader in the world." And this stuff has not been buried or removed from the internet since January 6. In fact, when Don Lynch, who had a doctorate from WLI, passed away in 2022, Dutch Sheets excerpted this exact clip and reposted it on YouTube as a tribute to him.[63]

Where was the media in all this buildup of charismatic fury? I have searched fruitlessly for even a single mention of Dutch Sheets's name in the mainstream media in the season between the 2020 election and January 6.

But millions of people were tracking Dutch Sheets's prophecies, including, evidently, some inside the White House. Millions of Christians were being inundated with this oratory of violent spiritual warfare during the season leading up to the Capitol insurrection.

The White House Meeting

Throughout late November and early December 2020, Dutch Sheets and his traveling band of prophets were building toward a fever pitch of charismatic anger and assurance that God would intervene. If Christians just pray and decree and declare enough, they claimed, *God was going to change this election*. Hundreds of thousands of charismatic Christians followed along online or showed up at stops on the contested-state tour.

But the miraculous intervention didn't come. None of Trump's legal challenges worked. The Supreme Court didn't throw the election to Trump, and all the states certified their slates of electors. By around mid-December, the wind seemed to have gone out of the sails of Dutch Sheets and his team.

Then it was time for the Christmas season, and the frenzy seemed to abate a little. A lull on social media and elsewhere suggested everyone was presumably focusing on family, decorations, presents, travel, and church services. But on December 19, Donald Trump tweeted out: "Big protest in D.C. on January 6th. Be there, will be wild!"

On Sunday, December 27, Don Lynch—he of the "chicken-legged Philistine" prophecy—had a dream about a "convocation of eagles" arriving in Washington, DC, and landing on different monuments. Eagles are a common symbol in NAR vocabulary for apostles—hence, the *Eagles'* Vision Apostolic Team. That night, Dutch and Tim Sheets and a couple of other members of the contested-state team had a conference call, and they decided that Lynch's dream was summoning them back to DC for one more boots-on-the-ground spiritual warfare assignment.

They had already intended to make another trip to DC before January 6, and they determined this must be the moment. So they sent word out to the team: everyone who could join should make their way to Washington, DC, the next day: Monday, December 28. They would convene at the Willard Hotel. Then, on Tuesday, December 29, they would pray at the monuments Lynch saw in the dream. Somehow, with just one day's notice, they were also able to procure a White House meeting room where they could gather with Trump administration officials on Tuesday afternoon.

It is very clear that the members of Sheets's spiritual warfare strike team were not supposed to publicly discuss the White House portion of this trip. So most of what we know about it comes from unguarded words spoken by Tim Sheets, Jacquie Tyre (a longtime WLI administrator and USSPN prayer coordinator), and Don Lynch to their respective churches after the fact.[64] Tyre would later narrate to her church that fifteen members of the team were able, on such short notice, to book travel to DC.[65] We also have social media posts from the group while they were in DC that allow identification of nine of the fifteen NAR apostles and prophets who were there. We know the meeting included Dutch Sheets, Tim Sheets, Jacquie Tyre, Don Lynch, Becca Greenwood, Gina Gholston (the prophet with the generals-charging-at-the-Capitol dream), and several other leaders from Sheets's contested-state team. The other six remain a mystery to me.

I requested the White House visitor logs for that day via the Freedom of Information Act to discover who was there and who arranged the meeting, but I was told by the Trump Presidential Library (the holder of these records) that the logs would be sealed to the public until five years after Trump left office. So we may yet discover more about this meeting.

Here's what we do know about the December 29 meeting: Tim Sheets mentions that the NAR group stayed at the Willard Hotel, which is a revealing detail. The Willard Hotel was the site of the war rooms where Trump advisers like Rudy Giuliani, Steve Bannon, John Eastman, and others were devising their machinations in the lead-up to January 6. One Trump administration official candidly called the Willard Hotel "the crime headquarters," vis-à-vis the Stop the Steal campaign.[66] I have no evidence that Sheets's team was directly tied to these war rooms. But their choice of that hotel, out of all the hotels in Washington, DC, that very week, raises questions.

Here is what Tim Sheets narrated to his church the following Sunday:

> We had a two-hour time to pray at the White House and make some decrees that God had given to us. It was a very strategic time . . .
>
> Things were exposed to us in the spirit realm. Strategy was given to us from people in the know around there that I cannot really talk about. And all of this was done on a secure site that we have had to develop because of hackers and different things. And we have a secure thread that we can communicate by now.[67]

He implies that, both before and after this meeting, there was ongoing secretive communication between these Trump administration officials and

Dutch's team through this "secure thread." This suggests that Sheets's government interlocutors were staying abreast of what the prophetic intercessors were doing. Who these "people in the know" were, and what "strategy" they were feeding to Sheets's team, is unclear.

Likewise, Don Lynch shared congruent details with his church:

> We ended up at the White House for much longer than we
> were scheduled to be there. It was a very powerful time. We had
> been praying. We knew we were going to be going into DC
> before the first of the year—before January 6—but we weren't
> sure when or how. But I guess that [my] dream was the trigger
> point. . . .
>
> We were at the White House for a couple of hours of things
> that are rather amazing. At the highest levels of our nation God
> is not only speaking, but he's being heard.[68]

Both men say "the White House," although members of the group posted photos that day on social media that make it clear the meeting was actually in the Eisenhower Executive Office Building, next door to the White House. It's there that many White House offices, including the Office of the Vice President, are located.

While the details we know about this meeting are scant, just pause and consider what all this tells us. For more than a month at that point, Sheets and his team had been spurred by people in the Trump administration into strategically traversing contested states and "marrying civil and spiritual government" through their prophetic decrees. And these same leaders were welcomed into the White House and allowed to offer similar decrees and declarations there. They met with "people in the know," "at the highest levels of our nation," and were given "strategy." At the very least, this reveals that part of the backstory to January 6 was that the Christian supremacy and Christian nationalism on display that day were actively cultivated by people within the Trump administration.

Don Lynch concluded his description of this meeting speaking to his church on December 31 by saying, "A necessary sacrifice may be made, but if your hands are dirty, then you need to be exposed. . . . We need a recon-stitution in our nation, and that's the level at which we are headed. . . . So buckle up your seatbelts on your horse that you're riding and get ready to gallop and get your sword bloody in the spirit of God."[69]

Six days later, thousands of Christians would descend on the Capitol, all geared up for that very purpose.

The Appeal to Heaven Flags on January 6

Before dawn on January 6, Dutch Sheets's Give Him 15 video appeared on his various channels. With his most sober, commander-in-chief delivery, he said, "Today is one of the most critical days in our history. . . . Many thou-sands of people, perhaps up to a million, have gathered in Washington, DC today to intercede onsite outside the US Capitol building, a Jericho March around the Capitol and Supreme Court grounds, and prayer in other loca-tions. Whether you are physically there or not, pray today as if the life of our republic depends on it. Indeed, it does."[70]

In light of everything that I've outlined above, I would argue that Dutch Sheets was the most effective drum major for Christian catalyzation and activation for January 6.

Indeed, one of the most overlooked and under-analyzed visual details of that day is just how many Appeal to Heaven flags there were in the crowds surrounding the Capitol. It's very difficult to get a comprehensive picture of what happened that day because the majority of frenzied images and record-ings come from social media photos and videos from within the crowds, and we don't get many wide-angle shots of the whole scene.

But having spent many hours poring through footage from that day, I'd estimate that there were dozens and potentially hundreds of Appeal to Heaven flags being carried by Trump supporters around the besieged leg-islators. This legion of Appeal to Heaven flags is a striking signal of how far Dutch Sheets's prophetic meme has spread. It speaks to his mobilizing potential and serves as one of the most visible markers of a connection between the NAR and the crowds of rioters and riot sympathizers that day.

As far as I can uncover, the vast majority of these flags in the crowds can be traced back to Dutch Sheets and the prayer movement he started around that meme. That's not to say that everyone carrying an Appeal to Heaven flag was intentionally referencing Dutch Sheets. After all, it is a meme, and memes can be appropriated and repurposed to diverse ends. I wouldn't be surprised if many flying the Appeal to Heaven flag then (or now) don't even know who Dutch Sheets is. That's how memes work.

But I have yet to find any cohesive group utilizing the Appeal to Heaven flag that *isn't* somehow tied back to spiritual warfare, prophecy, and Christian nationalism—and all of that traces to Dutch Sheets because that flag didn't carry those connotations when it was handed to him on stage at CFNI in 2013. Some reporters in the crowd on January 6 who interviewed people carrying Appeal to Heaven flags heard from them that "Trump has very clearly been prophesied to serve a second term."[71] And there were people who traveled to Washington, DC, that morning and posted a video of themselves on Facebook, flying their Appeal to Heaven flag and reading the January 6 Give Him 15 decrees from that day.[72]

If you look closely at the footage that rioters posted on social media, you can see Appeal to Heaven flags on the front lines as barricades are being torn down around the Capitol in the initial security breach.[73] You can even see an Appeal to Heaven flag at the central point where the crowds of rioters begin to clash with Capitol Police officers. The rioter uses the flag and flagpole to push their way through the police lines.[74] We know of at least one person who went into the Capitol wearing the Appeal to Heaven flag draped around his neck like a cape. When police later went to arrest him, they found the flag "dotted with 'blood and mace.'"[75]

Dutch Sheets and January 6

Dutch Sheets did not show up in Washington, DC, that day. The week before, he had been willing to pick up and go to DC because of a prophetic friend's dream, and he said that the life of the US republic hinged on that day. His friends Cindy Jacobs, Ché Ahn, Becca Greenwood, and Lance Wallnau were all there, but Dutch wasn't. Why?

After months of searching for an answer to this question, I believe I finally found one. Dutch and his closest team of apostles and advisers—including many of the members of his traveling team—had a daily prayer and spiritual warfare conference call scheduled every afternoon at 2:22 p.m., rooted in the 222 prophecies Sheets believed guided his life. These 222 conference calls were open to the public, but only Dutch and his team would speak or pray on them. Some of the recordings of these calls can still be found in obscure corners of the internet. Throughout late December, these daily calls were regularly getting two thousand people listening in. On January 6, it was four thousand people on the conference call acting as prayer warriors alongside Dutch and his team at the height of the Capitol Riot.

On January 6, at 2:20 p.m. eastern time, the US House of Representatives began to evacuate because the Capitol had been breached, and, starting two minutes later, we have a one-hour recording of what Dutch and his generals were saying and praying as they watched events unfold on their televisions. At the height of the Capitol Riot, spiritual warfare commander-in-chief Dutch Sheets was sitting at home in South Carolina—his dog bursts onto the call at one point—on a conference call.

What becomes clear, listening to these calls, is that Dutch Sheets did not believe that January 6 was going to be the apex of the contestation of the election. While hundreds of charismatic prophets had prophesied a Trump victory in 2020, Sheets's friend and prophetic wingman Chuck Pierce was a little cagier about whether Trump would win. But Pierce did issue one very specific prophecy. On November 2, the day before the election, Pierce prophesied publicly that "this will not fully be settled until January the 18th. It will be swampy. It will be nasty. And we must stand, praying until then."[76]

Sheets references this prophecy multiple times on the 222 calls, and this is the rationale he gives for why he did not travel to DC that day. He thought January 6 was just another waypoint—a crucial but not definitive skirmish in the cosmic war over the 2020 election. A true believer in prophecy, Dutch Sheets was still waiting for January 18.

At the top of the January 6 222 call, one of the members of Dutch Sheets's team begins by saying, "Lord, and as many of us are watching today, we see the Appeal to Heaven flags flying high in our nation's capital. And Lord, I thank you that you spoke to me that the word—the Appeal to Heaven word is what brought us to this moment, and it's gonna get us on the other side of this moment into your perfect will."[77] While most news analysts and reporting missed the import or origins of the Appeal to Heaven flags, Dutch Sheets and his team knew what the myriad pine-tree flags flying in DC that day signified.

One member of Dutch's team, Becca Greenwood, *was* there at the Capitol, alongside Cindy Jacobs, as we saw in chapter 3. In the middle of that January 6 222 call, as the riot was becoming increasingly violent, Greenwood texted Sheets to ask if he could speak by phone with Jacobs and her group. So Sheets decided to step away from the 222 call to phone in to the Capitol Riot. Jacobs and her group evidently did not think that their on-site spiritual warfare efforts were working, so they put Dutch on speakerphone over their PA system to decree and declare over the Capitol.

Here is what he prayed:

Lord, we just come into agreement with those on the ground
there in Washington. We ask you, by your spirit, to hover
over the Capitol now and bring order from the chaos. We ask
that, somehow, the spirit of peace will invade the atmosphere
and that the police would be able to do what they need to
do without loss of life. Lord, we pray for all of our team,
our friends there . . . [fading out] . . . This violence, and the
spirit of violence and the spirit of wrath, does not produce
righteousness, we take authority over it now. We declare peace
over the Capitol grounds this day.[78]

Sheets asserts that the riot was caused by a demonic principality, "the spirit of violence," "the spirit of wrath." But here's the rub: Sheets himself, more than any Christian leader in America, poured on the gasoline and lit the match of the Capitol Riot, with his violent oratory and systematic mobilization. After he makes his speakerphone decrees, Dutch comes back to the 222 call.

Capitol Police officers are being beaten, some within an inch of their lives. Rioters are parading around the senate chambers, praying their own Christian prayers. Mike Pence and many members of Congress and their staff are huddling in offices and hidden rooms, fearing for their lives. Ashli Babbitt is being shot and killed. Meanwhile, Dutch Sheets and his team of

NAR intercessors are watching it all on their screens while prophesying and decreeing Trump's triumph.

Toward the end of the call, one of the members of Sheets's contested-state prayer team, a prophet named Greg Hood, begins to prophesy:

> I hear the Lord saying, "America, I've heard your cries, I've heard your cries to return to your purpose. I've heard your cries to return to your destiny. . . ."
>
> "America, you're rising up, you're standing up. You're coming up out of the ashes," says God. "And you will be that nation that I've called you to be. . . ."
>
> "I've shaken you by the shoulders and I've looked you in the eye, America. And I've spoken to you today, and I say that you shall live. You shall be. You shall do. And you shall carry that thing that I declared over you, years and years ago."
>
> The Lord would say to his *ekklesia* today: "Oh you have been my mouthpiece, you have spoken well, and you are where you are today because you've been obedient to my word. I'm bringing you into a place of reward," says God.
>
> "For a shaking is released in this nation today, for those who have girded themselves up with my truth and stand in my kingdom will not be shaken. This is your day. This is the day I promised you," says the Lord. "Awakening is here."[79]

This bizarrely hopeful and uplifting prophecy is uttered by Greg Hood to the thousands of prayer warriors on Dutch Sheets's conference call just as chaos consumes the Capitol Building and rioters are stampeding in search of American elected officials. Sheets chimes in after the prophecy ends to say how encouraged he is:

> I just want to encourage everyone not to get too freaked out about what's happening. None of us like to see it. It all stirs up

emotion in us to see the chaos and the violence, but I do believe
the word of the Lord that just came forth. . . . I even feel like
what's happening in DC today, though God never orchestrates
evil or violence that is unlawful, but still I believe he's going to
use this to do some things.

So, Lord, we just thank you for your hand over all of this. We
know that you are hovering over that city, because we've asked
you to. We know you're working there, because you have told
us what to do and we have done it. We prayed thousands of
prayers in the last couple of months. Lord, all of us together,
asking you to do things. You have instructed us what to pray,
we have prayed it. You have instructed us where to go, we have
gone. We have boldly declared your words. Lord, I believe we
have been willing and obedient.

At no point in this hour-long prayer call is there any sense of even a
pang of conscience. Dutch's team knew what the Appeal to Heaven flags
that were everywhere in the crowds around the Capitol meant. They knew
that they had played a pivotal role in mobilizing people to be there in Washington, DC, that day. Dutch Sheets was literally hopping between prayer
calls and speakerphone calls with his friends who were boots on the ground,
doing strategic-level spiritual warfare outside the Capitol. At no point, it
appears, did anyone pause to say, "What are we doing here?"

In the midst of one of the worst crises the United States has ever faced,
this group of apostles and prophets of Christian rage takes solace in another
prophecy that reassures them that as bad as things may look on their TVs at
the moment, it's merely a shaking and all of their activities in the postelection season were righteous and have brought about the promised awakening.
It was, to borrow Sean Feucht's phrase, a literal Riot to Revival scenario
playing out in their imaginations.

"We Will NEVER Stop Fighting!"

This is how democracy is imperiled: not only by cynics and scrappers like
Donald Trump, Roger Stone, and Steve Bannon, who grasp for power and

connive to burn everything down around them, but also by true believers. Democracy is jeopardized by people so locked into the narratives of their own righteousness, their own certainty that they know what God wants, that they march right past the deadly conflagration they helped to instigate and never pause to consider the consequences.

Because Dutch Sheets was waiting for January 18, as Chuck Pierce prophesied, he and his team continued their efforts to mobilize the *ekklesia* in support of Donald Trump right up through Joe Biden's inauguration. Sheets even made another boots-on-the-ground spiritual warfare trip to Washington, DC, a few days after January 6 because he had received a prophecy that on his next trip to the nation's capital, God would release the archangel "Michael and his war army" to join Trump's cause.[80]

Eventually, as Trump agreed to leave the White House and plans for the Biden inauguration moved forward, Sheets and his team had to find some way to make sense of all of it—all the prophecy and warfare and imagined futures. In the aftermath of the riot and the inauguration, Sheets and his team did not say, "We must have been wrong about what we were hearing from the Lord" or "We missed the mark and our rhetoric got too heated." No. Built into their spiritual warfare worldview is a ready-made interpretation of defeat or unfulfilled prophecy; that is, we lost *this* battle, God's will was thwarted by the concerted efforts of Satan in *this* case, but God promises us victory in the larger governmental war over Planet Earth.

Sheets's daily Give Him 15 videos still flood the charismatic ether. His signature Christian supremacist optimism and Christian nationalist indignation still exhilarate his followers. In this sense, Sheets would agree with Sean Feucht: America is now in the midst of full-blown revival. Just look how much these charismatic practices are spreading; look how many people have embraced the Appeal to Heaven and the gospel of the *ekklesia*.

Dutch Sheets was, arguably, the most effective Christian leader in marshaling a Christian army to show up on January 6—and that wasn't even his endgame. He thought the real *denouement* would be twelve days later. So here's the disquieting thought that remains: What if he had really pulled out all the stops for January 6? How many more Appeal to Heaven flags would have been in the crowd if Sheets and his team had really put their shoulders into getting them there? How might a figure like Sheets have impacted that day if he himself had assumed boots-on-the-ground, battlefield command?

The other profoundly concerning aspect of the entire Dutch Sheets-January 6 saga is the harmonizing between Sheets's agenda and that of operators within the Trump administration. For all I know, Sheets's government interlocutors—both those who egged him on and who met with his team at the White House—may well have been true believers themselves, prompting him because they really hoped that strategic-level spiritual warfare might turn the tide in Trump's favor. Alternatively, while I would hesitate to say Sheets and his cohort were manipulated because they obviously had their own agenda and goals, what if members of the Trump administration were cynically utilizing Sheets to activate militant Independent Charismatic beliefs and networks and to throw a spanner in the works of American democracy? Either way, there are few more dangerous moments in a democracy than when the purported voice of God supplants the voice of the people.

In the fall of 2023, the Appeal to Heaven flag had its most prominent endorsement when it was discovered that the Republican backbencher who had been suddenly elevated to Speaker of the House, Mike Johnson, flies the pine-tree flag outside his congressional office. Knowing what I did about Sheets, I did a little digging and found that Johnson has close ties to the NAR and to Dutch Sheets, being longtime friends and political allies with one of Sheets's apostle mentees in Louisiana.[81] Johnson said in a statement that he had been given the flag by a pastor (who also has affiliations with NAR networks) and that he appreciated the "rich history of the flag."[82]

No one from Sheets's contested-state team has faced any legal consequences for what they did in the postelection season. If anything, they are more popular today than they were then. In July 2022, Sheets and Wallnau were in Atlanta for a special live taping of *FlashPoint* before a massive audience. Sheets led the thousands in attendance in collectively reading through a document he'd written titled the "Watchman Decree." The crowd recited (these are excerpts):

WHEREAS
   • we, the Church, are God's governing Body on the earth
   • we have been given legal power from heaven and now
exercise our authority

• we are God's ambassadors and spokespeople over the
earth . . .

. . . We declare that we stand against wokeness, the occult
and every evil attempt against our nation.

. . . We declare that we take back influence at the local
level in our communities.

. . . We decree that we take back and permanently control
positions of influence and leadership in each of the Seven
Mountains.

We will NEVER stop fighting!

We will NEVER, EVER, EVER give up or give in!

We WILL take our country back.[83]

If January 6 teaches us anything, it is that we ignore what people like
Dutch Sheets are doing at our own peril. If we don't pay close attention
to the theologies, prophecies, decrees, and declarations of far-right charismatic Christians, we may sleepwalk into another Christianity-inflected
insurrection.

CONCLUSION

THE ARC OF this story spreads out over decades and institutions and theologies and biographies. In case you have gotten a bit lost in the details, let me summarize the substance and sequence. Independent Charismatic leaders, particularly C. Peter Wagner, Cindy Jacobs, and Dutch Sheets, developed an aggressive and geographically tied vision of spiritual warfare that became very popular in the 1990s. Those leaders and many others congregated around Wagner, believing that they were divinely anointed apostles and prophets, empowered by the Holy Spirit to awaken the church into a great end-times revival. They believed themselves to be generals of spiritual warfare, equipped with special authority to destroy demonic strongholds and orchestrate campaigns of Christian prayer combat.

They built a far-reaching but low-profile set of leadership-networking institutions, which Wagner called the NAR, and they also assembled apostolic networks of nondenominational churches like Ché Ahn's HIM, which interlinked tens of thousands of these churches under the NAR spiritual oligarchy. Dominion theology—particularly as envisioned through Lance Wallnau's Seven Mountain Mandate—became integral to the movement in the late 2000s, leading them to conclude that they needed to "disciple nations" and take over whole societies to build the kingdom of God on earth. They entered into right-wing political circles in the United States to find legislative, executive, and judicial partners for this project.

No presidential candidate truly excited them until Donald Trump appeared on the scene. Lance Wallnau was the first NAR heavy hitter to fully champion Trump in 2015, but Peter Wagner followed shortly thereafter in early 2016, blazing the trail for the NAR leaders to become the premier Christian defenders and theologizers of Donald Trump in the 2016 presidential campaign. They mobilized their diffuse networks and developed prophetic memes (especially Wallnau's Cyrus Anointing concept) and biblical frames that made Trump more acceptable to the vast bloc of evangelical voters. They were rewarded handsomely by Paula White and Trump with positions of influence as evangelical advisers and interlocutors with the White House; in return, the NAR inner circle set in motion spiritual warfare campaigns on behalf of Trump's presidency and in sync with his policy agenda.

In the 2020 election, the NAR cohort worked even more hand in glove with the Trump campaign, inspiring and urging Paula White to launch the One Voice Prayer Movement and openly campaigning for Trump in their networks. Through Sean Feucht's Let Us Worship and Ché Ahn's anti-COVID-19-restrictions lawsuit coming to the Supreme Court, they aroused and agitated American Christians to defy local authorities and fight for Donald Trump. Hundreds of Independent Charismatic prophets, including many from the NAR networks, confidently and unanimously prophesied a Trump victory in 2020.

And when Trump lost the election but refused to concede, NAR leaders threw themselves into one of the most massive spiritual warfare campaigns in American history. *FlashPoint*, Give Him 15, Global Prayer for Election Integrity conference calls, Jericho Marches, Dutch Sheets's state-by-state prophecy tour: all of these were either built by or adopted as vehicles for NAR leaders to rapidly muster an army of Christian prayer warriors dedicated to seeing Trump reinstated for a second term. Some of this campaign was developed in coordination with people inside the White House. Through all of this, the NAR leaders truly believed that, should their mobilization of spiritual warriors be sufficient, God would intervene to transform America.

When nothing panned out, Trump inflamed and directed his throngs of supporters toward the US Capitol on the afternoon of January 6, and some NAR leaders likewise assembled in Washington, DC, that day: Cindy Jacobs, internationally acclaimed prophet and Wagner's original guide into strategic spiritual warfare; Ché Ahn, the most talented implementer of the apostolic governance model; Becca Greenwood, one of Wagner's most adept students and a veteran spiritual warrior; Lance Wallnau, who created the memes that made Trump palatable to many Christians; and Dutch Sheets, strategist extraordinaire, who barnstormed through every contested state using prophecy to enrage and radicalize untold masses of Christians.

Beyond the presence of these NAR captains on January 6, there were multitudinous markers of this NAR charismatic mobilization in the crowds surrounding the Capitol: Appeal to Heaven flags; Jericho Marchers blowing shofars as weapons of spiritual warfare; groups of people singing charismatic, warfare worship songs; prayer warriors speaking in tongues and pleading "the blood of Jesus"; apostles and prophets roving through the crowds, decreeing and declaring on behalf of the *ekklesia*; and accusations about demons and territorial spirits that were manipulating the election. Dozens of other Independent Charismatic religious leaders showed up that day, often following the lead of these NAR celebrities. The distinctive prophecy-driven, charismatic warfare spirituality of the NAR provided the Christian stage-setting to January 6, tying together what would otherwise seem like a bizarre array of Christian expressions.

After the NAR leadership, in collaboration with Paula White, broke down the wall between Independent Charismatic celebritydom and right-wing activist celebritydom, hundreds of other fourth-quadrant leaders have poured through. They are presently rebuilding and recalibrating the religious right in America and injecting charismatic worship and spiritual warfare practices directly into the heart of American politics.

All of this is demonstrated in depth in the preceding chapters. But that leaves us with the question: what do we do with this knowledge? Let me close with four reflections.

A Christian Problem

In the course of researching this book, interviewing numerous NAR and other Independent Charismatic leaders, and writing these chapters, I have had another voice in the back of my head that I have come to think of as the reasonable Christian objector. The reasonable Christian objector says, "Okay, these people you've identified were all present or influential among Christians in the crowds on January 6. So what? The NAR leaders didn't personally invade the Capitol or commit any physical violence that day." This is true—I have not found any NAR leader who committed physical violence or entered the Capitol on January 6.

"So how did these leaders respond after January 6?" the reasonable Christian objector proceeds. "Did they condemn the violence?" Well, yes, most of them did. Almost across the board, the main characters of this book, after the fact, condemned the violence perpetrated on January 6:

- Paula White: "I always have and will denounce violence, lawlessness, and anarchy in any and all forms."[1]
- Cindy Jacobs: "I condemn what happened inside the Capitol."[2]
- Ché Ahn: "I'm a very pro-life pastor, and I believe in peace. I don't believe in violence in any form."[3]
- Dutch Sheets: "I do, in the strongest terms, condemn Wednesday's [January 6] violence."[4]

The exception is Lance Wallnau, who has ridiculed how "everybody just stumbles over themself to say, 'We disapprove of this violence.'" Wallnau, starting on January 6 and continuing today, has perpetuated baseless conspiracy theories about how it was actually Antifa or "Democrat-funded anarchists" who instigated the storming of the Capitol.[5]

"And don't they, even Wallnau, have a First Amendment right to practice their religion unimpeded?" the reasonable Christian objector inquires. "Don't they have a free speech right to express their beliefs? As Christians, they believe in demons and principalities and territorial spirits, concepts that they find in the Bible. So as long as they personally aren't hurting anyone, what is the problem with them doing spiritual warfare around government buildings?"

Here we come to the crux of the matter. At the end of the day, this book is not about the physical violence that occurred on January 6. It is about the theologies of violence, the ideation of violence, and the romanticization of spiritual violence that have grown up in charismatic evangelicalism. It is about the culture of violent rhetoric that has spread from there into broader American Christianity and into American politics.

My objection to the NAR leaders is not that they believe in demons or practice spiritual warfare, which is fairly common across many forms of Christian belief and practice. My complaint is that they are spiritual warmongers, constantly expanding the arena of spiritual warfare, mapping it onto geographical territory and divisive politics in a deeply destabilizing and antidemocratic manner. Buttressed by latent American Christian entitlement and indignation, that impulse to violence is the iceberg from which the outcropping of violence on January 6 protrudes. And that iceberg still sits just under the surface of the waters of American Christianity.

Free speech and freedom of religious expression are core values of American democracy. With the possible exception of taxing these ministries and churches for violating the nonprofit rules against political campaigning, there is very little that can be done on a legal or government-policy level to rein in the NAR leaders' rhetoric and activities. This is a *civic* reckoning that we need to have within American Christianity and in American society. So let me briefly address my fellow Christians before broadening out to society as a whole.

The mobilization for the Capitol Riot was conducted—and the ongoing pageant of spiritual warfare in American politics is still being directed—by Christian ministers and Christian politicians. They are using Christian theology, Christian Bible citations, Christian worship, and Christian symbols; therefore, this story pertains to all Christians. Whether we are Independent Charismatics or not, NAR fans or not, we are our "brother's [and sister's] keeper" (Gen. 4); we all share in the same baptism and worship the same Lord in Jesus Christ (Eph. 4); we are part of the same body (Rom. 12). So if, as a Christian, you object to the activities and theologies I have outlined, it is your obligation to speak up. We will be complicit if we allow such things to be done in our name.

It is my opinion, informed by history, that Christianity in America has not been this divided—theologically, socially, regionally, or epistemically—since the eve of the Civil War. We desperately need intra-Christian and ecumenical conversations—perhaps some quite heated and contentious—that speak to these differences and bridge these divides. The best people to defang extremist Christianity are Christians.

So I urge my fellow Christians to find ways to talk about this, preach about this, and argue about this. I have no illusions that such confrontations will be easy or fast, but part of the reason that all of this extreme spiritual warfare ideation has evolved the way it has is that the rest of us have siloed it off and ignored it.

If you are an Independent Charismatic Christian or, even more pointedly, an Independent Charismatic leader, first, let me honor you for having the courage to read this far into this book! While I maintain that all Christians are responsible for correcting and challenging our fellow Christians, Independent Charismatics have an even more important and more difficult task: You can speak from the inside, using your credibility and shared vocabulary. You can persuade the persuadable in your community of the danger we see here.

This is a Christian problem, and we Christians cannot let ourselves off the hook or pretend that confronting toxic Christianity is someone else's job. It is our civic and, dare I say, our moral responsibility to face this antidemocratic radicalization, which has moved out of the fringe of American Christianity and become part of the carpet.

Beyond Homogeneous Understandings of Christian Nationalism

The investigation of this book also reveals the inadequacy of our current conversation about Christian nationalism or white Christian nationalism. In truth, there's no such thing as a generic American Christian nationalist; instead, there are regional varieties, theological subcurrents, sectarian identities, racial prejudices, and potent spiritualities that all feed into the phenomena we label "Christian nationalism."

While population-wide and demographic studies of Christian nationalism are valuable, we also need in-depth studies that chart the networks and locate the joints and sinews of this variegated trend. As I noted in the introduction, some modes of Christian nationalism are relatively harmless, indulging simplistic understandings of American history or blending American patriotism with Christian piety but not posing any sweeping threat to American democracy. Other forms of Christian nationalism—from the blending of white supremacy and Christian identity, to the Reformed Reconstructionist version of dominion theology, to these radicalized multiethnic Independent Charismatic networks—are poisoning American politics, accelerating extreme polarization, and sometimes sparking real-world violence.

In these pages, I have tried to gesture toward more nuanced ways of understanding the Christian nationalist phenomena: how arguments about religious freedom are often vehicles for Christian entitlement and Christian domination (a lá Feucht's Let Us Worship), how we can differentiate between more sentimental and domestically oriented Christian nationalism and organized transnational networks of Christian supremacy, how specific forms of Christian theology and Bible citation actually undergird many Christian nationalists' identities, and how charismatic spirituality and worship have become unifying forces in right-wing Christian circles.

Any religious nationalist movement operating in a polarized environment can be very dehumanizing. We see this in the NAR's impulse to assert that anyone who opposes them or any institution that resists their agenda must be possessed by demons or under the sway of malign territorial spirits, but we also see it in white Christian nationalists' antipathy to immigrants and ethnic minorities. Much of the challenge of living in a pluralistic, multiracial, multireligious democracy—which draws on the best values and best hopes for the American project—is to resist this gravitational pull toward dehumanization. This must even include not dehumanizing people who might be actively dehumanizing you.

The path out of polarization cannot be more polarization. Dehumanization must not be answered with dehumanization. Down that path lie madness and civil war.

The avenue to depolarizing our politics and building a more inclusive and collaborative American civil society is—and has always been—paved with further humanization, further inclusion, further alliances among people who may habitually and profoundly disagree about policy but who share a loathing of tyranny and a value for pluralism. Lord help us if we cannot find a supermajority coalition of Americans who are committed to that baseline.

Between Coincidence and Conspiracy

In my interviews with various NAR and Independent Charismatic leaders, I have occasionally pointed out to them how striking it is that so many from Wagner's circles were closely involved in the Trump campaigns and administration and also present on January 6. Several of them have shrugged this off as more or less a coincidence or just evidence of how invested the NAR leaders are in American politics in general.

Alternatively, some critics of the NAR have seized on my research to prop up their own conspiracy theories. This has contributed to wild claims about the NAR being a shadowy cabal lurking behind Republican politicians and clandestinely manipulating American politics to some nefarious and inscrutable end. Some have even attempted to use facts I've unearthed about the NAR and January 6 to claim that the NAR was the *real* force behind the Capitol Riot, as though this research supersedes or minimizes everything else we know about January 6: the Trump-aligned war rooms at the Willard Hotel, the entire Stop the Steal campaign of lies, the Proud Boys and the Oath Keepers' central role in the violence that day, and on and on.

Having spent an inordinate amount of time observing these folks and their activities, I have to say that I find both of these explanations simplistic and implausible.

On the one hand, it is no coincidence that the NAR and other apostles and prophets have been so closely tied to Trump. It is not a coincidence that five members of Wagner's EVAT were there on site at the Capitol Riot (Sheets by speakerphone), nor is it a coincidence that seven or eight additional EVAT members were involved in bolstering Trump's election denial cause in late 2020, hosting Dutch Sheets's contested-state prophecy sessions, encouraging their networks and churches to back Trump's lies, and amplifying the spiritual warfare crusade to overthrow the election. These spiritual warfare Independent Charismatic types were drawn to the spectacle and confrontation of January 6 like moths to a bright light.

On the other hand, while the NAR leaders cultivate auras of otherworldly insight and mysterious power, which is a huge part of their appeal to their followers, they also tend to exaggerate their real-world influence. These are not mysterious figures shrouded in intrigue. No, these are celebrities, prone to publicizing and trumpeting every new thought they have, every meeting or gathering they are invited to, every political leader whose favor they gain, every prophecy they offer. They cannot even pull off a secretive White House meeting because self-promotion is how they gain credibility in their world and keep their voracious audience's attention.

If there were some grand, orchestrated conspiracy by the NAR to instigate January 6, why did Dutch Sheets stay home that day? Why did Ché Ahn, by his own account, sleep through the Capitol Riot? Why, among the fifty or more Independent Charismatic leaders who were present at the riot, do you find expressions of surprise and serendipity on social media when they encountered each other that day—*Oh, you're in DC too? Did you know so-and-so is here right now?*

Between erroneous claims of coincidence, on the one hand, and misguided claims of conspiracy, on the other, I contend that the mass mobilization of charismatic Christians for January 6 is a great example of what we could call a *network effect*. In essence, Peter Wagner took a highly charged but disordered religious leadership culture—eccentric Latter Rain holdouts, hawkish dominion theology proponents, aspiring apostles and prophets, and ambitious spiritual warriors on the outskirts of the Independent Charismatic world—and wove them into a nation-spanning, globe-encircling mesh of networks. He bonded together key sets of these leaders through his mentoring circles (especially EVAT) and the leadership of his institutions that he called the NAR. He gave them enough sense of shared purpose and identity that they're still rowing together in the same direction but enough sense of autonomy and freedom to run their own oligarchic estates. *And* he brought into the center of that ecclesial infrastructure, in the mid-2000s, a vision for world domination via the Seven Mountains.

Claiming that Peter Wagner "radicalized" all these people would be a stretch because many of them were radical long before they crossed paths with him. But he knit them together, mentored them, raised their celebrity profiles, and boosted their epistemic confidence that they were the vanguard of the end times, meant to vanquish God's demonic enemies on the earth. I think a more accurate rendering of events would be to say that they all radicalized each other.

It was their shared theology and their Seven Mountains ideology that made these apostles and prophets gravitate toward politics and right-wing Christian activism. It wasn't a conspiracy that drew them to Donald Trump; it was an opportunity—an unprecedented chance to see their visions of revival and reformation with a top-down takeover of society accomplished.

We need to take stock of a new reality in our era of disenchantment with institutions and disillusionment with "organized religion." There is no such thing as disorganized religion. Nature abhors a (leadership) vacuum. The disintegration of more centrally organized religion merely creates new incentive structures and networked leadership cultures. It allows for the displacement of religious energy and epistemic claims into other arenas of modern life. It is definitely not the end of leadership abuses and megalomania.

The deinstitutionalization of Christianity has created a marketplace that rewards entrepreneurs and shrewd leaders who know how to corner their niche. It is a landscape of self-amplifying networks creating new eddies and subcultures. It is savvy operators climbing to the top of the pile, with little accountability or professional training. It is a religious celebrity culture built around fast-moving memes and flashy oracles. Deinstitutionalized Christianity is creating the conditions under which the apostles and prophets thrive.

The Future of American Christianity

Finally, the ambient context of this entire book is that, around 1990, American Christianity began hemorrhaging adherents. If you follow the General Social Survey, one of the most regular cross-sectional surveys in the United States, you may know that in 1990, approximately 90 percent of the US population identified as Christian. It dropped sharply to 80 percent by 1997 and remained stable there for about a decade. Then, around 2007, it began falling again, dropping to 63 percent of Americans identifying as Christians in 2022.[6] As sociologist Robert P. Jones has demonstrated, this drop-off was even more dramatic for white Christians, who started the Obama presidency in 2009 making up 54 percent of the US population and ended it in 2016 with only 43 percent.[7]

Put simply, for the past thirty years, America has been steadily becoming less demographically Christian. Without debating why this decline occurred, and obviously there were multiple factors, we can infer that the visceral awareness of this demographic shift fuels the sense of Christian nationalist desperation and the yearning for revival that we've seen play out among the NAR and Independent Charismatic circles.

The other side of that coin is that Peter Wagner was correct: nondenominational charismatic Christianity, what we've called the fourth quadrant, has proven the exception to this declining trend. Data from the World Christian Database show that the only segment of American Christianity that showed faster growth rates than Independent Charismatics in general (3.24 percent average annual growth from 1970 to 2010) was the subspecies of Apostolic charismatic Christians (3.66 percent average annual growth from the same period).[8] In other words, the fourth quadrant in the United States is growing, while the others all appear to be shrinking. This mirrors the global trend, where charismatics (of both the third- and fourth-quadrant varieties) are growing like gangbusters, while other forms of Christianity are holding steady or declining.

Perhaps Ché Ahn is right. Maybe the NAR is just the "next move," the next chapter in a global charismaticization and fivefold changeover in Christianity. This was clearly on Ché Ahn's mind when he went back to Harvest Rock Church the Sunday after January 6. He had invited his old friend Lou Engle to preach that day, but before he brought up Lou, Ché took fifteen minutes to address the elephant in the room.

After acknowledging he was in Washington, DC, that week and had attended Trump's rally at the Ellipse, he laughingly described taking that nap and missing the entire riot. He assured the congregation that "we condemn violence of any form or shape," to enthusiastic applause. He lamented that "some Trump followers got caught up in the excitement of the event, and they weren't mature, and they went into the Capitol," which went against Trump's status as "a president of law and order. Can we thank God for that?"

Then Ché Ahn began telling more of his January 6 story. He narrated being stuck in the crowd at the Ellipse for two hours, waiting for Trump's rally to begin. He introduced himself to the people around him, discovering a couple of other pastors in front of him as well as a Japanese Buddhist man from Hawaii and two Catholics behind him. Ché proceeded to evangelize to the Buddhist and Catholics, with help from his fellow Trump-supporting pastors, and all three "gave their lives to Jesus Christ."

He continued, describing his flight back to Los Angeles that week and being on a plane full of Trump supporters all returning from DC. He was seated next to a Trump supporter, a woman who was nominally Catholic, but he likewise evangelized to her, and, in Ché's telling, "she begins to weep, and she ends up giving her heart to Jesus Christ right there on the plane."

Then he broadened out:

> I'm thinking to myself, oh my goodness, the harvest has begun.
> And I want to tell you where the harvest is at: the harvest is
> with the 75 million, if not 80 million, of those who voted

for Trump. They have something in them—they know he's a pro-lifer, they have values that are similar, but they're not born again yet. . .

We're talking about 75–80 million [people], and there are a lot more out there. And they are so disappointed, they are brokenhearted over what happened this election. They are ripe. So I want to encourage you to reach out to your friends and family members who voted for Trump that are not saved. They are ripe for the gospel. The Spirit of God is moving upon them.

And that billion soul harvest that Bob Jones prophesied, I believe has started. And I believe we're going to see a great revival, a great harvest. And I still believe there is going to be transformation and reformation for our government and our nation.

We've got our work cut out. But now we know who to vote for and who not to vote for. And we now need to get more people registered [to vote]—the groundwork, the mechanics—all of that we've still got to do. But I'm optimistic that the kingdom of this world will become the kingdom of our Lord and of his Christ.[9]

For Ché Ahn, evangelizing people into his form of Christianity and mobilizing for the next election appears to be more or less the same thing.

So what happens if the long-awaited charismatic revival—the Third Great Awakening—comes to America but ends up being a partisan revival? What happens if the "good news" that is preached is the gospel of dominion, the *ekklesia*, and the Seven Mountains? What if new believers are baptized not only into Christianity but into being foot soldiers in a spiritual war fought on the battlefield of American politics?

The NAR leaders and their hyper-politicized Independent Charismatic celebrity colleagues have cornered the market on supernaturally steered Christian rage. They have brought their style of Christianity into the heart of right-wing politics.

It behooves us, in an era of charismatic revival fury, to ponder what will happen if the NAR's self-fulfilling prophecy actually unfolds. What will become of our pluralistic democracy if their Christian supremacist revival and reformation come to pass? In a way that few of us could have imagined before 2020, that possibility is now becoming distinguishable on the murky horizon.

ACKNOWLEDGMENTS

Doing this research and writing this book have brought me many new guides, friends, and conversation partners. I am especially grateful to the small but growing community of scholars who have served as my interlocutors in understanding the NAR and its environs, including Yvie Baker, Gordon Melton, Dale Coulter, Leah Payne, Caleb Maskell, Damon Berry, and Brad Christerson. Rachel Tabachnick is an encyclopedic resource on the NAR and was a key counselor to me at many stages of research. Bradley Onishi has been an exceptional ally and partner in figuring out how to introduce this complex material publicly and coherently.

I profoundly appreciate all of my colleagues and friends at the Institute for Islamic, Christian, and Jewish Studies who have supported this project. Special thanks goes to Madeline Dierauf, whose work as an intern helped organize and document some of the biographical sketches I included.

Broadleaf Books has been lovely to work with in bringing this book to fruition, and I'm overwhelmingly grateful for my editor, Valerie Weaver-Zercher, who believed in this project from the start and refined my writing and ideas countless times.

The Fuller Seminary library and archives staff was very helpful in allowing me to get access to C. Peter Wagner's papers. I also want to thank the dozens of Independent Charismatic and NAR insiders who agreed to be interviewed by me, not all of whom are named in this book and some of whom preferred to remain anonymous.

Finally, writing this book on what felt like an accelerated timeline (for an academic) has required sacrifices from me and my family, and I'm endlessly thankful for my wife and children and their willingness to roll with it and care for me. They give me purpose and hope in dark times.

NOTES

Introduction

1 Peter Manseau, Twitter post, January 15, 2021, https://twitter.com /plmanseau/status/1350251278186766337.

2 Bob Smietana, "Jericho March Returns to DC to Pray for a Trump Miracle," *Christianity Today*, January 5, 2021, https://web.archive .org/web/20210105214240/https://www.christianitytoday.com/news /2021/january/jericho-march-dc-election-overturn-trump-biden -congress.html.

3 Lena V. Groeger et al., "What Parler Saw during the Attack on the Capitol," Propublica, January 17, 2021, https://projects.propublica .org/parler-capitol-videos/?id=kk2ZFW9PB5w3.

4 Charlie Shamp and Darren Stott, "#Jan6 What Really Happened," YouTube, 48:20, https://www.youtube.com/watch?v=6on2LuKLpzc.

5 Groeger et al., "What Parler Saw," https://projects.propublica.org /parler-capitol-videos/?id=pp13Rljr67zI.

6 Groeger et al., "What Parler Saw," https://projects.propublica.org /parler-capitol-videos/?id=tfjhpJnZ8uOu.

7 Andrew Seidel, "Christian Nationalism and the Capitol Insurrection," written testimony delivered to the January 6th Select Committee, March 18, 2022, 17, https://andrewlseidel.com/wp-content/uploads /2022/07/Andrew-L.-Seidel-J6-Committee-testimony-Christian -Nationalism-and-the-Capitol-Insurrection.pdf.

8 See Philip S. Gorski and Samuel L. Perry, *The Flag and the Cross: White Christian Nationalism and the Threat to American Democracy* (New York: Oxford University Press, 2022).

9 These included leaders with direct ties to New Apostolic Reformation networks—Guillermo Maldonado, Mark Gonzales, Harry Jackson, Ramiro Peña, and Mario Bramnick—but also Independent Charismatic leaders who weren't as overtly aligned with the NAR networks, like Alberto Delgado, Alveda King, Samuel Rodriguez, Lourdes Aguirre, A. R. Bernard, Tony Suarez, and Mark Burns.

10 Andrew L. Whitehead and Samuel L. Perry, *Taking America Back for God: Christian Nationalism in the United States* (New York: Oxford University Press, 2020), 17.

11 Christians Against Christian Nationalism, "What Is Christian Nationalism?," https://web.archive.org/web/20220203003222/https://bjc online.org/wp-content/uploads/2021/01/WhatIsChristianNationalism .pdf.

12 Nikita Bakhru, "Leadership Lessons from Former White House Chief of Staff, Andrew Card," Dartmouth College—Rockefeller Center, November 2016, https://rockefeller.dartmouth.edu/news/2016/11 /leadership-lessons-former-white-house-chief-staff-andrew-card.

13 Adrienne LaFrance, "The New Anarchy," The *Atlantic*, March 6, 2023, https://www.theatlantic.com/magazine/archive/2023/04/us -extremism-portland-george-floyd-protests-january-6/673088/.

14 C. Peter Wagner, "The New Apostolic Reformation Is Not a Cult," *Charisma News*, August 24, 2011, https://web.archive.org/web/2011 0926203113/https://www.charismanews.com/opinion/31851-the -new-apostolic-reformation-is-not-a-cult.

Chapter 1: A Televangelist in the White House

1 US Religion Census, "Appendix B: Non-denominational Christian Churches," November 2022, https://web.archive.org/web /20230328031323/https://www.usreligioncensus.org/sites/default /files/2023-03/Appendix_B--Non-denominational_Christian_Churches .pdf.

2 Todd M. Johnson et al., "Christianity in Its Global Context, 1970–2020," Center for the Study of Global Christianity—Gordon Conwell Theological Seminary, June 2013, https://www.gordonconwell.edu /wp-content/uploads/sites/13/2019/04/2ChristianityinitsGlobalContext .pdf.

3 Brad Christerson and Richard Flory, *The Rise of Network Christianity* (New York: Oxford University Press, 2017), 5–6.

4 Ryan Burge, Twitter post, December 15, 2020, https://twitter.com /ryanburge/status/1338960279128993794.

5 Julia Duin, "She Led Trump to Christ: The Rise of the Televangelist Who Advises the White House," *Washington Post*, November 14, 2017, https://web.archive.org/web/20171115075716/https://www .washingtonpost.com/lifestyle/magazine/she-led-trump-to-christ-the -rise-of-the-televangelist-who-advises-the-white-house/2017/11/13 /1dc3a830-bb1a-11e7-be94-fabb0f1e9ffb_story.html?undefined= &utm_term=.8437afbc2fde&wpisrc=nl_most&wpmm=1.

6 Paula White-Cain, *Something Greater: Finding Triumph over Trials* (New York: Faith Words, 2019), 10.

7   Paula White, *Deal with It!* (Nashville: Thomas Nelson, 2005), 113.

8   White-Cain, *Something Greater*, 32–33.

9   White-Cain, *Something Greater*, 39.

10 White-Cain, *Something Greater*, 52.

11 Duin, "She Led Trump."

12 Shayne Lee and Philip Luke Sinitiere, *Holy Mavericks: Evangelical Innovators in the Spiritual Marketplace* (New York: New York University Press, 2009), 116–117.

13 Michelle Bearden, "Without Walls Church Is Hoping for a Revival," *Tampa Bay Times*, September 12, 2008, https://web.archive.org/web /20180805052548/https://tbo.com/news/nation-world/2008/sep/12 /without-walls-church-hoping-revival-ar-124369/.

14 Bearden, "Without Walls Church."

15 Bearden, "Without Walls Church."

16 Matthew Avery Sutton, *Aimee Semple McPherson and the Resurrection of Christian America* (Cambridge, MA: Harvard University Press, 2007), 3.

17 Sutton, *Aimee Semple McPherson*, 212.

18 Lee and Sinitiere, *Holy Mavericks*, 117.

19 White-Cain, *Something Greater*, 80–81.

20 Lee and Sinitiere, *Holy Mavericks*, 117.

21 John W. Smith, "A Church without a Building," *Reading Eagle*, September 25, 1999, https://news.google.com/newspapers?id=rSIyAAAA IBAJ&dq=paula-white&pg=2306%2C5742710.

22 Scott Thumma, "Exposing Megachurch Myths," Hartford Seminary, 2006, https://hirr.hartsem.edu/megachurch/ExposingMegachurchMyths .ppt.

23 Lee and Sinitiere, *Holy Mavericks*, 118.

24 White-Cain, *Something Greater*, 104.

25 White-Cain, *Something Greater*, 103.

26 Lee and Sinitiere, *Holy Mavericks*, 119.

27 Lee and Sinitiere, *Holy Mavericks*, 122.

28 Lee and Sinitiere, *Holy Mavericks*, 119.

29 Duin, "She Led Trump."

30 C. Douglas Weaver, *The Healer-Prophet: William Marrion Branham* (Macon, GA: Mercer University Press, 2000), 163.

31 David E. Harrell, "Healers and Televangelists after World War II," in *The Century of the Holy Spirit*, ed. Vinson Synan (Nashville: Thomas Nelson, 2001), 327.

32 Harrell, "Healers," 331.

33 Vinson Synan, "Oral Roberts," *Spiritus 2* 1–2 (2017): 11.

34 Harrell, "Healers," 325.

35 Interview with Mark Chironna and Dale Coulter, August 23, 2023.

36 Larry Eskridge, *God's Forever Family: The Jesus People Movement in America* (New York: Oxford University Press, 2013), 78.

37 Erskine, "1) Pastor Paula White and 2) Rick Gates," Erskine Podcasts, October 31, 2020, https://truthexpressradio.com/shows/.

38 Ed Boston, "Interview: Pastor Paula White—Praying and Worshiping Jesus at the Inauguration," Ed Boston Podcast Network, October 30, 2018, https://www.blogtalkradio-beta.com/edboston/2018/10/31/interview-pastor-paula-white--praying-and-worshiping-jesus-at-the-inauguration.

39 Doug Wead, *Inside Trump's White House* (New York: Center Street, 2019), 334.

40 Christopher Lane, "The Success Gospel of Norman Vincent Peale and Donald Trump," Yale University Press, November 23, 2016, https://yalebooks.yale.edu/2016/11/23/the-success-gospel-of-norman-vincent-peale-and-donald-trump/.

41 White-Cain, *Something Greater*, 179.

42 Lynda F. Simmons, "Senate Finance Committee, Minority Staff Review of Without Walls International Church | Paula White Ministries," January 6, 2011, https://www.finance.senate.gov/imo/media/doc/WWIC%20Whites%2001-05-11.pdf.

43 Deshayla Strachan, "Nasty Fight over Control of a Megachurch," Courthouse News Service, January 3, 2012, https://www.courthousenews.com/nasty-fight-over-control-of-a-megachurch/.

44 New Destiny Christian Church, "About NDCC," February 2010, https://web.archive.org/web/20100212070514/http://www.ndcc.tv/AboutNDCC/TheVision/tabid/2493/Default.aspx.

45 It's unclear how White met Duncan-Williams, though it is probable that T. D. Jakes was involved because he and Duncan-Williams have been close for decades. See Daily Guide, "Duncan-Williams Fights Wife," Modern Ghana, October 4, 2008, https://www.modernghana.com/news/162243/duncan-williams-fights-wife.html.

46 Paula White Ministries, "Season of Apostolic Reformation," YouTube, January 1, 2012, https://www.youtube.com/watch?v=t99ShTHxsCM.

47 Duncan-Williams's mentor Benson Idahosa was ordained by Latter Rain / healing evangelist Gordon Lindsay. Idahosa also attended Lindsay's Christ for the Nations Institute. Rume Kpadamrophe, "Apostle to the Nations: Archbishop Benson Idahosa," *Christian Today*, 2021, https://web.archive.org/web/20210802163710/https://christiantoday.com.au/news/apostle-to-the-nations-archbishop-benson-idahosa.html.

48 Leonardo Blair, "Paula White Installs Her Son as Pastor of Her Church," *Christian Post*, May 8, 2019, https://web.archive.org/web/20190508141602/https://www.christianpost.com/news/paula-white-installs-son-as-pastor-of-her-church-plans-to-plant-3000-churches-start-university.html.

49 Interview with Stephen Strang, October, 20, 2022.

50 White-Cain, *Something Greater*, 232–233.

51 Ryan Lizza, "Will Evangelicals Finally Dump Trump in 2024?," Politico—Playbook Deep Dive, June 23, 2023, https://www.politico.com/news/2023/06/23/pbdd-6-23-23-00103044.

52 White-Cain, *Something Greater*, 233.

53 Strang, interview.

54 White-Cain, *Something Greater*, 241

55 Strang, interview.

56 Religion News Association, "Panel: The New Revivalists," September 9, 2017, https://www.facebook.com/ReligionNewsAssociation/videos/10160001037885377.

57 Paula White, Benediction, Republican National Convention, July 18, 2016, https://www.c-span.org/video/?c4611566/pastor-paula-white.

58 Myrlie Evers-Williams was the first woman to do so at Barack Obama's 2013 inauguration, but she is not a minister.

59 Paula White-Cain, "Rally on Electoral College Vote Certification," Invocation, National Mall, January 6, 2021, https://www.c-span.org/video/?507744-1/rally-electoral-college-vote-certification.

Chapter 2: The Genesis and the Genius of the New Apostolic Reformation

1 Maggie Haberman, "Tears, Screaming and Insults: Inside an 'Unhinged' Meeting to Keep Trump in Power," *New York Times*, July 12, 2022, https://www.nytimes.com/2022/07/12/us/politics/jan-6-trump-meeting-screaming.html.

2 January 6th Select Committee, "Final Report," December 2022, 195, https://www.jan-6.com/_files/ugd/acac13_ffa28ed6c2694272a2 65860e447122c7.pdf?gad_source=1.

3 C. Peter Wagner, *Wrestling with Alligators, Prophets and Theologians: Lessons from a Lifetime in the Church—A Memoir* (Ventura, CA: Regal, 2010), 29.

4 See George Marsden, *Reforming Fundamentalism: Fuller Seminary and the New Evangelicalism* (Grand Rapids, MI: Eerdmans, 1987).

5 Wagner, *Wrestling with Alligators*, 36.

6 C. Peter Wagner, *Our Kind of People: The Ethical Dimensions of Church Growth in America* (Atlanta: John Knox Press,1979), back cover.

7 Wagner, *Wrestling with Alligators*, 113.

8 Wagner, *Wrestling with Alligators*, 120. I'm skeptical of these numbers, and he doesn't cite any source for this percentage.

9 Wagner, *Wrestling with Alligators*, 117.

10 Wagner, *Wrestling with Alligators*, 98.

11 Wagner, *Wrestling with Alligators*, 129.

12 Lewis B. Smedes, ed., *Ministry and the Miraculous: A Case Study at Fuller Theological Seminary* (Pasadena, CA: Fuller Theological Seminary, 1987), 15.

13 C. Peter Wagner, *The Third Wave of the Holy Spirit: Encountering the Power of Signs and Wonders Today* (Ann Arbor, MI: Servant Publications, 1988), 26.

14 Smedes, *Ministry and the Miraculous*, 70.

15 Interview with Kay Hiramine, July 19, 2023.

16 Rick Warren, "New Churches for a New Generation" (DMin Thesis, Fuller Theological Seminary, 1993).

17 Wagner, *The Third Wave*, 41.

18 Wagner, *Wrestling with Alligators*, 167.

19 Wesley Campbell, "The Conversion of Cindy Jacobs," YouTube, January 29, 2021, https://www.youtube.com/watch?v=yZWWWNx5R2I.

20 Johnson et al., "Christianity in its Global Context," 7.

21 Wagner, *The Third Wave*, 58.

22 Wagner, *Wrestling with Alligators*, 197.

23 This tripartite model of understanding the NAR ideology is partly inspired by Dale Coulter, "Neocharismatic Christianity and the Rise of the New Apostolic Reformation," *Firebrand*, January 18, 2021, https://web.archive.org/web/20210118120946/https://firebrandmag.com/articles/neocharismatic-christianity-and-the-rise-of-the-new-apostolic-reformation.

24 C. Peter Wagner, May 21, 1996, box 25, folder 04, C. Peter Wagner Collection, Fuller Theological Seminary, Pasadena, CA. Hereafter "Wagner archive (Fuller)."

25 C. Peter Wagner, "The New Paradigms of Today's Emerging Churches," *Ministries Today*, March/April 1996, Wagner archive (Fuller), box 34, folder 17.

26 Hiramine, interview. The people Hiramine recalls being at the meeting were Hayford, Wagner, Ted Haggard, Larry Stockstill, Frank Damazio, and himself.

27 Wagner, *Wrestling with Alligators*, 229.

28 Wagner, *Wrestling with Alligators*, 206. Emphasis his.

29 Interview with Becca Greenwood, August 31, 2022.

30 Wagner Leadership Institute, "Catalog," Wagner archive (Fuller), box 27, folder 2.

31 C. Peter Wagner, "ICA Presiding Apostle's Annual Report 2007," December 7, 2007, Wagner archive (Fuller), box 23, folder 1.

32 C. Peter Wagner, "Memorandum: Regional ICA Leadership Summits," April 9, 2001, Wagner archive (Fuller), box 22, folder 6.

33 C. Peter Wagner, "Apostolic Ministries," Wagner archive (Fuller), box 21, folder 2.

34 See Julie Ingersoll, *Building God's Kingdom* (New York: Oxford University Press, 2015); and Michael J. McVicar, *Christian Reconstruction: R. J. Rushdoony and American Religious Conservatism* (Chapel Hill: University of North Carolina Press, 2015).

35 Wagner, "ICA Presiding Apostle's Annual Report 2007."

36 Wagner, *Dominion! How Kingdom Action Can Change the World* (Grand Rapids, MI: Chosen Books, 2008), 118.

37 Todd Bentley, *Journey into the Miraculous* (Shippensburg, PA: Destiny Image, 2008).

38 Stephen Strader, *The Lakeland Outpouring: The Inside Story!* (Windermere, FL: Legacy Media, 2008), 143.

39 Ché Ahn, letter to Harvest International Ministry, June 2008, Wagner archive (Fuller), box 24, folder 3. Some of Ahn's close friends—who were respected apostolic and prophetic leaders but outside Wagner's NAR umbrella—were likewise squarely in support of Bentley. These included Bill Johnson, John Arnott, and Randy Clark, all members of the Revival Alliance network that Ahn created shortly before the Lakeland revival began.

40 Mike Jacobs, email, June 30, 2008, Wagner archive (Fuller), box 24, folder 02.

41 Churchwatcher, "Blessings, Impartations, Prophecies, and Comissionings [*sic*] at 2008 Lakeland Apostolic Alignment Ceremony," August 5, 2017, https://web.archive.org/web/20171215233421/https://churchwatchcentral.com/2017/08/05/blessings-impartations-prophecies-and-comissionings-at-2008-lakeland-apostolic-alignment-ceremony/.

42 Strader, *Lakeland*, 163–164.

43 Thomas Lake, "Todd Bentley's Revival in Lakeland Draws 400,000 and Counting," *St Petersberg Times*, June 30, 2008, https://web.archive.org/web/20080704145551/http://www.tampabay.com/news/religion/article651191.ece.

44 C. Peter Wagner, email to Global Harvest Ministries, August 25, 2008, Wagner archive (Fuller), box 24, folder 6.
45 Doris Wagner, email to Lee Grady, August 12, 2008, Wagner archive (Fuller), box 24, folder 1.
46 Wagner, "The New Apostolic Reformation Is Not a Cult."
47 Terry Gross, "A Leading Figure in the New Apostolic Reformation," *Fresh Air*, October 3, 2011, https://freshairarchive.org/segments/leading -figure-new-apostolic-reformation.
48 C. Peter Wagner, Facebook post, February 24, 2016, https://www .facebook.com/permalink.php?story_fbid=pfbid02MVrrS4jjL8z PbGzgzNyj5vEuJdjQ79p47jFr4RgYW4neLGYGcAipwpzus 5p13DT7l&id=1560633356.
49 Greenwood, interview.
50 Interview with James Nesbit, September 19, 2022.

Chapter 3: Generals of Spiritual Warfare

1 Campbell, "Conversion of Cindy Jacobs."
2 Empowered 21, "Cindy Jacobs," podcast interview, August 13, 2019, https://empowered21.com/podcast/cindy-jacobs/.
3 Campbell, "Conversion of Cindy Jacobs."
4 Empowered 21, "Cindy Jacobs."
5 Campbell, "Conversion of Cindy Jacobs."
6 Cindy Jacobs, *The Voice of God* (Ventura, CA: Regal Books, 1995), 36–37.
7 Campbell, "Conversion of Cindy Jacobs." This appears to be a para- phrase of Ralph Nader's, "The blasphemy of today is the commonplace of tomorrow."
8 Empowered 21, "Cindy Jacobs."
9 George Warnock, *The Feast of Tabernacles* (1951), 17, https://archive .org/stream/FeastOfTabernaclesByGeorgeWarnock/Feast+Of+Taber nacles+by+George+Warnock_djvu.txt.
10 Empowered 21, "Cindy Jacobs"; Campbell, "Conversion of Cindy Jacobs."
11 See Violet Kiteley, "Remembering the Latter Rain," *Charisma*, July 31, 2000, https://mycharisma.com/uncategorized/remembering-the -latter-rain/.
12 Jacobs, *Voice of God*, 82–83.
13 Jacobs notes her connections to CFNI several times in *Possessing the Gates of the Enemy* (Grand Rapids, MI: Chosen Books, 1991).

14 Cindy Jacobs, bio, National Symposium on the Postdenominational Church, Wagner archive (Fuller), box 25, folder 5.

15 Jacobs, *Possessing the Gates*, 31–32.

16 Cindy Jacobs, *The Reformation Manifesto* (Minneapolis: Bethany House, 2008), 34–35.

17 Wagner, *Wrestling with Alligators*, 157.

18 Jacobs, *Voice of God*, 112.

19 C. Peter Wagner, "Global Harvest Ministries President's Annual Report," September 6, 1996, Wagner archive (Fuller), box 21, folder 2.

20 C. Peter Wagner, "Battling the Strongholds of Darkness," *Ministries Today*, March/April 1995, Wagner archive (Fuller), box 34, folder 17.

21 Wagner, *Wrestling with Alligators*, 163.

22 C. Peter Wagner, "Confronting the Queen of Heaven," Wagner Institute for Practical Ministry, Colorado Springs, 1998, 34.

23 Wagner, *Wrestling with Alligators*, 207–208.

24 Wagner, *Wrestling with Alligators*, 207.

25 John Kelly, email to ICA, September 19, 2001, Wagner archive (Fuller), box 23, folder 3.

26 Wagner, *Wrestling with Alligators*, 246.

27 Hiramine, interview.

28 Angela Kiesling, "Cindy Jacobs: A General on God's Frontlines," *Charisma Magazine*, August 17, 2015, https://web.archive.org/web/20220707172902/https://charismamag.com/charisma-archive/cindy-jacobs-a-general-on-god-s-frontlines/.

29 Stephen Strang, "For Three Decades, Cindy Jacobs Has Been Raising a Prophetic Army through Generals International," *Charisma*, November 6, 2015, https://mycharisma.com/blogs/the-strang-report/cindy-jacobs-leads-the-charge-to-radically-change-our-world/.

30 Interview with James Goll, October 31, 2022.

31 Cindy Jacobs, "Word of the Lord for 2016," Generals of Intercession, January 6, 2016, https://www.generals.org/blog/word-of-the-lord-2016.

32 Tim Alberta, "Top Evangelicals Send Invites for Trump Meeting," *National Review*, May 24, 2016, https://web.archive.org/web/20190722200623/https://www.nationalreview.com/corner/top-evangelicals-send-invites-trump-meeting/.

33 Jennifer Leclaire, "Peter Wagner Was Truly One of God's Generals," *Charisma News*, October 24, 2016, https://web.archive.org/web/20161025232632/https://www.charismanews.com/opinion/watchman-on-the-wall/60760-peter-wagner-was-truly-one-of-god-s-generals.

34 By this time, Generals of Intercession had changed its name to Generals International. As One: A National Appeal to Heaven, "Partner Ministries," October 2016, https://web.archive.org/web/20161025194845 /http://prayasone.nationbuilder.com/partner_ministries.

35 Stephen Strang, "An 'Urgent, Pentecostal-type Prayer' Sparked Trump's Election as President," *Charisma News*, October 27, 2017, https://web .archive.org/web/20210304041516/https://charismamag.com/blogs /the-strang-report/34402-an-urgent-pentecostal-type-prayer-sparked -trump-s-election-as-president.

36 Right Side Broadcasting, "Jericho March LIVE from Washington DC," December 12, 2020, https://www.facebook.com/rsbnetwork /videos/188101792958083.

37 Paul Strand, "What This Faith Network Is Doing for President-elect Trump," CBN News, January 27, 2016, https://web.archive.org /web/20230609220648/https://www2.cbn.com/news/us/what -faith-network-doing-president-elect-trump.

38 Dutch Sheets, Facebook post, June 11, 2008, https://www.facebook .com/dutchsheets/posts/pfbid0327WPcoJq1SoBtzNRXygXUXY f2oZRLjwN3NKpxejM8duAznAmgYR2eGywRE89Me5Yl.

39 Jon and Jolene Hamill, *White House Watchmen* (Shippensburg, PA: Destiny Image, 2020), 4–5.

40 Wagner Leadership Institute, "Divisions Worldwide," June 2002, https://web.archive.org/web/20020610051855/http:/www.wagner leadership.org/divisions_worldwide.phtml.

41 James Goll (God Encounters), Facebook post, August 21, 2019, https:// www.facebook.com/watch/?ref=search&v=463406111056218 &external_log_id=dde2d2d8-d666-41f2-8bc7-744d741426d3 &q=one%20voice%20prayer%20movement.

42 One Voice Prayer Movement, November 2019, https://web.archive .org/web/20191111033432/https://onevoiceprayermovement.com/.

43 Adam Wyatt Schindler, Facebook post, December 28, 2020, https:// www.facebook.com/AdamWyattSchindler/posts/pfbid035uzX4Lm PEeW5cRkvHp8n3Ae2DsH33uwpNfiYpczJARz8yQYxA9XP pnHbX41y7bvTl.

44 Intercessors for America, "One Voice Prayer Movement," December 1, 2020, https://www.facebook.com/IFAPray/videos/16420820543 5753/.

45 Intercessors for America, "IFA Webcast Wednesday, January 6," January 6, 2021, https://www.facebook.com/IFAPray/videos/350083 4713362601.

46 Right Side Broadcasting, "Jericho March LIVE."

47 Leah Asmelash and Melissa Tapia, "Protesters Ripped and Set Fire to BLM Signs at Two DC Churches," CNN, December 14, 2020, https://web.archive.org/web/20201215002427/https://edition.cnn .com/2020/12/14/us/protest-dc-blm-asbury-metropolitan-ame-trnd /index.html.

48 Jacobs explained to a group on December 31 that she had just decided to be in DC on January 6. Glory of Zion, "Starting the Year Off Right (12/31)," https://tv.gloryofzion.org/videos/starting-the-year -off-right-12-31-7pm-session-3.

49 Jon and Jolene Hamill, *Turnaround Decrees* (Shippensburg, PA: Destiny Image, 2022), 87.

50 Records indicate that Jacobs's clearance was requested by a William Hallisey, ostensibly at the behest of Allison Hooker, a deputy assistant to the president assigned to the National Security Council. It is unclear if Hooker was the person who requested prayer.

51 US Capitol Police, "Demonstration Endorsement Sheet: Women for a Great America/50+ Days of Blessing," December 18, 2020, https://www.justsecurity.org/wp-content/uploads/2021/09/january -6-clearinghouse-us-capitol-police-protest-permits-january-6-common -law-release.pdf.

52 Women for a Great America, Facebook post, January 6, 2021, https:// www.facebook.com/watch/live/?ref=watch_permalink&v=4013534 24303676.

53 Becca Greenwood, Interview, August 31, 2022.

54 Ron DeSantis, "Take a Stand against the Left's Schemes," *Recount*, https://therecount.com/watch/incumbent-gov-ron-desantis-rfl/26458 84669.

55 Aila Slisco, "Steve Bannon Ridiculed after Suggesting John Fetterman Is 'Satanic,'" *Newsweek*, August 17, 2022, https://www.newsweek .com/steve-bannon-ridiculed-after-suggesting-john-fetterman-satanic -1734652.

56 Right Wing Watch, Twitter post, March 7, 2022, https://twitter.com /RightWingWatch/status/1500915977726439431?s=20&t=1bGk IpQVCXHqtbw7K8ruPw.

Chapter 4: The Second Apostolic Age

1 Ché Ahn, "Pastor Ché Ahn in Freedom Plaza at a Prayer Rally for President Trump," January 5, 2021, https://ugetube.com/watch/pastor

-che-ahn-in-freedom-plaza-at-a-prayer-rally-for-president-trump_llj
2aCCMvRPAUn7.html.

2 Interview with Ché Ahn, September 30, 2021.

3 Janet Wells, "The Love of a Father," CBN News, December 10, 2022, https://www1.cbn.com/700club/love-father.

4 Interview with Brent Detwiler, January 20, 2023.

5 Jon Hamill, "God's Fire Starter," *Charisma Magazine*, November 30, 2001, https://charismamag.com/spiritled-living/gods-fire-starter/.

6 See Tiffany Stanley, "The Sex-abuse Scandal that Devastated a Suburban Megachurch," *Washingtonian*, February 14, 2016, https://www.washingtonian.com/2016/02/14/the-sex-abuse-scandal-that-devastated-a-suburban-megachurch-sovereign-grace-ministries/.

7 Quoted in Margaret M. Poloma, "Reviving Pentecostalism at the Millennium: The Harvest Rock Story," Paper presented at the Pentecostal and Charismatic Movements in California: Historical and Contemporary Perspectives, October 9–10, 1998, Costa Mesa, CA, http://hirr.hartsem.edu/research/RevivingPentc.pdf.

8 Margaret M. Poloma, "Gamaliel's Admonition and the Toronto Blessing: A Theo-Sociological Report," Hartford Institute for Religion Research, July 5, 2000, http://hirr.hartsem.edu/research/pentecostalism_polomaart7.html.

9 C. Peter Wagner, email to Strategic Warfare Network, December 8, 1995, Wagner archive (Fuller), box 29, folder 2.

10 Gross, "A Leading Figure."

11 Wagner, "ICA Presiding Apostle's Annual Report 2007."

12 Hamill, "God's Fire Starter."

13 Lou Engle, "Receiving the Call," *Inside GI News*, January–February 2000, https://web.archive.org/web/20001209092200fw_/http://www.generals.org/gi_news_2k.htm#gi%20news%20the%20call.

14 Radiant Ministries, "The Call DC 2000," YouTube, https://www.youtube.com/watch?v=83lh6m93ZKw.

15 Hamill, "God's Fire Starter."

16 Ché Ahn, *Modern-day Apostles: Operating in Your Apostolic Office and Anointing* (Shippensburg, PA: Destiny Image, 2019), 48

17 Ahn, *Modern-day Apostles*, 67–71, 99–101.

18 Beni Johnson passed away in 2022.

19 Wagner Leadership Institute, "Regionals," December 2010, https://web.archive.org/web/20101229114907mp_/http:/wagnerleadership.com/regionals.htm.

20 Ché Ahn, Facebook post, October 13, 2020, https://fb.watch/fOOzlUin4D/.

21 Melissa Quinn, "Supreme Court Sides with Church Challenging California's COVID Restrictions," CBS News, December 3, 2020, https://web.archive.org/web/20201203170014/https://www.cbsnews.com/news/supreme-court-covid-restrictions-california-church/.

22 Ahn, interview.

23 Gregory A Smith, "45% of Americans Say U.S. Should Be a 'Christian Nation,'" Pew Research Center, October 27, 2022, https://www.pewresearch.org/religion/2022/10/27/45-of-americans-say-u-s-should-be-a-christian-nation/.

24 Ché Ahn, Facebook post, January 12, 2021, https://www.facebook.com/watch/?v=749314475706895.

25 Ché Ahn, "Senator Josh Hawley & Wife Erin Morrow Hawley," YouTube, November 29, 2021, https://www.youtube.com/watch?v=blPdkLLWqRU.

26 Revive California, "Leadership Summit & Gala," September 16, 2023, https://revivecal.kindful.com/e/leadership-summit-gala.

Chapter 5: Seven Mountains

1 Jessica Martinez and Gregory Smith, "How the Faithful Voted: A Preliminary 2016 Analysis," Pew Research Center, November 9, 2016, https://www.pewresearch.org/short-reads/2016/11/09/how-the-faithful-voted-a-preliminary-2016-analysis/.

2 Ed Stetzer and Andrew MacDonald, "Why Evangelicals Voted Trump: Debunking the 81%," *Christianity Today*, October 18, 2018, https://web.archive.org/web/20181030115016/https://www.christianitytoday.com/ct/2018/october/why-evangelicals-trump-vote-81-percent-2016-election.html.

3 National Association of Evangelicals, "NAE Denounces Insurrection at the US Capitol," January 7, 2021, https://web.archive.org/web/20211016063942/https://www.nae.org/nae-denounces-insurrection-capitol/. Emphasis added.

4 Terry Mattingly, "New Podcast: New York Times says 'Christian Nationalism' Tied to White 'Evangelical Power,'" *Get Religion*, January 13, 2021, https://www.getreligion.org/getreligion/2021/1/13/thus-saith-the-new-york-times-christian-nationalism-now-tied-to-white-evangelical-power.

5 Mark Galli, "Looking for Unity in All the Wrong Places," in *Still Evangelical? Insiders Reconsider Political, Social, and Theological Meaning*, ed. Mark Labberton (Downers Grove, IL: InterVarsity Press, 2018), 140.

6 The Oak Initiative, "Lance Wallnau—Board Member Bio," January 2012, https://web.archive.org/web/20120106212022/https://www.theoakinitiative.org/lance-wallnau.

7 Legacy.com, "Carl N. Wallnau, ESQ.," Obituary, https://www.legacy.com/us/obituaries/name/carl-wallnau-obituary?pid=189443061.

8 Phoenix University of Theology, "College Credit for Experiential Learning," April 2016, https://web.archive.org/web/20160410043314/http://www.phxut.org/life-experience-credit; Warren Throckmorton, "Phoenix University of Theology and the Federal Definition of a Diploma Mill," February 25, 2017, https://web.archive.org/web/20201129162933/https://wthrockmorton.com/2017/02/25/phoenix-university-theology-federal-definition-diploma-mill/.

9 Lance Wallnau, Facebook post, May 14, 2017, https://www.facebook.com/LanceWallnau/videos/10155360551579936.

10 The nonprofit was originally titled the Pneuma Institute (*pneuma* is Greek for "spirit" or "breath").

11 Lance Wallnau, Articles of Amendment to the Articles of Incorporation of Pneuma Institute, March 30, 1998, Rhode Island Secretary of State, Corporations Division.

12 Lance Wallnau, "Lance Wallnau GZI TV," Glory of Zion TV, December 31, 2016, https://tv.gloryofzion.org/videos/lance-wallnau.

13 Loren Cunningham, "The Seven Spheres of Influence," podcast, February 16, 2016, https://ywampodcast.net/shows/teaching/the-seven-spheres-of-influence-loren-cunningham/.

14 See Loren Cunningham, *Making Jesus Lord* (Seattle: YWAM Publishing, 1988), 123.

15 Wallnau, "Lance Wallnau GZI-TV." Wallnau admits that when he attempted to track down the details of this near-death experience story, even the person whom he claimed relayed the story to him disavowed it.

16 Kelly Head, "Get Out of Church," *The Voice: Christ for the Nations Institute*, Spring 2013, https://resources.cfni.org/resources/voicemagazine/CFNI_Magazine_201303.pdf.

17 Paul Djupe, "How Many Americans Believe in Modern-day Prophets? What Does That Entail?," *Religion in Public*, April 10, 2023, https://web.archive.org/web/20230410140604/https://religioninpublic.blog/2023/04/10/how-many-americans-believe-in-modern-day-prophets-what-does-that-entail/.

18 Paul Djupe, "Is Modern Prophecy Leading Its Followers to a Religious State?," *Religion in Public*, April 26, 2023, https://web.archive.org

/web/20230426151823/https://religioninpublic.blog/2023/04/26
/is-modern-prophecy-leading-its-followers-to-a-religious-state/.

19 C. Peter Wagner, "Global Harvest Ministries—President's Annual Report," November 16, 2007, Wagner archive (Fuller), box 21, folder 3.

20 Wallnau, "Lance Wallnau GZI-TV."

21 Wagner, "Global Harvest Ministries—President's Annual Report."

22 Wallnau, "Lance Wallnau GZI-TV."

23 Wagner, *Wrestling with Alligators*, 256.

24 C. Peter Wagner, New Apostolic Roundtable meeting notes, April 23–25, 2003, Wagner archive (Fuller), box 25, folder 7.

25 C. Peter Wagner, "KFI—How to Shift into a Kingdom Mindset," Glory of Zion TV, accessed December 7, 2023, https://tv.gloryofzion.org /videos/kfi-how-to-shift-into-a-kingdom-mindset-peter-wagner-ses-2.

26 C. Peter Wagner, "ICA Presiding Apostle's Annual Report 2007," 1.

27 Lance Wallnau, "The Lakeland Revival—What's Really Going On?," July 2, 2008, Wagner archive (Fuller), box 24, folder 2.

28 Peter Horrobin, letter to Peter and Doris Wagner, July 2008, Wagner archive (Fuller), box 24, folder 2.

29 Max Blumenthal, "Inside Sarah's Church," *Daily Beast*, September 5, 2009, https://web.archive.org/web/20170704171606/https://www .thedailybeast.com/inside-sarahs-church.

30 C. Peter Wagner, "ICA Presiding Apostle's Annual Report 2008," Wagner archive (Fuller), box 23, folder 1.

31 Wagner, "ICA Presiding Apostle's Annual Report 2008."

32 Department of Treasury—Internal Revenue Service, "2008 Return of Organization Exempt from Income Tax (Form 990): Lance Wallnau Ministries," https://projects.propublica.org/nonprofits/display _990/61481481/2010_05_EO%2F06-1481481_990R_200812.

33 Sarah Pulliam Bailey, "Which Presidential Candidate Leads among Evangelicals? Right Now, It's Donald Trump," *Washington Post*, August 6, 2015, https://web.archive.org/web/20150813011424/https:// www.washingtonpost.com/news/acts-of-faith/wp/2015/08/06/which -presidential-candidate-leads-among-evangelicals-right-now-its-donald -trump/.

34 Anthea Butler, "Video: Peril to Democracy: Racism and Nationalism in America," Harvard Divinity School, February 28, 2022, https:// cswr.hds.harvard.edu/news/peril-to-democracy/2022/2/10.

35 Wallnau initially tried out a different version of the phrase, hearkening back to a hit pop song from a couple years prior, "Trump is Heavens [*sic*] Miley Cyrus Wrecking Ball to the Spirit of Political

Correctness." Lance Wallnau, "Meeting Donald Trump an Insider's Report," LanceWallnau.com, October, 3, 2015, https://web.archive .org/web/20160129050802/http:/lancewallnau.com/2015/10/meeting -donald-trump-an-insiders-report. He later dropped the pop music reference.

36 The Jim Bakker Show, "Two Election Choices: Soros or Cyrus (with Dr. Lance Wallnau)," YouTube, October 21, 2016, https://www.youtube .com/watch?v=WfIn60tBYK0.

37 Christine Sneeringer, "Lance Wallnau on Donal [*sic*] Trump," You-Tube, February 20, 2016, https://www.youtube.com/watch?v=wXvH 0R45xLk.

38 Marvin Olasky, "The Sixty Years' War: Evangelical Christianity in the Age of Trump," *National Review*, June 27, 2022, https://www .nationalreview.com/magazine/2022/06/27/the-sixty-years-war -evangelical-christianity-in-the-age-of-trump/.

39 Wagner, Facebook post.

40 Greenwood, interview.

41 Mina's Heaven, "Lance Whitaker Wallnau on Trump," YouTube, https://www.youtube.com/watch?v=hPp9P7_JpCs.

42 Wallnau, "Lance Wallnau GZI-TV."

43 Victory Channel, "Home," December 28, 2020, https://web.archive .org/web/20201228190919/https://www.govictory.com/.

44 Comscore/Shareablee, "Victory Channel 01/01/2000–09/30/2023," retrieved October 19, 2023. Mike Hixenbaugh (NBC News) found this data.

45 Right Side Broadcasting, "Jericho March LIVE."

46 *FlashPoint*, "SPECIAL God's Unfolding Plan! (January 6, 2021)," https://*flashpoint*.govictory.com/episode/special-gods-unfolding-plan -jan-6-2021/.

47 Ché Ahn, Instagram post, November 23, 2020, https://www .instagram.com/p/CH8T1kxhVAd/?utm_source=ig_web_copy_link &igshid=MzRlODBiNWFlZA==.

48 Right Wing Watch, "Johnny Enlow Says Trump Can Impose Martial Law, Arrest & Execute Those Stealing the Election," YouTube, https:// www.youtube.com/watch?v=kjz9xlMeMsM.

49 Truth and Liberty Coalition, "About," February 2021, https://web .archive.org/web/20210205085357/https://truthandliberty.net /about/.

50 Stefani McDade, "'How Could All the Prophets Be Wrong about Trump?,'" *Christianity Today*, June 21, 2021, https://web.archive.org

/web/20210621173922/https://www.christianitytoday.com/ct/2021/july
-august/trump-prophets-election-jeremiah-johnson-reckoning-charisma
.html.

Chapter 6: Worship Is a Weapon

1 Sean Feucht, *Brazen: Be a Voice, Not an Echo* (Redding, CA: Newtype Publishing, 2020), 24.

2 Feucht, *Brazen*, 25.

3 Feucht, *Brazen*, 27.

4 Feucht, *Brazen*, 29.

5 Sean Feucht, "Perspective, Prayers & a Nigerian Dream about the End of *Roe v. Wade*," *Hold the Line* podcast, May 3, 2022, https://podcasts.apple.com/eg/podcast/perspective-prayers-a-nigerian-dream-about-the-end/id1572540011?i=1000559486274&l=fr.

6 Feucht, *Brazen*, 41.

7 Feucht, *Brazen*, 41.

8 Burn 24-7, "What Is The Burn?," August 2009, https://web.archive.org/web/20090804134644/http://burn24-7.com/about/what-is-the-burn.

9 Feucht, *Brazen*, 98.

10 Feucht, *Brazen*, 99.

11 Burn 24-7, "Apostolic Council," August 2009, https://web.archive.org/web/20090804135037/http://burn24-7.com/about/apostolic-council.

12 Feucht, *Brazen*, 131. Emphasis removed.

13 Sean John [Feucht], Facebook post, October 31, 2016, https://www.facebook.com/permalink.php?story_fbid=pfbid0gX5mrHpkDDLwGJ3ZMUv3XjHyBMVW9sXQUbSMPSQfdRE32y9eK7SxrnREAEram4ySl&id=608060175.

14 Bill Johnson, "My Encounters with Revival: Preparing for Glory," Destiny Image, October 2, 2014, https://www.destinyimage.com/blog/2014/10/02/my-encounters-with-revival-preparing-for-the-glory.

15 Interview with Bill Johnson, January 18, 2023.

16 Bethel School of Supernatural Ministry, "Home," March 2015, https://web.archive.org/web/20150301032436/http://bssm.net/.

17 Christerson and Flory, *Rise of Network Christianity*, 36.

18 Bill Johnson, "Glory Clouds and Gold Dust, Signs and Wonders," YouTube, December 21, 2015, https://www.youtube.com/watch?v=eZwWLvpC8GY.

19 Bethel School of Supernatural Ministry, "Academic Life," March 2014, https://web.archive.org/web/20140331130321/http://bssm.net/academic-life/academic-life.

20 Bob Smietana, "There's a Reason Every Hit Worship Song Sounds the Same," *Religion News Service*, April 11, 2023, https://religion news.com/2023/04/11/theres-a-reason-every-hit-worship-song-sounds-the-same/.

21 Christerson and Flory, *Rise of Network Christianity*, 106.

22 Mark James, "What Is Bethel Music? 5 Top Examples & History," Music Industry How To, March 29, 2022, https://www.musicindustry howto.com/what-is-bethel-music/.

23 Feucht, *Brazen*, 142.

24 Feucht, *Brazen*, 148.

25 Feucht, *Brazen*, 156.

26 Feucht, *Brazen*, 165.

27 Feucht, *Brazen*, 159.

28 David J. Harris Jr., "Schiff and Obama Admin Exposed and Guest Sean Feucht," September 30, 2019, https://archive.org/details/youtube_-_UC62KZJ1mShIQ-14rjzVYt9A_2019/20190930+-+gYhn_apZjOU+-+Schiff+and+Obama+Admin+Exposed+and+Guest+Sean+Feucht!/20190930+-+gYhn_apZjOU+-+Schiff+and+Obama+Admin+Exposed+and+Guest+Sean+Feucht!.mkv.

29 Jared Laskey, "'Worship Inside the White House': Sean Feucht Prays over President Trump as Christian Musicians Perform," *Faithwire*, December 9, 2019, https://www.faithwire.com/2019/12/09/worship-inside-the-white-house-sean-feucht-prays-over-president-trump-as-christian-musicians-perform/.

30 Feucht, *Brazen*, 180.

31 Ché Ahn, "Modern-day Superheroes | Sean Feucht & Jay Koopman," *Equipping the Saints*, April 13, 2022, https://www.youtube.com/watch?v=YgcX0x593VI.

32 Ahn, "Modern-day Superheroes."

33 Life to the Fullest, "A NEW Jesus People Movement," YouTube, July 21, 2021, https://www.youtube.com/watch?v=SFtEbUlX81w.

34 Sean Feucht, *Bold: Moving Forward in Faith, Not Fear* (Washington, DC: Salem Books, 2022), 18–19.

35 Ahn, "Modern-day Superheroes."

36 Feucht, *Bold*, xvii.

37 Feucht, "The Ziklag Moment," *Hold the Line* podcast, June 28, 2023, https://youtu.be/4_sYDtcnF6o?si=dsT6-_8W3NXug5Bm.

38 Samuel Smith, "Police Prevent Sean Feucht and Team from Setting Up for Worship Night in Chicago," *Christian Post*, September 18, 2020, https://www.christianpost.com/news/police-prevent-sean-feucht-and-team-from-setting-up-for-worship-night-in-chicago.html.

39 Feucht, *Brazen*, 131.

40 Feucht, *Bold*, 38.

41 Kyle Iboshi, "Hundreds Gather at Portland Waterfront Saturday Evening, without Masks, to See Controversial Worship Leader," *Oregonian*, August 9, 2020, https://www.oregonlive.com/portland/2020/08/hundreds-gather-at-portland-waterfront-saturday-evening-without-masks-to-see-controversial-worship-leader.html.

42 Feucht, *Bold*, 64. Emphasis his.

43 Marisa Iati and Sarah Pulliam Bailey, "Christian Worship Leader Brings Controversial Prayer Rallies to Cities Roiled by Protests," *Washington Post*, September 16, 2020, https://www.washingtonpost.com/religion/2020/09/16/sean-feucht-prayer-rallies-kenosha-chicago/.

44 Feucht, *Bold*, 77.

45 Aimee Herd, "Sean Feucht in Seattle: The Church Refused to Be Intimidated and God Kept Pouring Out!," *ElijahList*, August 11, 2020, https://web.archive.org/web/20201117233015/https://www.elijahlist.com/words/display_word.html?ID=24108.

46 Feucht, *Bold*, 146.

47 Feucht, *Bold*, 169.

48 Sean Feucht, "#LETUSWORSHIP—Washington, DC," YouTube, November 2, 2020, https://www.youtube.com/watch?v=i3p8oPrn-Cg.

49 Feucht, "#LETUSWORSHIP."

50 Sean Feucht, "Expanding Spiritual Territory," *Hold the Line* podcast, June 21, 2022, https://www.youtube.com/watch?v=bLYplYR7QRM.

51 Brandie Barclay, Facebook post, October 30, 2022, https://www.facebook.com/brandie.barclay/videos/1134273903859934.

52 Sean Feucht, "Worship and Warring," Glory of Zion TV, December 31, 2020, https://tv.gloryofzion.org/videos/starting-the-year-off-right-12-31-worship-and-warring-1.

53 John Fea, "The Court Evangelicals Are Now Linked to Yet Another 'National Embarrassment,'" *Current*, November 23, 2020, https://web.archive.org/web/20211020235711/https://currentpub.com/2020/11/23/the-court-evangelicals-are-now-linked-to-yet-another-national-embarrassment/.

54 Feucht, *Brazen*, 175; Department of Treasury—Internal Revenue Service, "2020 Return of Organization Exempt from Income Tax

(Form 990): Sean Feucht Ministries," https://projects.propublica.org/nonprofits/organizations/273357455/202123089349300412/full.

55 iTunes Charts, "Sean Feucht—'Let Us Worship,'" November 12, 2020, http://www.itunescharts.net/us/artists/music/sean-feucht/albums/let-us-worship-washington-dc/.

56 Sean Feucht, Facebook post, January 1, 2022, https://www.facebook.com/sean.feucht/posts/pfbid02makPcWgkqx7qM8QWUPHrp9d
TWt8XxcN7gURkXW662M5jcqZmcmRevPYpcEysGKUsl.

57 Shawn Schwaller, "Evangelical Bethel Church Devotee Speaks at Neo-fascist Event," A *News Cafe*, December 31, 2021, https://anewscafe.com/2021/12/31/redding/the-continuing-story-of-sean-feucht-evangelical-with-ties-to-bethel-church-speaks-at-turning-point-usa-americafest-moves-to-orange-county-continues-raking-in-the-bucks/image-4-feucht-and-trump/.

58 Sean Feucht, "Virtual Prayer Meeting with General Michael Flynn," YouTube, February 24, 2022, https://www.youtube.com/watch?v=_4Qk
RH7_cms.

59 Movieguide Staff, "Worship Leader Sean Feucht Announces Upcoming Documentary, Superspreader," *Movieguide*, July 5, 2022, https://www.movieguide.org/news-articles/worship-leader-sean-feucht-announces-upcoming-documentary-superspreader.html.

60 Sean Feucht, Facebook post, June 24, 2022, https://www.facebook.com/sean.feucht/posts/pfbid02VbSwPqRuFn55jjcfotJ1A22Hs
gT1YSfdHtCSEeUuuMfm2RP4bAMKt2zN68VFSWnHl.

61 Sean Feucht, "We Are Living in a Spiritual War," YouTube, August 8, 2023, https://www.youtube.com/watch?v=5qR5_55hHcI.

62 Sean Feucht, "Worship Is Our Weapon," *Hold the Line* podcast, October 17, 2021, https://holdtheline.live/podcasts/.

63 Alejandra Molina, "Hate Watch Groups Voice Alarm about Sean Feucht's Portland Security Volunteers," *Religion News Service*, August 13, 2021, https://religionnews.com/2021/08/13/hate-watch-groups-look-into-worship-leader-sean-feuchts-security-team-for-extremist-ties/.

64 Leonard Ravenhill, *Why Revival Tarries* (Minneapolis: Bethany House, 1987), 117.

65 PRRI Staff, "Competing Visions of American: An Evolving Identity or a Culture under Attack?," Public Religion Research Institute, November 1, 2021, https://www.prri.org/research/competing-visions-of-america-an-evolving-identity-or-a-culture-under-attack/.

66 Paul Djupe, "Prophecy Believers and Election Fraud: A Match Made in Heaven," *Religion in Public*, November 8, 2022, https://web.archive.org

/web/20221108212745/https://religioninpublic.blog/2022/11/08/prophecy-believers-and-election-fraud-a-match-made-in-heaven/.

67 Fanhao Nie et al., "The Future of 'Born-again Evangelicalism' Is Charismatic and Pentecostal," Public Religion Research Institute, June 29, 2023, https://www.prri.org/spotlight/the-future-of-born-again-evangelicalism-is-charismatic-and-pentecostal/.

68 Nie et al., "The Future of 'Born-again Evangelicalism.'"

69 Stephanie Hammer et al., "Modeling the Future of Religion in America," Pew Research Center, September 13, 2022, 20, https://www.pewresearch.org/religion/2022/09/13/how-u-s-religious-composition-has-changed-in-recent-decades/.

70 Gregory A. Smith, "About Three-in-Ten US Adults Are Now Religiously Unaffiliated," Pew Research Center, December 14, 2021, https://www.pewresearch.org/religion/2021/12/14/about-three-in-ten-u-s-adults-are-now-religiously-unaffiliated/.

71 David French, Twitter post, June 29, 2023, https://twitter.com/DavidAFrench/status/1674439090115080192.

72 National Association of Evangelicals, "Most US Evangelical Leaders Expect Persecution in Coming Years," October 2016, https://www.nae.org/u-s-evangelical-leaders-expect-persecution-coming-years/.

73 PRRI Staff, "Is Religious Liberty a Shield or a Sword?," Public Religion Research Institute, February 10, 2021, https://www.prri.org/research/is-religious-liberty-a-shield-or-a-sword/.

74 Pew Research Center, "Religious Landscape Study: Adults in California," 2014, https://www.pewresearch.org/religion/religious-landscape-study/state/california/.

75 Feucht, *Brazen*, 28–29.

76 For example, groups can be heard singing "Raise a Hallelujah" a Bethel song (*FlashPoint*, "SPECIAL God's Unfolding Plan!") and "Revelation Song" by Kari Jobe, another worship leader from the 2019 White House visit. Ashton Pittman, Twitter post, January 10, 2021, https://twitter.com/ashtonpittman/status/1348446136709898240.

77 Elizabeth Dias and Ruth Graham, "The Growing Religious Fervor in the American Right," *New York Times*, April 6, 2022, https://www.nytimes.com/2022/04/06/us/christian-right-wing-politics.html.

Chapter 7: A Governmental War

1 I was the first researcher to discover and publicize this meeting. Matthew D. Taylor and Bradley Onishi, "Evidence Strongly Suggests Trump Was Collaborating with Christian Nationalist Leaders before

January 6," *Religion Dispatches*, January 6, 2023, https://religion
dispatches.org/evidence-strongly-suggests-trump-was-collaborating
-with-christian-nationalist-leaders-before-january-6th/.

2 Tim Sheets, "Air Raid Sirens," Oasis Church, January 3, 2021, https://
www.youtube.com/watch?v=6HCylscRj3Q.

3 Dutch Sheets, "End 2020 Well and Keep Fighting," *Give Him 15*, December-
ber 31, 2020, https://www.youtube.com/watch?v=1MltuGSdiQA.

4 Denise Goulet, "Kingdom Come (Feat. Dutch Sheets)," *Revealing
God's Heart* podcast, February 2, 2021, https://directory.libsyn.com
/episode/index/show/revealinggodsheart/id/17741573.

5 Dutch Sheets, "The Power of Honor," *Give Him 15*, June 13, 2022,
https://www.youtube.com/watch?v=15nfYZB-NAc&t=12s.

6 This CFNI staffer prefers to remain anonymous.

7 Jacobs, *Voice of God*, 113. The nature of Stennett's relationship to Sheets
and Hodges is unclear, but he was listed in Hodge's apostolic network
in the earliest sources I can find. Federation of Ministers and Churches
International, "West Regional Churches," July 2001, https://web
.archive.org/web/20010720190443/http://www.fmcapostolicnetwork
.com/westregionalchurches.htm.

8 Jacobs, *Voice of God*, 138.

9 Goulet, "Kingdom Come."

10 Dutch Sheets, *Intercessory Prayer* (Bloomington, MN: Bethany House,
1996), 39.

11 Sheets, *Intercessory Prayer*, 37. Emphasis his.

12 Wagner, *Wrestling with Alligators*, 219–221 and 225–230.

13 Wagner, *Wrestling with Alligators*, 229.

14 C. Peter Wagner, ed., *Destiny of a Nation: How Prophets and Intercessors Can Mold History* (Colorado Springs, CO: Wagner Publications,
2001), 12.

15 Wagner, *Destiny of a Nation*, 38–39.

16 Wagner, *Destiny of a Nation*, 51.

17 Dutch Sheets, "Prayer Alert for This Nation," October 2000, https://
web.archive.org/web/20001109160700/http://www.dutchsheets.org
/Prayer_Alert.htm.

18 Wagner, *Destiny of a Nation*, 74–76.

19 Wagner, *Destiny of a Nation*, 12.

20 Wagner, *Destiny of a Nation*, 57.

21 Dutch Sheets, *Authority in Prayer* (Minneapolis: Bethany House,
2006), 72–73.

22 Wagner, *Destiny of a Nation*, 80–83.

23 Wagner, *Destiny of a Nation*, 84.

24 Maureen D. Eha, "In the Eye of the Storm," *Charisma*, September 30, 2006, https://mycharisma.com/charisma-archive/in-the-eye-of-the -storm/.

25 Dutch Sheets and Chuck Pierce, *Releasing the Prophetic Destiny of a Nation* (Shippensburg, PA: Destiny Image, 2005), 18–19.

26 Chuck Pierce, "Aligning for Reformation," in *The Reformer's Pledge*, ed. Ché Ahn (Shippensburg, PA: Destiny Image, 2010), 235–236.

27 Sheets and Pierce, *Releasing the Prophetic Destiny*, 175–176.

28 Dutch Sheets, email to Peter Wagner, June 6, 2008, Wagner archive (Fuller), box 23, folder 3.

29 Dutch Sheets, "A Statement and Appeal Regarding Lakeland," August 21, 2008, Wagner archive, box 24, folder 8.

30 Dutch Sheets, letter to Peter Wagner, August 5, 2010, Wagner archive, box 26, folder 1.

31 C. Peter Wagner, letter to Dutch Sheets, August 9, 2010, Wagner archive, box 25, folder 1.

32 C. Peter Wagner, handwritten notes, January 2, 2007, Wagner archive (Fuller), box 26, folder 1.

33 C. Peter Wagner, handwritten notes, November 9, 2009, Wagner archive (Fuller), box 26, folder 1.

34 Dutch Sheets, "The Rising Ekklesia," March 14, 2015, https://www .youtube.com/watch?v=uSUCYCANQuo.

35 Dutch Sheets, USAR Leadership Gathering, February 26, 2010, Wagner archive (Fuller), box 26, folder 1.

36 Feucht, "Expanding Spiritual Territory."

37 Jennifer LeClaire, "EXCLUSIVE: Dutch Sheets Shares Vision for Christ for the Nations," *Charisma News*, February 29, 2012, https:// web.archive.org/web/20120302213242/https://www.charismanews .com/us/32920-exclusive-dutch-sheets-shares-vision-for-christ-for-the -nations.

38 John Locke, *Two Treatises on Civil Government* (London: Routledge and Sons, 1884), 280.

39 Dutch Sheets, *An Appeal to Heaven* (Dallas: Dutch Sheets Ministries, 2015), 43.

40 Dutch Sheets, "Dutch Sheets Tells the Story behind the Appeal to Heaven Flag," *Charisma News*, January 28, 2015, https://web.archive .org/web/20150131075045/https://www.charismanews.com/opinion /48051-dutch-sheets-tells-story-behind-the-appeal-to-heaven-flag.

41 Marcus Yoars, "Dutch Sheets Resigns from Christ for the Nations, Cites Limited Window for Change in US," *Charisma News*, May 7, 2014, https://web.archive.org/web/20140510195117/https://www

.charismanews.com/us/43767-dutch-sheets-resigns-from-christ-for-the
-nations-cites-limited-window-for-change-in-us.

42 Dutch Sheets, memo, April 16, 2009, Wagner archive (Fuller), box 26, folder 1.

43 Bruce Wilson, "Dutch Sheets: 'The President Is a Muslim,'" October 31, 2011, https://www.youtube.com/watch?v=wD7OIjjALlI.

44 Wendy Griffith, "'It Ain't Over!' Christians Appeal to Heaven," CBN News, November 18, 2015, https://www2.cbn.com/news/us/it-aint-over-christians-appeal-heaven.

45 Ishaan Jhaveri, "The Pine Tree Flag: How One Symbol at the Capitol Riot Connects Far-right Extremism to Christianity," Tow Center for Digital Journalism, February 24, 2021, https://web.archive.org/web/20210303173008/https://towcenter.medium.com/the-pine-tree-flag-how-one-symbol-at-the-capitol-riot-connects-far-right-extremism-to-christianity-f02314a5f759.

46 Sarah Palin, "Exclusive—Sarah Palin: An Appeal to Heaven," Breitbart, June 27, 2015, https://web.archive.org/web/20191127145252/https://www.breitbart.com/politics/2015/06/27/exclusive-sarah-palin-an-appeal-to-heaven/.

47 As One, "Partner Ministries."

48 Stephen Strang, *God and Donald Trump* (Lake Mary, FL: Charisma House, 2017), 20.

49 Dutch Sheets, Facebook post, October 21, 2016, https://www.facebook.com/dutchsheets/videos/1170821679647384.

50 Dutch Sheets, Facebook post, November 2, 2016, https://www.facebook.com/dutchsheets/photos/a.320431614686399/1189366501126235.

51 Dutch Sheets, "Dutch Sheets GZI TV," Glory of Zion TV, December 31, 2016, https://tv.gloryofzion.org/videos/dutch-sheets-6.

52 Dutch Sheets, Facebook post, September 5, 2018, https://www.facebook.com/photo/?fbid=1903557146373830&set=a.320431614686399.

53 International Church of Las Vegas, "ICLV Sunday Church Online 1st Service," Facebook video, October 18, 2020, https://www.facebook.com/iclvglobal/videos/346351929970015.

54 Dutch Sheets, Facebook post, October 19, 2020, https://www.facebook.com/dutchsheets/photos/a.320431614686399/3453761598020036.

55 Jack Jenkins and Maina Mwaura, "Trump, Confirmed a Presbyterian, Now Identifies as 'Non-denominational Christian,'" *Religion News Service*, October 23, 2020, https://religionnews.com/2020/10/23/exclusive-trump-confirmed-a-presbyterian-now-identifies-as-non-denominational-christian/.

56 Dutch Sheets, "A Strategic and Defining Dream," *Give Him 15*, December 20, 2020, https://www.youtube.com/watch?v=xRIc7RZVGnY.

57 Dutch Sheets, "Running with the Horses," *Give Him 15*, January 1, 2021, https://www.youtube.com/watch?v=RTH3DpN6NHM.

58 Stephen Strang, "Dutch Sheets Says Dreams Revealed Prayer Strategy to Destroy Plot to Take over America," *Strang Report* podcast, https://www.charismapodcastnetwork.com/show/strangreport/ea31 c7fd-6407-4cf4-8a9a-1aa56c6a779f/Dutch-Sheets-Says-Dreams -Revealed-Prayer-Strategy-to-Destroy-Plot-to-Take-Over-America.

59 Dutch Sheets, "Recapping 2020," email to supporters, December 30, 2020, https://mailchi.mp/dutchsheets.org/recapping-2020?e=94 af5bde94.

60 The team included Joseph Garlington, a longtime ACPE member; Rodney Lord and Hope Taylor, who were connected to Sheets from his time working at Church of the King in the 1980s; USSPN state coordinators Regina Shank, Jacquie Tyre, Tom Schlueter, and Ken Malone; and Sheets's own Network Ekklesia International apostolic network leaders Don Lynch, Clay Nash, Gina Gholston, and Greg Hood.

61 Dutch Sheets, "Pray for the Nation from Pennsylvania," livestream, December 1, 2020, https://www.youtube.com/live/ednhkskD2ys?si =fGs-XNs-t-XCm1b-.

62 Dutch Sheets, "Pray for the Nation from Arizona," livestream, November 23, 2020, https://www.youtube.com/live/3IjCOc1QgtY?si=WB Xlvgd8HiyGF8xh.

63 Dutch Sheets, "Don Lynch," February 21, 2022, https://www .youtube.com/watch?v=jeNiSc4ZsqE.

64 While I interviewed Becca Greenwood, that was before I discovered the existence of this White House meeting, so I was unable to ask her about it.

65 Jacquie Tyre Ministries, "1-3-21," CityGate Atlanta, January 10, 2021, https://www.youtube.com/watch?v=jVfuKOmGsZw.

66 Asawin Suebsaeng and Adam Rawnsley, "Special Counsel Probes Team Trump's Jan. 6 'War Room,'" *Rolling Stone*, July 10, 2023, https://www.rollingstone.com/politics/politics-features/trump-jan-6 -jack-smith-willard-war-room-1234792827/.

67 Sheets, "Air Raid Sirens."

68 Don Lynch, "FreedomHouse New Year's Eve Service," FreedomHouse Jax, December 31, 2020, https://www.facebook.com/fhjax /videos/827289248108532.

69 Lynch, "FreedomHouse New Year's Eve Service."

70 Dutch Sheets, "Today History Is Made," *Give Him 15*, January 6, 2021, https://www.youtube.com/watch?v=Qer3gk836v4.

71 Michelle Boorstein, "For Some Christians, the Capitol Riot Doesn't Change the Prophecy: Trump Will Be President," *Washington Post*, January 14, 2021, https://www.washingtonpost.com/religion/2021/01/14/prophets-apostles-christian-prophesy-trump-won-biden-capitol/.

72 Tami Barthen, Facebook post, January 6, 2021, https://www.facebook.com/tami.barthen/videos/3647958945250939/?sfnsn=mo.

73 Groeger et al., "What Parler Saw," https://projects.propublica.org/parler-capitol-videos/?id=HS34fpbzqg2b.

74 Groeger et al., "What Parler Saw," https://projects.propublica.org/parler-capitol-videos/?id=xM8CXfu9pQHk.

75 Marisa Sarnoff, "Delaware Man Previously Known to FBI after 'War Crimes in Bosnia' TikTok Post Charged with Jan. 6 Crimes," *Law and Crime*, January 11, 2022, https://lawandcrime.com/u-s-capitol-breach/delaware-man-previously-known-to-fbi-after-war-crimes-in-bosnia-tiktok-post-charged-with-jan-6-crimes/.

76 Chuck Pierce, "On the Verge of Growing in a New Way," Facebook post, November 2, 2020, https://www.facebook.com/watch/?v=3411687658939458.

77 Clay Nash, "222 Prayer Call Recording," My Large Conference, January 6, 2021, https://www.mylargeconference.com/wall/recorded_audio?audioRecordingUrl=https%3A%2F%2Frs2941.freeconferencecall.com%2Fstorage%2FsgetHD%2FHWh34%2F7kR.

78 Women for a Great America, Facebook post, January 6, 2021, https://www.facebook.com/watch/live/?ref=watch_permalink&v=401353424303676.

79 Nash, "222 Prayer Call Recording."

80 Dutch Sheets, "God of the Impossible, Our Hope Is in You!," *Give Him 15*, January 11, 2021, https://youtu.be/fhqhRakLKuo?si=OixJlhm_X7zIPLCW.

81 Matthew D. Taylor, "Mike Johnson, Polite Extremist," The Bulwark, October 30, 2023, https://plus.thebulwark.com/p/mike-johnson-polite-extremist.

82 Matthew D. Taylor and Bradley Onishi, "The Key to Mike Johnson's Extremism Hangs Outside His Office," *Rolling Stone*, November 10, 2023, https://web.archive.org/web/20231110162314/https://www.rollingstone.com/politics/political-commentary/mike-johnson-christian-nationalist-appeal-to-heaven-flag-1234873851/.

83 The Victory Channel, "Watchman Decree," Facebook post, September 15, 2022, https://www.facebook.com/watch/?v=6150430864973

099; and *FlashPoint*, "Watchman Decree," GoVictory, 2022, http://*flashpoint*.govictory.com/wp-content/uploads/sites/7/2022/06/WatchmanDecree.pdf.

Conclusion

1 Paula White-Cain, Twitter post, January 6, 2021, https://twitter.com/Paula_White/status/1346938401757540354.
2 Cindy Jacobs, Facebook post, January 6, 2021, https://www.facebook.com/cindy.jacobs.16144/posts/pfbid027mPhx3EST9Gjpgk1NQrue3HB94TB7e3yPXUfeFAkCcz5CP3ba5XsWRNHZ9D87fDEl.
3 Ché Ahn, "Encouragement for 2021 from Ché Ahn," January 7, 2021, https://www.youtube.com/watch?v=2seoDL98u38.
4 Dutch Sheets, "The Warrior's Heart," *Give Him 15*, January 8, 2021, https://www.youtube.com/watch?v=FXEwNo2TxP0.
5 Lance Wallnau, Facebook post, January 8, 2021, https://www.facebook.com/LanceWallnau/posts/455172258994646/.
6 Hammer et al., "Modeling the Future of Religion."
7 Robert P. Jones, "The Rage of White, Christian America," *New York Times*, November 10, 2016, https://www.nytimes.com/2016/11/11/opinion/campaign-stops/the-rage-of-white-christian-america.html.
8 Christerson and Flory, *Rise of Network Christianity*, 5–6.
9 Ché Ahn, "My Perspective on the Events of January 6, 2021," January 12, 2021, https://www.youtube.com/watch?v=TWtKvZEwOzY.

INDEX